UNDER THE CHANGING SKIES

Under the Changing Skies

The Best of the *Guardian*'s Country Diary, 2018–2024

First published by Guardian Faber in 2024
Guardian Faber is an imprint of Faber & Faber Ltd,
The Bindery, 51 Hatton Gardent
London ECIN 8HN

Guardian is a registered trademark of
Guardian News & Media Ltd
Kings Place, 90 York Way, London N1 9GU

Typeset by Faber & Faber Limited
Printed and bound by CPI Group (UK) Ltd, Croydon, CRO 4YY

Compiled and edited by Paul Fleckney
Illustrations by Clifford Harper

A CIP record for this book
is available from the British Library

ISBN 978-1-783-35310-1

MIX
Paper | Supporting
responsible forestry
FSC
www.fsc.org   FSC® C171272

Printed and bound in the UK on FSC® certified paper in line with our continuing
commitment to ethical business practices, sustainability and the environment.
For further information see faber.co.uk/environmental-policy

2 4 6 8 10 9 7 5 3 1

Contents

Introduction

Each day, at the tail end of my early-morning strolls – which begin in different kinds of light and are accompanied by different compositions of birdsong, depending on the time of year – I buy my *Guardian* from the shop that's just up the street and across the main road from my house.

Sometimes I arrive at the same moment the papers do, and I help to carry them inside as the van drives off. The woman who does the morning shift sorts out my *Guardian* and passes it to me. 'Country Diary?' she smiles today. I nod and say, 'Country Diary.' I've told her in the past which bit of the paper I turn to first, and those two words have become our sometime greeting and occasional goodbye. I like to believe I'm known as 'The Country Diary Man', which is better than some nicknames I could have.

I wander home and I can feel by the weight in my hand that the news is heavy today, but there is a still and shining centre in this whirling vortex: The *Guardian* Country Diary. Three hundred and fifty words of glittering prose that have graced these pages for well over a hundred years, words that for me, rather than being a green-tinged antidote to the news, are central to how the world works and to how language works, especially in these times of dire climate emergency when the Earth can often seem to be sleepwalking into the future with its pyjamas on fire.

Country Diary takes a stand for description, poetry and narrative, for continuity, a personal point of view and, more importantly, for how these things can help the planet. These words feel more important, more monumental, more crammed with possibilities than the space they take up.

I spread the paper on the table, opening it at the right page. A squirrel runs across our garden, scaring a blackbird that's been pecking at a discarded apple, living examples of the sentences I'm about to read. I don't want to suggest from this that I live in some rural idyll reached only by a muddy track when the weather is good. I've lived all my life in a pit village near Barnsley that's now a former pit village, and I'm lucky enough to have a garden and some trees at the back of said garden.

I think I'm the sort of reader Country Diary is meant for. I like to walk in the open air but I don't know much about the names of the birds or the trees. I like reading good writing, and I'm interested in how sentences work and how you might use a brilliant and unexpected image to illuminate something. I like to read people who can articulate how I feel about the world around me.

The squirrel is on the bird table now, and there's a robin on one end of my grandchildren's seesaw. I use Country Diary as my calendar, my almanac, my commonplace book and, yes, my diary. For me it's a daily miracle and a tone poem, as well as a series of urgent dispatches from the front line.

The first Country Diary, then called A Country Lover's Diary, appeared in 1904; it was put on hold at the start of the First World War, before being reinstated a few months later. This could have been because people wanted relief from reports of the fighting, but I prefer to believe – though I could be on my own here – that people wanted to bathe in words that would make them understand themselves and the world more fully, even if those words were seemingly only about blackbirds or sycamore trees.

I first read it when I was a teenager, at my Uncle Jimmy's house in Peebles in the borders of Scotland. At the time I was amazed – imagine me saying 'I'm amazed' in a voice that was cracking and breaking and running up and down the scales – that such a piece could co-exist with the news. In those days, the *Guardian* was a broadsheet, and it was like reading a flag or a picnic blanket, and because your teenage years are impressionable it felt totally natural to have the (ahem) natural world next to news of wars and famines and the latest films and shows. Uncle Jimmy wasn't impressed: 'Country stuff in the *Manchester Guardian*?' he would say from behind the wide pages of his *Scotsman*. 'I didn't think you'd be able to see the fields for the smoke.' I didn't care. I carried on reading it, and I've carried on reading it since.

Of course, if this introduction were a Country Diary piece, I would now be way past the end of it. I would have to start again and set a scene, develop an argument, take the reader on a journey in muddy boots and give them a safe landing by the time I powered down to the last full stop. I would have written some transcendent sentences and created some images that would stay with the reader all day. And I would make it all seem effortless, with no hint of the many drafts floating around like waste-paper-bin palimpsests.

In this book you'll find entries from the last few years arranged month by month. You'll be able to wander through the year and marvel at the way the writers present it to you. Sometimes I dream of using their words as a guidebook, leading me by the hand across the nation, a soundtrack of voices introducing me to a huge diversity of places I might not otherwise visit. Each of the Country

Diary writers have their own style. This is my personal internal and external landscape, they say, in the way they shape their sentences. Well, thanks to them it's my landscape too. And it belongs to all of us.

Ian McMillan, January 2024

JANUARY

Farewell, dear Kite, my companion among these hills

NORTH WESSEX DOWNS

*In front of me, a short-eared owl quarters in the
golden hour, goth-eyed and paddle-winged.
But my mind is on the space by my side*

Golden hour on the downs, and the light is pouring through a slow
eyeblink of lowering cloud over Wiltshire. Quartering low in front
of me is a short-eared owl, filled and fringed with silver, then gold.
Its long paddle wings flick upwards; then it pivots on a wingtip,
folds itself up, lands, misses its target and looks straight at me with
goth-eyed surprise. It raises then lowers its 'ear' tufts, and continues hunting. Sitting on a damp, grassy anthill, I put my hand out to
my side, seeking warm fur. Something is missing.

The sweetest, happiest, most biddable soul has left us: our be-
loved dog Kite was put down, just before her twelfth birthday – a
last kindness we owed her. Dad had picked her out of a new year,
mother/daughter double litter of twenty-two unplanned puppies –
the product of a happy 'farm accident' between the shepherd's col-
lie and the gamekeeper's labradors.

She was with us in almost all we did and had a great 'work ethic'
and discipline. A hare could bolt from under her nose and she'd
look the other way.

I miss her terribly, this most tireless of soul companions:
her brown, bright, clever eyes, her salt-and-pepper paws, the
kite-frame cross on her chest, and the smell of her paws, which
have inspired many a writing workshop I've led (what *do* they
smell of? Grass and galloping, kite-flying on the headland, wild
thyme, winter fires). She taught herself to stop, lie down and wait

if I raised my binoculars. We've watched many an owl like this.

The short-eared owl turns into the light and disappears as the lid of cloud closes. Another winter storm is due and a late flock of linnets parachutes into the sanctuary of the gorse. As I reach the lane, there is the clicking of claws behind me. I spin round to see the rolled cigarillos of dry hornbeam leaves, chasing at my heels.

Nicola Chester, 2024

Weeds, glorious weeds

POYLL VAAISH, ISLE OF MAN

*One particular field on the island is a throwback to
the post-war heyday of mixed farming. The resulting
biodiversity is astonishing*

On the south coast of the Isle of Man there exists a field so impossibly teeming with birds that I don't know where to begin. I was last there on Christmas Day – an odd day to go birding perhaps, but not here. The island's annual Bird Race, a collective effort to find as many species as possible, runs between Christmas and the new year. In 2022 we set a record: 121 species, three of which were found in this field and nowhere else.

So what's this field got that makes it so popular for birds? Weeds, glorious weeds. Aren't they wildflowers too? The field is a throwback to seventy years ago, to the heyday of mixed farming, when every farm had an acre of vegetables – and lots of weeds.

Today I make a visit. A flock of twite is busy doing the rounds – this is the only place where you can hear them on the island this winter. They are joined by skylark, greenfinch, linnet and lesser redpoll. In five minutes I see more reed bunting than I saw throughout 2022. Yet there is something altogether more rewarding hidden here. I am hoping to see a tree sparrow.

On our island, this overlooked yet handsome bird is our most threatened, thanks to our hatred of weeds. But this weedy field of veg is supporting two tree sparrows this winter. Such is their perilous state, they caused a small twitch on Christmas Day.

Today I catch only the briefest glimpse of one. Content enough, I pop into the farm shop, thank Mrs Gawne for her conservation efforts and compliment her on her weeds. If we're going to save tree sparrows, we must support farmers to provide a lot more fields like this.

Economics have forced our farmers to specialise and to hate weeds, and we are losing biodiversity as a result. On our island we have 90,000 acres of grazing, yet just 45 acres of veg. This explains the plight of most farmland birds, and why there's one I did not see today. Once common, we recently lost our yellowhammer. They would have liked this field.

David Bellamy, 2023

My paean to the hawthorn, feeder of many

ALLENDALE, NORTHUMBERLAND

In my garden, this small but generous tree is a vital winter food source to redwings, goldcrests, squirrels and mice

The garden looks monochrome in a pale grey mist, the hawthorn outside my kitchen window two-dimensional. A lone blackbird is up early to feed on the berries strung like beads along spiny branches. I hold my breath as a shadowy hare lopes along, and I can just make out the bouncing white rumps of two roe deer. Otherwise, everything is still.

As the day warms, the berries colour to a dull red and more birds arrive. At one time I count seven blackbirds, wings flapping, tails dipping as they teeter on twig ends to snatch with pincering beaks. On other days there have been winter visitors from Europe, redwings and fieldfares, or our native plump wood pigeons flashing white neck patches, drawn by the haws, which are rich in antioxidants.

This little tree is barely twice my height, yet it feeds so many. A grey squirrel pauses to snack. Heaps of chewed berries on the ground show where mice have fed. In spring, hawthorn leaves are the first to emerge in the valley, followed by blossoms, plentiful in nectar and pollen for bees and hoverflies.

Parties of long-tailed tits move restlessly between the garden trees, gathering other species of tits into their circus act. My little hawthorn is a favourite place to feed as they swing through it, picking off the aphids, spiders, tiny insects and moth caterpillars. Today among the blackbirds there's a goldcrest, and on the mossy stones below, a wren, as fast and slight as a blown leaf.

I've photographed the angular branches backlit by the west, when ice balls knock together against a pink sky, or lurid sunsets flame in late summer. In the flower borders, I find spiky seedlings, progeny to make a note of and transplant somewhere new in winter.

This then is my paean to the hawthorn. January is a good month to plant a bare-rooted tree, costing little, quick to establish while dormant. The blackbirds are joined by a song thrush, brown spots on its creamy white breast, and I'm struck by what a difference one small tree can make.

Susie White, 2022

Gently, quietly, these cows are doing vital work in the forest

ABERNETHY FOREST, STRATHSPEY

Introduced to mimic the habits of the extinct aurochs,
only the jangle of their bells gives them away

These first few days of the new year have been blustery, and the wind has scoured most of the snow off the hilltops. During a lull from the wind and rain, I take a chance and head out to a remoter path in the Abernethy Forest. The track is strewn with small, wind-torn branches and twigs, lichen and pine needles. Clouds scud across the sky and the forest is an ever-changing mosaic of light and shade. A stiffening breeze drowns out any birdsong that may be about, including the flock of finches that fly over, which I know will be crossbills.

From somewhere among the trees, I hear an odd sound of metal against metal, a hollow jangling that doubles and trebles, each tone a slightly different pitch. From within the trees I see a cow, then another, and more still – one is black, another grey; a few are sandy brown. They turn to look at me with a mixture of vague curiosity and nonchalance, before turning back to continue munching on the heather.

This herd, a mixture of breeds, has been introduced to this forest to mimic the work that aurochs – the extinct native wild cattle that used to roam here – would previously have done. They'll eat the heather and churn up the ground with their hooves, creating more opportunities for biodiversity and giving space for new flushes of the blaeberries and crowberries that are such important food sources for capercaillies, those elusive and threatened birds that I always hope to see.

There's something quite magical about their stillness and size. Usually, any larger animals in this place will be deer, which will startle and spring away, but these cows are going quietly about their business; were it not for their cowbells, I may not even have noticed them. I turn back to take another path, watching them from afar as they lumber off, their jangling receding as they disappear further into the woods, lost among the Scots pines once more.

Amanda Thomson, 2022

Winter finally comes to these woods

STAPLE HILL, SOMERSET

*The icy air quickens the blood and tautens
everything with its astringent sting*

Finally, a winter's day that actually feels like one. Crisp air, blue sky, frost – just what the doctor ordered. For months, it has felt as if the Earth itself has been suffering from a low-grade fever – it was a depressingly record-breaking 16°C on New Year's Day here and has been grumbling along in low double figures ever since.

Today, though, the icy air quickens the blood, tautening everything with its astringent sting. I want to feel it against my skin, as you might test a knife's sharpness with your thumb. I head to Staple Hill, where the footpath skirts the conifer plantations: mostly Scots pine, Norway spruce and the occasional magnificent cedar. There are also oaks, beech and silver birch, and under the trees a tussocky jumble of bracken, moss and brambles. The whole area is a delightful patchwork of evergreen and deciduous, straight rows and rambling woodland, tarmacked pathways and animal tracks, open glades and spooky fairy-tale forests where a gruffalo would feel right at home.

The tree trunks look painted in colours squeezed fresh from the tube. A trick of the eye? Surely this much iridescent green belongs in the summer and in the leaves of the canopy, not on the trunks and branches of the naked trees? Lichen reigns supreme at this time of year, in every shade of jade, emerald, pistachio and chartreuse. Each variety the result of a particular blend of fungus, bacteria and algae.

The sun has been out all day, but in the dips and shadows, frost still lingers. Tiny white globules adorn each blade of grass. I pick one up, expecting it to crumble, deliquesce or pop; but it stays on the tip of my finger, a pearl of solid water, supercooled dew. I put it in my mouth and it melts deliciously on my tongue.

I cross a glade of plantation trees, their tall shadows spreading on the grass as precisely as a barcode, and enter the forest. Fallen pine needles cushion the ground, putting a spring in my step. The air is drenched with phytoncides. I can almost feel my immune system bucking up.

My walk back is a slow strobe – two steps dark, two steps dazzle – as though the sun has decided that this perfect crystal day must end in a blaze of glory.

Anita Roy, 2022

I ask the dark sky to show me a nice bird today – it obliges

STOKE-ON-TRENT, STAFFORDSHIRE

My vision isn't good at the moment, but this old railway line grants me bullfinch, fungus and blood-ripe berries

There is a long, hidden path that runs through the industrial estate where I live. It's as straight and narrow as a railway line and, a hundred years ago, that's what it was. Now it is full of dog walkers and cyclists with cold breath, steaming through its dark tunnels, vests as neon bright as the graffiti. Dog walkers, cyclists and me.

I am particularly unwell at the moment, but all I want is to be outside. I love the path in winter: the stunted, skeletal trees that line it; all those gorgeous, branching fractals overhead. I like the mud; the dark otherworlds glimpsed in puddles; the deep browns of leaf litter pushed to the edges; the unexpected architecture of scruffy hedgerow plants, frozen in decay.

As the light dims, my boyfriend sets up my wheelchair with fleece-cosy and hot-water bottle, helps me in, and pushes me along the path until it gets dark. Up and down: a slow, watchful locomotive. My vision isn't great, and I struggle to take it all in at once. Instead, I use my camera to focus on small windows of interest.

And we find so much. A hazel branch grown into a tight red knot; a sudden, thick carpet of green apples. The damp, sawn stump of a tree glowing like a headlight while clumps of orange fungus spatter its fallen trunk like fairy umbrellas. Blood-ripe berries hang on, and the last of the light turns the odd yellow bramble leaf gold. I am enchanted, serenaded by robin song, preserving each detail: click.

On our last walk, I make a request. 'Show me a nice bird today?' I call to the dark sky. I'd have been content with another robin, but it is a bullfinch that finds my lens, sitting still and watchful, bright as a bauble.

Even in winter, in the urban gloom, even in darkness, nature is so generous. I take each photo to look at later, thankful, back in bed.

Josie George, 2022

The rising river threatens to overtake the road

MARSHWOOD VALE, DORSET

The lane ahead floods often, and I've learned
to respect the water's power

The road ahead is covered with sliding sheets of toffee-brown water. I wonder if it is worse further on and whether we'll be able to get through. For now, it's shallow, so I proceed cautiously, past the big orange willow in the hedge and down to the bridge over the River Char.

This lane floods frequently. I've learned to read the signs and re-spect the water's power. One wet winter's night, coming back from bell-ringing practice in the village, the torrent was stronger than I realised. It lifted my car so that, for a second, I was steering a boat, adrift in the starless dark.

It's perilous to ignore the solar-powered warning sign that flashes when the flood is deep. Once we turned back when the river was coiling over the bridge, only to meet the vicar, late for a service. 'Don't cross!' we warned, but he hurried on, got stuck and wrote off his four-by-four.

The river is rising, but it's not quite over the road yet, as it has been many times recently. The grass on the banks is flattened in snaky runnels where water poured only twenty-four hours ago, and a serpent of torn branch has been washed against the bridge rails.

Being less than three miles from the sea, the Char is affected by tidal surges. The river was once navigable – in the ninth century it brought a pack of Vikings inland, seeking plunder. Legend says that a local wise woman led the villagers in battle. The peasants won, but the wise woman was killed in the fight. She was declared a saint and her bones were enshrined in the church.

Heavy rain, saturated ground and high tide at Charmouth in an hour mean the bridge will soon be impassable again. As I edge by, a couple of goldcrests flit along the stump-cut hedge, peeping in alarm. They've been searching for tiny insects, probing the nubs of hazel catkins that are beginning to cluster along the streams, side by side with last year's rosehips.

Sara Hudston, 2021

The camera captures a world curtained by fog

SANDY, BEDFORDSHIRE

*There are no edges, tree trunks are filmed in a milky
wash and branches dissolve into the white*

There is a vague hump shape, like a sleeping dinosaur under the trees, and the camera is hunting for it. I catch the 'tick-tick-tick' whirr of anguished electronics by my side as it struggles to find an edge on which to focus.

My eyes learn from the camera about how we see at a distance in freezing fog. Normally dark tree trunks are not dark at all but are filmed with a milky wash, and the spread of branches dissolves into the white of the white. Outside our immediate bubble of clarity, there are no edges, only gradations and blur.

The clear clop of a horse's hooves on a hard track brings the camera to the left of the trees. Rider and beast appear out of the mist as one animal, and the world walks slow. A single click fixes the lift of a hoof. Another click, then another, before the rider's face comes into sharper focus and the camera hangs respectfully limp as she passes.

'Grim, isn't it?' she ventures. I mutter something about 'but isn't it beautiful?' She doesn't appear to hear. 'And people wonder why my nose is red,' she adds, thrown from above the horse's retreating rump.

We make it to the shelterbelt of trees where our giant lies. The camera has no trouble with the close beauty of the bush here, water pearling beneath alder catkins in frozen drips that will not drop. Glass chains of reinforced spiders' webs link twig to twig, a crystal foreground to a backdrop of ploughed loam fields and a curtain of fog.

The giant, a red excavator with its neck bowed towards a collapsed rabbit hole, was eating trees here all day long yesterday, and shreds of wood poke out of its clamped metal jaws. A heavy-duty giraffe, it rode with a tyrant's whim down the track, pulverising the hardcore base under a heavy caterpillar tread. It swung its head from side to side, a curved thumb insinuating itself around branches and trunks, guillotine blade slicing them off – trees to stumps, bricks to dust.

Now, with an empty cab, it dozes. The camera, though, is awake. Click.

Derek Niemann, 2021

Blackbirds feast on the food of the gods

LANGSTONE, HAMPSHIRE

*A rare sight in British gardens, persimmons
have the waxy, smooth-skinned appearance
of oversized tomatoes*

When my neighbour, a keen plantsman, moved out last winter, the landlord razed the garden, dismantling the vine-laden greenhouse, chainsawing the apple and acer trees, and ripping from the fence the tapestry of clematis, honeysuckle and rambling roses.

The sole survivor was a scrubby persimmon. The tree existed in obscurity throughout spring and summer. But in autumn it came to my attention again, when its leaves flamed red and gold. When they finally dropped, vibrant orange fruit were revealed.

Though persimmons are now a common sight on supermarket shelves, the hardy, self-fertile trees are rarely grown in British gardens. The fruit have the waxy, smooth-skinned appearance of oversized, squat tomatoes, and, like tomatoes, morphologically they are actually berries. The genus name, *Diospyros*, is often translated as 'food of the gods', but due to its high tannin content, the unripe fruit is mouth-puckeringly bitter. It wasn't until mid-December, when the pale, custard-like flesh had softened and sweetened, that blackbirds began to flock to the laden boughs.

Male blackbirds establish a breeding territory during their first winter, but when natural food sources are scarce, they are driven by their need to feed and are therefore more tolerant of rivals, so it's also common for birds to cross boundaries. The first to arrive were the resident individuals, sporting matt-black breeding plumage, with bright yellow eye-rings and bills. They were soon joined by brown-feathered females and several males with duller bills and no eye-rings – winter visitors from northern Europe.

As I watched one male enthusiastically peck the pulpy innards from a wizened outer shell, I wondered how persimmons taste to a blackbird. It's fundamental for most birds to be able to detect bitter, to avoid ingesting toxins, but only a small number of species, such as hummingbirds and parrots, can perceive sweet tastes in a similar fashion to us. While the human mouth contains around 10,000 taste buds, birds possess far fewer – between 50 and 500, depending on the species. So though the blackbirds gorge with gusto, it's unlikely that they savour the slightly earthy, honeyed tang of the fruit in quite the same way I do.

Claire Stares, 2021

Wild clematis in winter is a magical plant

INKPEN, NORTH WESSEX DOWNS, BERKSHIRE

Traveller's joy, old man's beard, smokewood –
whatever you call it, it has a phantom quality

Within the hour, the fog seeded itself, took root and wound an alchemy through the hedgerow. Wild clematis (*Clematis vitalba*) has become a familiar companion, roping together every dog walk, ride, run and drive in my home counties of Berkshire, Hampshire and Wiltshire.

This most magical of chalk plants has an ability to appear and disappear, seemingly at will – though really this is weather related. In wet weather, the sodden, damson-coloured seedheads turn spidery and go unnoticed. In dry weather, the feathery plumes fluff and curl in on themselves, forming globes that catch the light. Then they form an ethereal smoke blossom in silver, gold or bronze, appearing at the same hour for days before vanishing, then reappearing. The plant has a phantom quality.

Halfway between the two weathers, particularly in fog, the seedhead centres of the globes hold a pearl of light in a drop of water. Diffused by the fronds, they glow like tiny Victorian gas lamps.

Wild clematis has many names: traveller's joy, old man's beard, shepherd's delight, smokewood. My preferred name is bedwine, from the old Berkshire border dialect. Adam Thorpe revived the name in his novel of this place, *Ulverton*. Bedwine twines through the centuries and chapters of his book. It's a curious name; the trick is to say 'betwined' in the accent, dropping the 't', then the 'd' so it becomes 'bedwine'.

This winter, I used the thick vines hanging from tall trees as a swing. Hanging like ropes in a school gymnasium, the great, twisted cables seemed to suggest that I should. I stepped nervously into a creaking loop, half a metre off the ground. A hank uncoiled. It did not break, but I was tipped upside down, scattering wood pigeons, caught by an ankle and the unyielding, twisted vine, which had somehow slipped around my waist. I wriggled free and made a slow, undignified fall into the safety net below.

Nicola Chester, 2020

In this buffeting wind, we are light as lichen spores

CHAPEL FELL, WEARDALE

Giddy from the gales, we lean against a stone wall.
Something here is in its element

The weather for today's walk, judged according to Sir Francis Beaufort's wind force scale, feels like force 7 – a near gale. The relevant definitions seem to fit.

'Whole trees in motion'? Branches of a gnarled mountain ash on the fellside, hunched in its own wind shadow after decades of bending before prevailing south-westerlies, clatter together as we pass.

'Inconvenience felt when walking against the wind'? Something of an understatement: strong gusts bring us to a halt and send us staggering back on several occasions as we labour up the steep, stony track.

It is a relief to finally lean over a wall, breathless, to admire the view that we have come to see: a panorama encompassing most of the upper dale, magnificent on any clear day, but exceptional this morning. Today's gale seems to invest it with giddy energy, as if the ground under our feet is shifting.

The north side of the valley is drenched in sunshine and swept by racing shadows of torn stratus drifting overhead, trailing behind it rooster tails of fine rain that become ephemeral rainbows, dissolving and reappearing when the sun breaks through gaps.

The wall we rest against is encrusted with lichens in innumerable shades of green, yellow, orange and grey, which always seem more vivid after rain. These strange amalgams of alga and fungus, ingrained into bare rock surfaces, first arrived here in the wake of the melting glaciers that sculpted this landscape. Winter is their season, wind their conveyance. An encrustation of *Lecidea lithophila* – the texture and colour of a ripe tangerine – is speckled with small, black, jam-tart-shaped apothecia that release microscopic spores, destined to be whisked away across the valley, over the fells.

The showers become heavier. We retreat downhill, holding on to our hats as the wind shoves us in the back. It seems to have moderated a little, perhaps to a strong breeze – force 6: 'Whistling heard in telegraph wires; umbrellas used with difficulty'; had we dared to raise one, it would have surely followed in the wake of those lichen spores.

Phil Gates, 2020

January is a cautious month, the year's story yet to yield

WENLOCK EDGE, SHROPSHIRE

The robins and great tits are still circumspect in their songs, the catkins hang stiffly, anticipating bad weather

January's cautionary snowdrops open in the lee of a stone wall; they are as white as splashes of wood pigeon droppings under their roost tree, as white as snow that has not yet come. Instead, the day is bright and smack-in-the-face cold. Yesterday it rained and smelled of damp sheep; tomorrow will be different. There are emergency sirens on the main road, several: something bad has happened. There is the wave-rumble of a passing aeroplane, going somewhere under a waxing gibbous moon. There is the clacking of jackdaws in tall trees, agitated by something. All this is swallowed by a north-westerly breeze.

A stream passes through culverts underground and can be heard flowing beneath iron inspection hatches in the road. Yesterday's rain, the flush from fields, ditch trickles, all spliced into a watery hawser and dragged through clay and limestone down to the brook, through red roots of alder to the Severn: 'A stone fountain weeping out my year,' as John Donne wrote in his poem 'Twickenham Garden'.

January is cautious about the passing of time, and this end of the year has more to lose. The robins, great tits, song thrushes – they ease themselves from sub-songs into the shine of day on the shoulder of wind, but are still circumspect. There is something lodged in the birds' syrinx, close to the heart, hungry and stern, that holds them back; their evening half-song is now half familiar. Catkins hang stiffly, anticipating bad weather, reluctant to let loose their golden clouds of pollen yet; light catches in the hazel's metallic sheen. In the black buds of ash, purple of birch, bronze of oak and red of hawthorn, the leaves are wrapped tight around a punctuation mark in a story yet to yield.

'You're a caution!' once meant you were astonishing or amusing; January's character is that: fugitive and odd. I dreamed last night that I was given a handful of white pills and swallowed them without thinking, without asking why. The pills were like snowdrops in the lee of the wall, returning as they always do in the comedy of weathers. As it darkens now at five and the forecast is uncertain, owls call the January cautions.

Paul Evans, 2019

We thank Fanny Talbot for this fine view of a wine-dark sea

BARMOUTH, GWYNEDD

The gorse-covered hillside of Dinas Oleu was the National Trust's first acquisition in 1895

You descend towards the holiday delights of 'Brummagem-on-Sea' by the southernmost ridges of the Rhinogydd. This long chain of hills is a byword among hill-goers for craggy roughness, but here at their seaward end they relent to greensward. You skitter down through steep footpaths and alleys, to debouch instantly into the crowded pub-and-chip-shopped streets of Barmouth itself.

Somehow it's fitting that the National Trust's first acquisition, in March 1895, was not a tax-avoidance stately home bequest destined ever more to attract frocks-and-frolics film-location advisers, but a four-and-a-half-acre stretch of hillside above this scruffy little Victorian town. It's called Dinas Oleu – fortress of light – an epithet perfectly descriptive of this bluff that rears up above Afon Mawddach, looking out to the mountain of Cadair Idris, and across Porthmadog Bay to the long northern peninsula of Wales, with the full stop of Ynys Enlli (Bardsey Island) at its sunset end.

These few acres were given by Fanny Talbot (1824–1917), benefactor and friend of John Ruskin, so that the poor and ordinary people of the town might have 'a beautiful sitting room in which to take pleasure and delight'. It still fulfils that purpose. I come here often on fine afternoons, saunter up from the station, perhaps call in at St John's Hall Gallery to muse on Bernard Barnes's vast, visionary canvases, which are unlike anything else in contemporary art, before climbing on by zigzag ginnels to emerge breathless through a mountain gate on to the gorse-flamed moor above.

Beneath me this week, the Mawddach roiled and eddied under the railway bridge. Breakers unfurled against wide beaches with a regular, hissing beat that reached even to this height – as did the frying aromas of the town. High encircling hills of Snowdonia were cloud-palled northerly. Far out west, Ynys Enlli swam whale-like through a band of golden light between cumulostratus and the wine-dark sea. The curving shores of Cardigan Bay led the eye south, south, to the distant headland of Penmaen Dewi in Pembrokeshire.

Cadair was mist-helmeted, the wind gusted cold. I crouched behind a wall, opened my flask, warmed my hands and felt gratitude for Fanny Talbot's generosity.

Jim Perrin, 2019

We have reached an arrangement with the mole

CLAXTON, NORFOLK

The front lawn has been contested territory between
the humans who assume they own it and the creature
that truthfully has possession

After heavy rain, our front lawn looks nothing more than a level, evenly cut sward devoid of interest. Yet its singularity lies precisely in that flatness.

For the past four months that same turf has been the setting for a contest between the humans who assume they own it and the 100-gram creature that truthfully has possession. It is a mole that arrived last autumn and then proceeded to pile up – in about ninety molehills to date – about a quarter of a ton of soil.

How mole numbers can be estimated I'm not sure, but our national total was put at 31 million in 1995, and such a figure implies a cumulative earth-moving operation involving millions of tons every year. Given that moles are virtually universal below an elevation of 1,000 metres, it means these little parcels of the underworld are heaved out over much of Britain. How strange that a creature that barely sees or visits the Earth's surface has so much impact upon it.

In return for all this labour, we have made a bitter enemy of old Moley. For centuries, a whole human lineage – the professional mole-catcher – was and is still devoted to his slaughter. True, it did once cause the death of a monarch – William of Orange's horse threw its charge when it stumbled in a mole-hole – and true, the soil bacteria in molehills are said to ruin silage crops. Yet is the killing really necessary? I vividly recall scenes in the Derbyshire lanes of my childhood where every tine on the barbed wire carried a desiccated mole corpse, with fifty in a row a personal record.

I have worked out that the best way to live in harmony with our mole is to remove the earth as soon and as carefully as possible. If you shovel it up any old how, it seems to trigger the beast into more earthworks and you end up with as many new hills as you originally cleared. Over time the excavations have subsided to a minimum, the lawn has resumed its even temperament, and we have been supplied with the best topsoil for our veg-growing patch.

Mark Cocker, 2018

The quiet scrape of reed on reed

BORTH, CEREDIGION

*Stymied by high tide, I turn inland, to a wonderfully
wild landscape of reed, river and peat bog*

As soon as I reach the top of the sea wall, I realise that I have badly misjudged the state of the tide. Instead of miles of firm sand,
exposed by the retreating sea, I am faced with a jumble of storm
waves breaking against the cobbles at the back of the beach. My
destination, the dunes of Ynyslas a couple of miles to the north,
is temptingly visible through a shroud of misty salt spray – but,
stumbling across the shifting, irregular stones, I make only slow
progress. Cursing my cursory examination of the tide tables, I realise I have read the time for high water, rather than low.

After half an hour, the dunes look as far away as ever. I begin
to consider alternatives. Looking east, I spy the Afon Leri, and
beyond that the great flat expanse of Cors Fochno – a rare survival of raised peat bog, and part of the UNESCO-recognised Dyfi
Biosphere. With a backdrop of steep, open hills, this diverse wild
landscape is an important ecological resource, protected both by
statute and by sheer inaccessibility.

I take a raised track towards the river, the noise of the breaking
waves diminishing with each step. Altered by reclamation but still
valuable, the matrix of reed beds and pools here forms a buffer
zone for Cors Fochno. In the still air, the only local sounds are the
creak of reed scraping on reed, and occasional soft footfall as one
of a group of grazing white horses changes position. As a single
rook guardedly watches my approach, patches of sunlight appear,
leaving the bog mottled and multicoloured.

Arrow-straight as a result of canalisation in the early nineteenth century, the Afon Leri once had a meandering path into the open sea; a small portion of this is still visible as a shallow, weed-choked channel. In the late afternoon sunshine, the surface of the water is tranquil enough to perfectly reflect both the reeds and the blue sky above, until the rising wind – chill and penetrating – breaks the illusion.

John Gilbey, 2018

FEBRUARY

Return of the butterscotch humbugs

*This flock of chattering farmland birds is delightful
enough in itself. It's also the sign of a
conservation success story*

Up ahead, beneath dried splinters of cut kale, the ground appears
to shift. A ripple of small birds is working its way through the
stubble in the morning sun, foraging on fallen seed. Occasionally,
they raise their heads, striped like humbugs, the colour of cara-
mel or butterscotch, and I count quickly, scarcely able to believe
my luck.

I came to this sloping stretch of farmland on the south Devon
coast in the hope of spotting just one of these rare, sparrow-sized
birds. Instead, I'm watching a chattering flock of at least a dozen.

They are cirl buntings – pronounced 'sirl' – and these close relatives of the yellowhammer have every reason to sound chirpy.
Once spread across thirty-nine counties, cirl buntings drained
from the countryside during the twentieth century as agricultural
practices intensified, leaving just over a hundred pairs in the West
Country. In the 1990s, the RSPB launched a desperate bid to save
the species from UK extinction, working with local farmers to ensure hedge-lined fields and coastal scrub were providing sufficient
food and nesting sites.

It worked – these yellow and brown buntings now number
more than a thousand pairs, strung out along the southern edge
of Devon and Cornwall. And while still far from common (they
remain the UK's rarest resident farmland bird), the cirl bunting
embodies something every bit as scarce these days: a wildlife good
news story.

They fly to a nearby blackthorn bush overlooking the sea, perching in the sunshine, seeming to enjoy the mild weather and companionship of their kind. Among them, a handsome male in brighter breeding plumage, sporting stencil-sharp black-and-lemon head stripes.

The cirl bunting may sound like an obscurity for the ornithological connoisseur, with its peculiar name of Italian origin and restricted range, but this is now a species anyone can encounter along the South West Coast Path, well accustomed to passing hikers and dog walkers.

Every one of these little beacons of hope, lighting up the hedgerows, is a cause for optimism. Roll out the bunting and celebrate this conservation success.

Charlie Elder, 2022

Trouble beneath the blackthorn

LONG DEAN, COTSWOLDS

Despite the air of contentment among our small herd
of North Devons, one of them is not well

The cattle are scattered across the top of the bank, their winter coats burnished russet by the light. They know this south-facing side receives the fullness of the sun. Below me, a pheasant senses disturbance, hunches low and scuttles. I note with apprehension the freshly scratched-up patches where a badger has rummaged through the dung for worms – TB is a constant concern.

From the empty ring feeder comes the scent, redolent of a beach at low tide, of the mineral supplement we add to the hay each day.

Fed before dawn, the beasts now lie cudding, eyes half closed, content. A calf from last year stands alone, nibbling bramble leaves, more bored by the idleness than hungry.

I move among them familiarly; all were born on the farm, handled from an early age. These are heifers and cows at varying stages of pregnancy, and the core of our small suckler herd of North Devons. From time to time they will lean back, tilting their bulk of calf-containing belly to the sky, then right themselves again with a great exhalation.

I approach one, examining her eyes, feet, nascent teats. I move her tail aside and see a thick strand of dark, discoloured membrane hanging from her vulva. Her breathing continues with patient rhythm, but mine catches. She has aborted. I rest my hand on the soft warmth of her haunch, and sit with her for a moment in the stillness of the morning.

A blood sample identifies a parasitic organism called *Neospora*. Carried by the canine species and shed in their faeces, this is increasingly an aggravation for farmers who graze livestock on land with public footpaths. It is without cure; once infected, the animal remains infected and will repeatedly abort. Her breeding life is over.

Farming is subject to many variables and, as in life itself, not all exposure to risk can be controlled. There are rich benefits for a herd that is permanently at pasture, but the close cohabitation with nature sometimes has a cost. How we delighted in the summer to see a vixen rearing her cubs in an abandoned badger sett; how we now rue that she chose to make her den there, beneath the tunnelled blackthorn, where the cattle so often sought sanctuary from the tyranny of flies and heat.

Sarah Laughton, 2022

A tranquil scene that masks a dark contest

MORELAND'S MEADOW, BELFAST, COUNTY ANTRIM

The sex life of mallards is aggressive and highly unusual among birds, and has led to a remarkable evolutionary development

An eruption of quacks from a female mallard draws my gaze up the River Lagan. Two pairs. Further on, two single males. Familiarity can breed a dismissive 'Oh, it's just a . . .' but the mallard drake is a splendid creature – the bottle-green head; the primary-yellow bill; the thin white collar over his chocolate-coloured breast. The finely vermiculated porcelain-grey and taupe that sweep down to the rump, with its upturned kiss-curls and white wedge of tail. His mate's plumage is an embroidery of browns, but she shares with him a bright blue flash on the wing's secondary flight feathers, called the speculum.

The reeds stir. Three more drakes emerge on to the open water. A loitering female swims away quickly to catch up with her mate. Her caution is wise. This tranquil scene masks a dark contest.

The sex ratio of mallard populations is skewed towards males, and surplus males gang up to bully females into what biologists coyly term 'forced copulation'. It's something I still find disturbing. Female mallards usually resist, but can even end up drowning. Sticking close to one's mate offers some protection until the ducklings hatch, whereupon their father decamps, perhaps to join a gang of marauding bachelors.

Drakes succeed in mating with unwilling females partly because, as an evolutionarily ancient group, duck species have retained the avian penis, which is highly unusual among birds (for most species, sperm transfer relies on a co-operative genital 'kiss').

But that's not the whole story. Nature has contrived to provide female mallards with inbuilt contraception. The vagina has a spiral that counters unwelcome penetration by a male's corkscrew-shaped penis (the spiral apparently relaxes when a female solicits copulation). It also has dead-end 'pouches' to receive unwanted sperm. An undesired male may win the battle, but he usually loses the war.

So, while some mallard matings may be forced, only a tiny proportion of such matings successfully father ducklings. The female's discerning choice prevails. And it's that choice – what gladdens her eye and, over the generations, likewise gladdened her fore-mothers' – that has evolved to this extravagant male beauty.

Mary Montague, 2022

The strange tranquillity of an aqueduct

PONTCYSYLLTE, WRECSAM

It is a dreamlike experience to watch a narrowboat
float in the impossible space between the treetops

There is a shadow-life to things. From the iron rail at the edge of the aqueduct, the abyss plunges through trees down to the river. Low winter sunlight casts shadows of the piers (pillars), like the ribcage of some great creature straddling the gorge. This massive shadow seems to move, to have a life, an animus free of the stone and iron that make this wonder of the industrial age.

At 38 metres above the River Dee, Pontcysyllte is the highest navigable aqueduct in the world. Its eighteen piers span 307 metres, carrying the 'stream in the sky' – the Llangollen Canal – across the Vale of Llangollen. Yes, it is an engineering feat worthy of its UNESCO World Heritage Site status, but it is not just the genius of engineers such as Thomas Telford that should be recognised, but the lives of all the workers and their families who toiled for years after the first stone was laid in 1795, a dangerous place where many died.

It also stands for those bargees and their horses and canal folk who plied the waterways around the country. Wood smoke rises from the narrowboats of those who inherit that nomadic life. There is a piddling sound as water leaks from a cast-iron joint into the void below. The canal's water level is maintained by Horseshoe Falls, a weir on the Dee beyond Llangollen. Water diverted into the canal, through nature's shadow engineering, is returning to the river.

The aqueduct's shadow is the kind of spirit thing that in superstitions changes the destiny of what, or who, it touches. Local people say that the aqueduct has a strange kind of tranquillity for such a huge construction. To see the shadow of a narrowboat float softly through that impossible space across the treetops is a dreamlike experience. Only birds can fly through the same space. The light changes by the minute. The River Dee has a song of restless travel. The aqueduct is also not so fixed; it has a shadow-life, a thing that roams the valley – moody, ephemeral and transformative.

Paul Evans, 2022

A mini tornado wrapped itself around our house

MARSHWOOD VALE, DORSET

The kitchen window came in, roof tiles smashed and a
15-metre fir tree was felled – all in about two minutes

It was the ash twigs, speared into the lawn like arrows, that made me think again about the nature of the storm the previous evening. It was unlike any weather event I have experienced in Dorset.

It happened after dark, a little before 8.30 p.m. Rain was hurling down outside, the wind singing over the fields. Then the gale transformed itself, wrapping around the house with a screaming roar. It was as if we were inside a gigantic washing machine, water sloshing in all directions, spindle squealing with the weight.

The kitchen window came smashing in, high notes of splintering glass backed by the deeper crash of breaking roof tiles. Flying objects battered and thumped the walls so hard that the house shook and the timbers groaned. Outside, the air was filled with a whirling snow of earth, moss, lichen, bark and ripped plastic. It lasted two or three minutes – and then it stopped.

Agitated and confused, we began to clear up, blocking the broken window with cardboard and parcel tape. By midnight, the rain had ceased too, and we went to check the damage, splashing through puddles, watched by an angry, black-clouded moon.

A big ash tree was down, blocking the road; a tall fir had been uprooted; strong branches had been torn off the oaks and hornbeams. Bramble briars, forcibly blown out of the tangled hedge, hung in bouffant masses like displaced comb-overs. The phone line had snapped and the loose end was whipped tightly around a treetop.

Collecting debris in sunshine the next morning, I found ash shafts, some as long as my forearm, driven into the ground, all pointing the same way. A few metres to the right were some more – aligned in the opposite direction.

How could the wind have blown with such strength in two ways at once? Then I realised: it had been moving anticlockwise in a circle.

Between thirty and fifty small tornadoes hit Britain every year, mostly in the Midlands. Generally short-lived, they usually measure no more than 1 on the Fujita scale, with wind speeds of up to 112mph. It seems we endured a typical example.

Sara Hudston, 2021

A fantasy escape for when lockdown ends

PUMLUMON FAWR, CEREDIGION

One day again I will come to this wild peak, perhaps by way of the moorland lakes of Glaslyn and Bugeilyn

What will I do when lockdown is over? I'll pack a small tent, a sleeping bag, a stove, and – depending on how much rain there's been – will make my way to the north side of Pumlumon, the highest point in the Cambrian Mountains.

'The grand Plynlimon' is how writer and traveller George Borrow's personal guide described it to his eccentric client in 1854. And from the north side, the epithet is fitting. The windfarms that mar the southerly views are hidden from here. I'll pitch camp on a small grassy shelf above the confluence pool of the Hengwm and Hyddgen streams – my favourite wild site in Wales.

Two wide valleys converge here, and they are as desolately expansive as any in the Welsh hills. Perhaps I'll arrive by way of the moorland lakes of Glaslyn and Bugeilyn to the east, along the track from the old gibbet above Dylife. The track fades out after the shepherd's lake and ruined *tyddyn* (homestead), into expanses of bare peat where blanched trunks of rowan trees punctuate the dark terrain.

Or maybe I'll come at it by the rock-spined belvedere of Fainc Ddu, its sky-reflecting pools braided with bogbean, and look north into what Borrow's guide called 'an *anialwch* [wilderness] to a vast distance. Pumlumon is not a sociable country, sir. Nothing to be found in it, but here and there a few sheep.'

It's not changed much since Borrow's day – if anything it's become lonelier, for the old farmhouses and mine workings are ruinous now, shelter only for kestrels or barn owls. If I choose a full-moon night for my visit, peering out across the valley to the hillside beyond, at this time of year I'll see the glimmer of two blocks of white quartz – the covenant stones of the Welsh warrior-chieftain Owain Glyndŵr. The first victory in his great uprising against English rule was gained here in 1401, against massive odds.

Hyddgen is as significant in Welsh history as Hastings is to its English counter-narrative. Early-fifteenth-century court rolls testify how many pledged allegiance to Glyndŵr and his cause, the wild spirit of which lives on in this place.

Jim Perrin, 2021

There's little so charming as the wood pigeon mating ritual

CROOK, COUNTY DURHAM

The male hops and struts, bowing until his beak touches the roof tiles, pursuing his disdainful consort

If their plumage was gaudy, if they lived in tropical jungles, then the family life of wood pigeons would be the subject of a TV documentary. It was dawn in early February, and the cooing outside my window was a sign that breeding – not just feeding – occupied the mind of the resident male wood pigeon. Heavy snowfall soon cooled his ardour, but after the thaw his courtship routine began.

First, wide, parabolic flights across the garden, sometimes accompanied by wing clapping, like pistol shots. Then, hopping and strutting, pigeon-chested, bowing until his beak touched the roof tiles, pursuing a disdainful consort. Eventually, she too thawed. Once he captured her attention, I could watch his *pièce de résistance*, performed in the lime tree at the end of the garden.

They nodded to each other several times, from branches about a metre apart. Encouraged, he gripped his perch, leaned forward until facing almost vertically downwards, and fanned his tail feathers, like a gambler laying a winning hand. A gust of wind nearly blew him off his perch. He managed four performances before she lost interest, but his moves must have worked their magic; next time I saw them, they were side by side, beaks interlocked, sharing regurgitated food.

Today, she is staring down at me from her nest in the willow-leaved pear at the centre of the garden. The rudimentary nest is a flimsy affair, a platform of twigs used (with perfunctory repairs) nine years in succession, often twice annually. I've never seen an egg or chick fall out.

The enchanting culmination of this annual cycle will come in May, when the squabs flutter down from the nest, still helpless, still clad in spiky pin feathers, with thin, soft beaks that they push down their mother's throat to drink regurgitated liquid food. They draw her close with a wing stretched across her back.

It's one of the most charming spectacles in British natural history.

Phil Gates, 2021

The kingfisher's brilliance manages to lift the morning gloom

PURWELL NINESPRINGS, HERTFORDSHIRE

It's out on a stem, eyeing the pond.
Appetites need sating

Everywhere, water is seeping. Filling the ditches and field margins, submerging the paths. The moist air feels heavy and the sedge beds look flat and lifeless as I squelch across North Meadow in my wellies. I've heard reports of kingfishers and snipes in the wetlands, so I'm hoping for an avian encounter to lift the morning gloom.

In the shelter of a hawthorn, I scan a small pond, fringed all around with sedges and reeds, as if all the water's a stage. Tuning in to the ambient sounds (dripping in the brambles, seesawing of a great tit), I wait.

As if on cue, a kingfisher whirrs low over my head and takes centre stage, alighting on a tall reedmace stem at the far side of the pond. In relief against the sepia backdrop, all burnt-umber alder trunks and tawny sedges, the kingfisher is cast in warm copper and jade.

It flicks its head, then plunge-dives into the pond. It reappears with a tiny fish – likely a three-spined stickleback – swallowing it in one fluid motion, not even pausing to stun its prey.

Entranced by the virtuoso performance, I'm unprepared for the jolt as the kingfisher disappears in a blur of brown streaks. It calls in alarm, a series of short, shrill squeaks that tail off as a sparrow-hawk emerges from the sedge, gleaming body in its talons. Stowing the kingfisher in its undercarriage, the hawk sweeps across the meadow and exits through a pinprick of sky into the alder canopy.

I'm left reeling from the speed and impact of the attack, staring open-mouthed at the deserted pond above which a void now shimmers, radiating a manifest absence.

I half expect the kingfisher to blaze back out of the water, but the surface lies impassive. There's no escaping the finality of this dramatic act.

Nic Wilson, 2021

A dazzling array of daffodils

ST DOMINIC, TAMAR VALLEY, CORNWALL

This region used to be known for its variety of narcissi, including some dating to pre-1930 that still appear in their old plots

A succession of blossoms cheers the prevailing grey, belying the fact of winter in my semi-wild garden. Perfume wafts from the thicket of *Daphne bholua*, spread from a single bush acquired more than thirty years ago. Wren and goldcrest seek out insects among the lichens on bare branches. A blackbird, in between gobbling ivy berries, prospects nest sites in the overgrown privet before the next bout of cold.

Several camellias are showing too: the tall *Camellia x williamsii*, whose glossy leaves set off the whiteness of the Cornish Snow on elegant arching twigs, the Saint Ewe with its shocking pink petals and yellow stamens, and the flamboyant double blossoms of Debbie and Donation. Some blooms are singed and dulled by frost, and should be replaced in the next milder period by yet more opening buds.

The adjoining slope to this garden was laboriously cultivated until the mid-twentieth century, when similar areas in the Tamar Valley produced a variety of narcissi for up-country markets. Even the earliest-appearing daffodils were grown out of doors, then picked, bunched, boxed and sent away by rail to be bought as omens of spring, successors to the valley's winter crop of anemones. Some old-fashioned daffodils, dating from pre-1930, still appear in their original plots in the orchard and around the withered hart's-tongue ferns in the regenerating woodland.

Today, the dainty trumpets of Henry Irving have already broken bud, soon to be followed by the larger flowers of the prosaically named The First. Van Sion, known locally as the Double Lent and dating from the seventeenth century, remains in a tight bud; it was once valued for Mothering Sunday's demand for cut flowers. In the parish's abandoned market gardens – which have evolved into woodland – the hardiest, long-lived daffodils coexist in the underlying leaf mould along with bluebells, ferns and dog's mercury.

The few remaining flower growers here mostly concentrate production in polytunnels, sheltered from the wind and rain. Most popular on the local roadside stalls are bunches of multi-headed tazettas – flowers such as Grand Primo, Grand Soleil d'Or and paper-whites, ten sturdy stems each arranged with a sprig of eucalyptus.

Virginia Spiers, 2021

The starling murmuration is beyond any human art

STONEY MIDDLETON, DERBYSHIRE

*Black fireworks, an octopus, a silk scarf in the breeze . . .
it is all these things and more, somehow all at once*

All starling roosts are wonderful, but some are more wonderful than others – a matter determined by numbers, their location, the prevailing light and wind, and one's capacity to get close to the birds. This one was slow to build, and by 4.47 p.m. I was beginning to wonder if it would happen at all. Then there was suddenly an evolving genie of birds.

Soon there were multiple genies, and as these formations re-volved there were convulsive downward movements as hundreds entered the roost and vanished. Yet if thousands disappeared, thou-sands arrived, and the sky became a self-filling vessel.

It is difficult to define precisely why murmurations are so cap-tivating, but perhaps it's this. As they passed, the gyrations sug-gested to me the following: a flock of knots, a shoal of minnows, an army-ant colony in hunting spate across the rainforest floor, an octopus, an anaconda wound in round coil, a broad river's flow but also its arching bridge, an ocean tide, a silk scarf in a breeze; they were autumn leaves torn down by a strong wind, black fireworks, a black rainbow and an amoeba in phagocytosis.

These were not in sequence; they were all manifest simultaneously. I could perhaps describe it best if I took all the letters from all those words and made a single construction that conjured all parts at once. Yet for every observer that imaginary word would have to be unique, because for each of us starlings summon different things.

Bear in mind also that a roost is not an inherited entity shaped by genes. It is a cultural phenomenon, passed on, one to another. Perhaps we should think of it as art involving movement and music, since one has both the geophony of the wind through trees and the biophony of their voices and wings. The closest might be a ballet with orchestra – but recall that there is no rehearsal, and it is entirely functional. Perhaps it's more than any human art. It is starling art: made in soil of earthworms and leatherjacket mash, conceived in the moment, delivered in real time and unique each evening.

Mark Cocker, 2020

In death, the hare had never looked more alive

SANDY, BEDFORDSHIRE

Huge, yellow-rimmed black eyes gave me a hard, bird-like stare. This was ugly evidence of a criminal 'sport'

The warning signs first appeared last autumn on an estate five miles west, mounted on the kind of boards that might advertise a village fete. Two had been banged into the ground at the points where footpaths through woods spilled out into open farmland. Call the police if you see anything suspicious, they said.

Just before Christmas, the threat came closer; a gamekeeper on another estate three miles away told me he had confronted a gang of men. And now, in fields a ten-minute walk from home, we were being wagged at and licked by a Rottweiler–mastiff cross. The dog's big feet suggested the owner was not exaggerating when he said it was only half grown.

Despite its boisterous affection, the dog had more gratifying things on its mind, the scent of blood in its nostrils. It was ducking and twisting, trying to nudge past us to a shape on the ground that we had found lying there minutes before.

In death, the hare had never looked more alive. Huge, yellow-rimmed black eyes gave me that hard, bird-like 'I can see you' stare – the pupils looking back, as if at the last thing it had seen. The animal's forelegs were stretched, ready to run. Its back legs were bent and cramped in the manner of a supreme athlete, hunched haunches betraying the piston power of limbs that could spring from ungainly to sprint in an instant. Its ears, though, looked oddly crimped, as if they were blackened leaves of corn on the cob, and its fur was wet through.

There was an absence of fur along its lower back and rump; instead, a raw-red stain, which the dog was now sniffing. My wife caught its collar before its jaws made a grab for the hare's bloodied flanks.

'Hare coursing,' said the dog's owner. 'It's for the sport. They set lurchers on the hare, then bet on which one kills it.'

The animal's still-bright eyes and bloody wound suggested it had died that morning or the night before. Not killed to be eaten, but killed for killing's sake. We took pictures, went home and called the police.

Derek Niemann, 2020

Forward into spring, back to pre-Raphaelite days

*Urban sprawl has engulfed the farm where
Millais and Holman Hunt spent an idyllic
summer capturing rural Surrey*

The Ordnance Survey app on my phone tells me where I am, but I'm finding the question of *when* I am much trickier. In travelling 250 miles south to a south-western suburb of London, I've hopped almost two weeks forward in the schedule of blossom, bulb and birdsong, and 170 years back in the company I'm keeping.

The first morning, I heard my first song thrush, mistle thrush and blackbirds of the year, saw blackthorn, primrose and alkanet in flower. But at Worcester Park there's no sign now of the farm where members of the young pre-Raphaelite brotherhood spent an idyllic summer in 1851, capturing rural settings *en plein air* with tiny brushes and obsessive attention to nature's detail – rejecting nothing, selecting nothing and scorning nothing.

Back then, the route I'm walking now – part unadopted road, part footpath – was an avenue of elms that led downhill to Malden. The trees are gone. The farmhouse is gone, the ivy-covered door William Holman Hunt used as a setting for *The Light of the World* and the wall where John Everett Millais set *A Huguenot* have also gone.

Having read of these locations in their lively diaries, I'm almost as disorientated by the urbanisation that has engulfed their idyll as they might be. At the crest of the hill, though, there's a swatch of open amenity land with a view just expansive enough to let me imagine the rolling Surrey landscape this used to be.

Near the bottom of the hill, close to the spot on the Hogsmill River where Millais painted the background for his drowning

Ophelia, is a brick and flint church both artists would recognise. I pause under a huge holm oak by the lychgate that looks easily old enough to span the intervening decades. Straggly catkins in luminous yellow shimmying at the tips of the branches acknowledge spring, but the canopy of evergreen leaves evokes high summer. Courtesy of a break in the clouds, I'm granted a sudden sun-dappled moment of light and warmth that is both February 2020 and July 1851.

Amy-Jane Beer, 2020

Winter bees are busy in my garden

LANGSTONE, HAMPSHIRE

The profusion of non-native winter flowers and shrubs in urban gardens, plus climate change, are changing bumblebee behaviour

There was still a dusting of snow atop the fence on the day that I spotted an unmistakable plump-bodied, gold-banded insect flying towards my winter honeysuckle. It was the poet John Clare's 'black and yellow bumble first on wing / To buzz among the sallow's early flowers' – a queen buff-tailed bumblebee (*Bombus terrestris*).

Buff-tailed bumblebees typically have one colony cycle a year, with queens mating in late summer, hibernating underground throughout the winter months and emerging in early spring to found a new colony.

Over the past twenty or so years, entomologists have observed that the species is becoming winter-active in urban areas of southern Britain. Instead of seeking out hibernation sites, a small number of newly mated queens establish nests during October and November. These second-generation colonies are able to survive due to a combination of factors – milder winters, spring advancement and the foraging niche provided by parks and gardens.

There are very few native winter-flowering plants, making it unlikely that colonies could survive in the countryside, but the profusion of non-native winter-flowering shrubs and perennials planted by gardeners provides nectar to fuel their flight and pollen as a source of protein. Buff-tails forage on a large variety of species, and studies show that winter-active bumblebees can attain foraging rates for nectar and pollen that match – or even surpass – those recorded during the summer. During the past two weeks, I have observed several queens and smaller 'worker' females visiting my rosemary, sweet box, forsythia, mahonia, cyclamens and daphne.

It is estimated that a full honey stomach gives a bumblebee just forty minutes of flight time, so when I spot an immobile queen clinging to an unopened snowdrop, my first thought is that she's in a state of torpor, suffering from the cold and depleted energy reserves. I then realise she is 'nectar robbing' – feeding without pollinating the plant.

Short-tongued bumblebees find tubular flowers problematic, as they can't reach the nectaries concealed deep within. Undeterred, this queen has bitten a hole near the base of the petals, poking her proboscis through to suck out the nectar.

Sated, she flies away, leaving a pinhead-sized perforation in the corolla as evidence of her floral larceny.

Claire Stares, 2019

This young grey heron has been hanging out with the grebes

TINSLEY, SOUTH YORKSHIRE

*I was admiring this manic-eyed juvenile, when it
does something I've never seen a heron do before*

Threads of mist are still rising off the water as I cycle under an old railway bridge and spot the familiar shape of a grey heron poised at the river's edge. I haul on the brakes and stop to watch. At my back is the roar of traffic from the double-decker viaduct that lifts the M1 into the sky. To my right are the old Templeborough steelworks, a mile long, where 10,000 people once worked. It's a museum now.

Across the river to the north is the Blackburn Meadows sewage works, one of the largest in England. There's willow here, and a generous stand of bulrushes, but no one would call this the country. Tell that to the heron. Framed against wilderness or motorway, it is no less itself.

This heron is clearly a youngster. Mature adults carry a handsome plume that sweeps back from a black stripe above the eye, a contrast with the dazzling white crown. The head of this one has no plume and is murky grey, emphasising the manic yellow of the iris.

Herons have an angular, almost ponderous grace while hunting, levering each long leg slowly in and out of the water as they stalk their prey. Mine is having none of that. It turns its head with a frown and then does something I've never seen a heron do before, plunging under the surface of the water, like a grebe on steroids, its broad arse bobbing up in the air before it disappears completely.

After what seems an age, the heron resurfaces on the far bank among the cover of reeds and swallows hard. Then it hunkers down, glowering at me like a moody teenager.

I can't fault its attitude. Centuries ago, herons were considered good eating, especially the young ones, known in those days as 'hernsews' or 'hearnshaws'. When angling became popular, they were persecuted as competition. After industrialisation, the River Don was simply too toxic for fish or herons. Now they're moving back in with us, taking up ruined spaces we no longer seem to want. I pedal off towards Rotherham and leave the fisher king to its new demesne.

Ed Douglas, 2019

The winter coat of the stoat is no camouflage now

ALLENDALE, NORTHUMBERLAND

*Efficient killers they might be, but stoats in late winter
are vulnerable to predation themselves, their patchy
white pelt giving them away*

I'm eating my breakfast when I see a flash of white hurtling down the garden path. Reaching for the binoculars on the kitchen table, I see it's a stoat, part ermined, starkly revealed now the snow has gone. Its fur is a rich red-brown with white patches, the brilliant winter coat contrasting with the jet-black tip of its tail. Flowing lightly over dormant flower beds, it streaks over a wall and disappears into the field.

Minutes later, I see the stoat again, limp vole in its mouth. It runs around the square of the garden, keeping to the inside of the boundary, before slipping between the stones of one of the dry-stone walls. It emerges without the vole, which it has cached, storing as surplus food for later. For the next half hour I watch it hunting, undulating along coping stones, its neat little face popping out from under the topiary. As the sun comes up, a mistle thrush sings and backlit winter gnats take to the air.

My garden is undermined with vole runs, the soil sinking as I walk on the borders. There are dark round holes in the thick mats of thyme and chamomile. Handfuls of dianthus pull away where the base of its stems has been nibbled. However, the voles provide food for the stoats and their annual spring litter of kits, as well as for the tawny owls that nest in the sycamore or for the heron that stalks the field.

The stoat's species name, *Mustela erminea*, refers to its valued pelt, which was seen as a symbol of purity and used for ceremonial robes. Efficient killers, they bite through the back of the skull or neck of their prey, able to tackle rabbits far larger than themselves. In turn, one of their main predators is the domestic cat; an ermine will be particularly vulnerable now the snow has gone. It does have a defence trick, though: like a skunk, the stoat can repel attack with a powerful sulphuric stink from its anal glands.

Susie White, 2018

MARCH

I swim on behalf of the life in this river

GRASSINGTON, YORKSHIRE DALES

*The water is dark and choppy, and still
carries the bright bite of snow*

I'm not far from the car when I hear the first rumbles of thunder. I could probably get back before the heavens open. But it's months since I've been in the Dales, and the promise of time with the river has been sustaining me all week. So I continue.

Ten minutes later, my commitment is wavering; glad of my wellies but regretting the jeans. Do I really want to swim?

It's an act of faith to keep going. Faith and a hint of rebellion. The Wharfe was recently listed as one of the most polluted rivers in England, yet part of it – at Ilkley – is also an official swimming site. For its name to be synonymous with filth is an outrage. Even this stretch in Grassington, miles upstream from the better-known polluted part, is not completely safe. Still, I swim, at my own risk and at least partly in protest. After all, I have a choice whether or not to be in this river, but the life that exists in it does not.

The mood of the water matches my own: dark and choppy. Rain hammers on my hood, forcing my head down so that my eye is caught by a swatch of colour at the water's edge. It's a sherd of bright blue china. I ruminate on broken plate, broken river, broken system, broken trust.

A trickle of curlew song, fluid as rain, brings my gaze skywards, and up there is another fragment of blue. By the time I reach the rocky constriction of Ghaistrill's Strid, the overhanging sycamores glitter with sunlit raindrops, and a chaffinch delivers his version of water music – a cascade of notes with a musical trip at the bottom.

My swim is short – the water still carries the bright bite of snow – but the sun is warm enough that I can potter on the rocks afterwards, air-drying for the first time this year.

The next thing to make me look up isn't a sound, but an inkling. A barn owl is sliding over the water at head height – perhaps the darkness of the storm has roused it early. It turns its alabaster doll-face and we're present to each other for an unfathomable moment.

A lucky break, a break in the clouds, a breakthrough.

Amy-Jane Beer, 2023

A funeral for a farmer, returned to the land he knew so well

TEBAY, CUMBRIA

He lived and worked here for fifty years before he handed me the keys. Today we say goodbye

The sun is breaking through the early-morning mist and the ground is frozen solid. It's the sort of morning that sheep farmers dream of: cold and frosty to 'kill off bugs', with sunshine on the sheep's backs. I stand by the side of the road squinting into the sun, waiting for the funeral cortège. The mountains are so steep that at this time of year, we only see sunlight in the very middle of the day.

When we bought our farm four years ago, the previous farmer had to leave through ill health, and while he was happy that it had been bought by a family who wanted to farm, he had already had to move out and did not want to meet us. He wanted to remember the farm as it was, having lived and worked there for fifty years.

This morning is the morning of his funeral, and he is being driven through the farm one last time. The cars crawl down the hill and stop at the entrance to the farm lane. For a minute the cars stay there, giving him a final chance to say goodbye. 'I'm looking after it for you,' I whisper, and the cars drive on.

I feel suddenly very moved by the passing of the farm from one generation to the next, just as I did when his brother handed me the keys, a shepherd's guide and some horn-branding irons. I am strangely affected by saying goodbye to someone I have never met but whose legacy is all around me every day. Ownership of land is just a fleeting thing. As a farmer, I don't feel that the farm belongs to me; I belong to it and am part of it.

Later in the day, as I walk to the post office, there is activity in the church graveyard as the family grave is closed again. The farmer has become part of the land itself. I wonder if he was buried with sheep's wool between his thumb and first finger, as is the local tradition, so that when he arrives in the next world, he has the excuse that his flock kept him tied to the land and out of church on Sundays.

Andrea Meanwell, 2022

Ten days of isolation, and the world is transformed

BADENOCH, CAIRNGORMS NATIONAL PARK

It's still a cool 5°C, but the air is alive with birds, twittering and calling, piping and singing

It's my first walk after Covid. Here in Scotland we still have to self-isolate for ten days, and because I live with a GP husband and a lodger, that meant sticking to a couple of rooms and only sneaking down to the kitchen with a mask and disinfectant spray when they were out. I even stopped patting the dog.

On my last walk before my positive test, the strath (valley) was deep in snow, every tree cloaked in white, the forest silent. Now I'm out again, the world is transformed. Scraps of snow still linger on the hills, but the valley is clear. Today the sun beams from its pale-blue sky and the cohorts of clouds look too lazy to do very much.

Though still only 5°C, the air feels fresh and light on my house-bound skin. I never lost my sense of smell, so I bask in the fragrances of soil and trees again, of the earth opening. Most of the forest near me is deciduous; the aspens, birches and oaks hold all their new life in tight fists, skeleton limbs stark against the sky.

But the birds! The difference in a fortnight is striking, as though they all found their voices when I lost mine. The tracery of branches quivers with them, flitting and bobbing, twittering and calling, piping and singing. Here are all the tits, tiny but insistent, the chaffinches with their downward tumble of notes, the corvids still quarrelling and ruffling feathers, and a lovely mistle thrush, singing its heart out. Doves flute, gulls carry the sea in their cries and a high buzzard pierces the blue. Somewhere, a hidden woodpecker drums.

Down at the marsh, the water's edge is fringed with delicate ice patterns, suspended in the rushes just above the surface. Beyond, a half-frozen slush melts back to water, and further still two swans are feeding, their necks slipping down into the dark and rising again in graceful curves; all of it caught by the sunlight.

I am blessed beyond measure to have come through Covid so easily, to be alive and free in a time of troubles, to hear the world sing on a day like this.

Merryn Glover, 2022

High dales will heal again after the storms

SETTLE AND GORDALE SCAR, NORTH YORKSHIRE

*The winter has taken an astonishing toll here, with
dieback-afflicted ash and shallow-rooted beech
the worst affected*

There are new colours flying from the flagpole on Castleberg
Crag in Settle: summer-sky blue and sunflower yellow. I see them
everywhere now: hyacinths and daffodils outside the supermarket;
black-faced sheep on Warrendale Knotts with blue and yellow smit
marks, the combination no less powerful even where it is uninten-
tional.

The woodland adjacent to Castleberg is a scene of devastation,
wreaked by a different kind of airstrike. It's the same all over the
high dales – the winter has taken an astonishing toll on the most
statuesque trees, with dieback-afflicted ash and shallow-rooted
beech the worst affected. Many have been sectioned and stacked
alongside roads and bridleways. Others lie where they fell.

There are old farmers here who have never seen such winds, I'm
told. The worst came, unusually, from the north, so trees that have
stood firm against prevailing gales found themselves stressed in unfamiliar ways. Post-Covid, I can relate to that. I'm grateful for the
vaccines that primed my immune system, but I'm still taking time
to recover. Hills are a challenge, so I pick routes carefully, contour-
ing, following the lines of dry-stone walls. Some walls have fallen
under toppled trees, and will be reassembled using only what is to
hand. They make me think about resilience, and how we will find
it as the storms keep coming.

I go to a place that I think might have some answers. They call
them scars – limestone pavements, crags and clefts, places where

the Earth shows its bones. Attermire Scar, Yew Cogar Scar, Loup Scar, Great Scar and this one, Gordale. A scar looks like damage, but it actually means healing. The characteristic vegetation on the most challenging parts of the scars is yew – slow-grown, long-lived, winter-green, offering shelter and sustenance, but also poison. They know a thing or two about resilience, these old ones, but also about resistance. They show me how they hold tight with their roots to what is most sure and certain, and open their branches to all that life throws at them. As darkness falls, they whisper that poison, in the right dose, can be a cure.

Amy-Jane Beer, 2022

The last farm in Britain to be worked by horses

SILLYWREA FARM, NORTHUMBERLAND

Two huge Clydesdales are working a field – in 1900,
there were a million horses on our farms

A large grey cat squats in the cobbled yard. Around him is a range of stone-built barns. Protruding from one is a blue and red painted cart. There's no sign of mechanisation, just wisps of hay lying across the cobbles. This is Sillywrea, high above the Tyne Valley, and the last farm in Britain to be worked by horses.

I walk along a track where the mud is studded with hoof prints. Either side, curlews bubble over the fields. Ahead, through a gap in a hawthorn hedge, I spot two horses powering up the slope. Behind them, the figure of a man, bent to the plough. Wheeling above is a flock of white gulls, like one of Rowland Hilder's pre-war paintings of British landscapes. The team works up and down the slope, creating corduroy lines of turned soil, curved and smooth on one side where metal has sliced through the earth.

Stopping to turn at the hedge line, the horses nudge one another, shaking their massive heads, ears pricked towards me. A pair of Clydesdales: one is Alfie, the other is Archie. Brown and white roans, their dark shaggy manes are the same colour as the padded leather collars that let them pull to their full strength. Two horses working a field in Northumberland – in 1900, there were a million working Britain's farms.

Richard Wise makes an adjustment to the plough. Born and brought up on this family farm, his grandfather was John Dodd, who died last year aged ninety-one. The film by Charles Bowden, *The Last Horsemen*, is the story of John and his family, and this, the farm that never converted to tractors. Alfie and Archie pull a sledge in winter to feed the sheep, they cut and turn the hay, they lead the hay into the barn and cart out muck for spreading on the field. Just a borrowed tractor is brought in for baling.

Rope coiled in his hands, Richard clicks to the team and they move off. With an 'Away, Archie, to the gate', they turn into the next field. Rhythmical plods come from their thickly feathered hooves. The sounds are slight: a faint squeak of metal, nodding heads against leather, the song of peewits and skylarks. No diesel fumes, no tractor noise; Sillywrea means 'quiet corner'.

Susie White, 2021

The creature I'm after lurks at the very bottom of the pond

CROOK, COUNTY DURHAM

I should be pond-watching with my grandchildren,
but we're reduced to sending photographs instead

Almost seventy, on my knees, and staring at life below the surface of our garden pond – it's a childhood pleasure that you never really outgrow. Perhaps, too, a subconscious urge to eavesdrop on the lives of ancestral life forms from our evolutionary past, still thriving in an environment that we left behind aeons ago.

I wish I could be pond-watching with our grandchildren, but this year Covid precautions have put paid to that. Sharing discoveries with them digitally is the only option now, so I need some photographs.

Mosquito larvae, hanging from the surface film by their breathing tubes, wriggle away, down through a cloud of pinhead-sized water fleas. Below them, palmate newts, prowling like weightless astronauts, predators poised to pounce with a swish of their tail.

But the creature I'm looking for lurks at the very bottom: the water slater, an aquatic cousin of the woodlouse with an unglamorous job. *Asellus aquaticus*, also bearer of the unlovely name 'water hoglouse', is a recycler of dead plants and animals, and thrives in this oxygen-depleted ooze. The Victorians, who popularised aquarium-keeping, recommended water slaters – more tolerant of neglect than tadpoles – for children to keep and study.

The water is still bone-achingly cold when I plunge my arm in, but the net, full of decaying leaves, emerges teeming with my quarry.

Back indoors, the slaters scuttle across the bottom of the aquarium, dazzled by bright light. Some larger males carry a female under them, ready to mate as soon as she moults her exoskeleton. Within a couple of weeks, these little recyclers from the abyss will carry brood pouches swollen with eggs, then young. With their long antennae, seven pairs of legs and overlapping armoured plates extending on either side of slender bodies, they could be the design inspiration for medieval siege engines.

I upload photographs and press 'send', then wait for questions that young minds will surely ask. There will be lots to talk about when we compare our catches.

Phil Gates, 2021

The last of the redwings slip away

WEST NORWOOD, SOUTH LONDON

These sharp little thrushes have been a tonic to this long winter lockdown – but they've taken off without a murmur

The least they could do is say goodbye. Just a head round the door and 'see you in October'. But that's not the redwing way. They slip off without a murmur, leaving me scanning the trees for one last sighting. Rude.

These sharp little thrushes have been an antidote to this endless winter. Sometimes they've disguised themselves as a patch of grass before flurrying away. Sometimes I've responded to a mysterious instinct and looked up just in time to see one dashing overhead. They've taunted me with their invisibility, the only clue to their presence a chorus of thin *tseeps* from the canopy. But now they've gone, and the new season is finally upon us.

The venue for these encounters is West Norwood Cemetery, one of the 'magnificent seven' – large, private cemeteries established across London in the 1830s – and the heart of my local patch. WeNoCem (as those in the know never call it) is the perfect length for my daily walk. Here among the grand mausoleums and dramatic statuary are well-established trees, areas allowed to grow over, shady paths inviting a slowing of pace. It's a pocket of peace in the south London bustle, an advert for the benefits of urban nature. As I walk through the arched entrance, the rumble of traffic recedes and stress falls away.

Spring is here, bursting at the seams. And boy, is it ever welcome. You can almost hear things growing: dense blizzards of blackthorn; magnolia buds, pert pink candles slowly unfurling; slender, droop-headed narcissi, quivering with energy.

Birds are clamouring. Great tits, a two-note repertoire with variations – the Status Quo of birdsong; a wren – tiny shouter – its machine-gun trill bouncing off lopsided gravestones. An invisible goldcrest pipes up – *tsee-bada-tsee-bada-tsee-bada-scabba-diddle-oo*. Bubble of goldfinch, shriek of jay, plangent screech of angle grinder. Peace is a relative term.

I complete my lap, head for the exit. A *tseep* catches the ear, so faint I might have imagined it. Up with the binoculars, a scan, and there they are. Four of them. The last redwings. See you in October.

Lev Parikian, 2021

Little Ginge is now the mother of ten squealing piglets

HEWOOD, DORSET

*There were silvery-pink ones, black-splodged ones
and a tiny white one – and number seven
nearly didn't survive*

The sow lies on her side, quivering. Along her belly, a double row of blubbery udders judders and shakes. This is Little Ginge's first litter, and we are watching closely in case she needs help.

A pointed tip of pink hoof appears, only to slide back from view. This happens a few times – and then Ginge grunt-shoves and the first piglet flops, wet and liver-coloured, on to the straw. Within seconds it struggles to its feet, wobbling wildly, eyes open and making a quacking noise.

Ginge heaves herself on to her haunches and peers downwards. She lowers her head to sniff, her triangular ears flapping as she gives a series of fast snorts. This is a crucial moment; we step back and wait.

It doesn't take long. Ginge pushes the piglet with her snout and collapses back on her side, exposing all thirteen of her stoppered teats. The piglet noses them clumsily.

A few minutes later, she gives birth again, this time to a strong, silvery-pink piglet trailing a thick umbilical cord. Pig uteruses are forked and embryos form in each half. During birth, the two horns contract alternately, pushing piglets out from one side and then the other. There's usually about twenty minutes between each, but sometimes two are born at once – as happens next, when a pair of black-splotched piglets tumble out together.

The next ones after that come easily: one tiny and white – the runt – and another spotty. But the seventh piglet, a ginger with small spots, is born lifeless. Alexa picks it up and it hangs limply in her hand. She wipes its nose and shakes it gently. No reaction.

'Come on, pig,' she says, clearing its airways. No response. She rubs it with straw – nothing. And then, just when it seems certain it is dead, the piglet retches, gasps and begins to breathe, life inflating its crumpled body.

Ginge produces ten piglets in total. As night falls, we leave them rooting and squealing and slurping around her under the rosy contentment of a heat lamp.

Sara Hudston, 2021

Catch these twinkling stars before their lights go out

LOWER BENEFIELD, NORTHAMPTONSHIRE

*Glow-worms must now go on to the
'last chance to see' list*

In the hedgerows the blackthorn is shooting sprays of small white blossom upwards, thus signalling the end of the winter. If this is so, then we have had an exceptionally warm and wet season.

Perhaps counter-intuitively, such weather can spell disaster for many insects, adapted as they are to sitting out a season, their biggest enemies becoming mould and bacteria that may proliferate in their dormant tissues. Concern turns to the potential impact on struggling populations of insects that have already faced so many challenges, most blatantly the fragmentation and pollution of their habitats. We must firmly add climate change to this list, the most recent evidence coming from a long-term study of glow-worm populations in Essex that found a 75 per cent fall across nineteen sites.

Glow-worms are enigmatic and intriguing animals at every level. I can recall camping near Hastings as a child and seeing one glowing in the vegetation; on investigation, the mysterious light blinked out and the source could not be discovered.

The larvae and the wingless female, *Lampyris noctiluca*, are brown segmented animals, not as instantly recognisable as beetles; they feast on snails and possess a white spongy appendage that extrudes from their rear end and wipes away snail slime. The eyes of the adult male beetle are also fantastic: two great hooded orbs, aerial searchers for the cool, green lights of the females.

'Bright scatter'd, twinkling star of spangled earth,' the Northamptonshire poet John Clare wrote of them in 1820, 'Thy pale-fac'd glimmering light I love to see.' But everyone who is anyone has written about glow-worms; they are in *A Midsummer Night's Dream* and Blake's 'A Dream', as well as Wordsworth, Coleridge, Pliny, Dr Johnson and William Cowper. 'We are all worms,' Churchill stated, 'but I do believe that I am a glow-worm.'

Like coral reefs, glow-worms must now go on to the 'last chance to see' list. There are still places in Northamptonshire and further afield where they can be found, and perhaps this June we should go and see them, while we can.

Matt Shardlow, 2020

Accepted into the fellowship of frogs

BUXTON, DERBYSHIRE

There is something funny and gloriously shameless
about the amphibians' mating behaviour

What is it about mating common frogs that is so humorous? Part of it is surely their physical comedy, such as the winking white throats bellowing in and out as the males chorus at the surface. Then there are the old man's skinny legs on all frogs. My mother-in-law mentions the ear-to-ear grin across every frog face.

Another friend talks about an aura of 'smugness' about them and, indeed, there is something faintly ridiculous about the way one will climb across the spawn lolling at the surface and stand on top, full square, head raised proudly as if in ownership of the entire hoard.

There is also something gloriously shameless about frogs: how they will clamber over their fellows, briefly smothering them or working with those immense hindlegs against a neighbour's face, forcing each gold-rimmed black eye to close, then reopen after it finally passes. None seems to mind either the inconvenience or these levels of familiarity.

The thing I love most, aside from the song, is the animals' collective willingness to accept me. Make a sudden move and you are left with an empty pond; yet slow your pace to a heron's stalk and you can get right down among them. In fact, I can vouch that a human thumb and four fingers at the water's surface can seem highly attractive to an amorous frog.

At that range you can watch each pinhole nostril, billowing air in and out, working precisely as it has done for the last 200 million years. And to kneel in my waders among the pond's abundance, to be accepted on equal terms by its owners, provided a special kind of reward. For a moment, amid the wider church-bell-ringing song of song thrushes and the chiming of great tits, surrounded by the fellowship of frogs, I was allowed to feel that March 2020 was like any other spring, and that all would soon be well with the world.

Mark Cocker, 2020

A flicker of litter turns into a jewel

LANGSTONE, HAMPSHIRE

A suburban sighting of a kingfisher is both surprising and wonderful – I'm surprised to see it so far upstream

Before it reaches Southmoor Nature Reserve, the Langbrook Stream passes through the town of Havant, flowing past a supermarket and several fast-food outlets. As I walk into town, I'm unsurprised to find the bank strewn with sandwich and burger packaging, while midstream the resident moorhen pair pick their way across a raft of discarded soft-drink bottles and crisp packets.

Up ahead, a flicker of turquoise blue catches my eye. At first glance I assume it is a piece of litter snagged on a twig, but as I draw closer, the smudge of colour morphs into a kingfisher (*Alcedo atthis*). Sensing my approach, it turns to face me, its burnished copper breast-feathers glowing in the late afternoon sun.

Kingfishers are a fairly common sight in Langstone Harbour throughout winter. At this time of year these sparrow-sized birds need to consume their own body weight in fish every day, and often move from inland rivers and lakes to the coast in search of food. In Germany, they are called *Eisvogel* – or ice bird – perhaps alluding to this migratory behaviour, though there may be a more macabre origin to the name: on the continent, kingfishers have been found entombed beneath the surface of frozen ponds and canals, perfectly preserved in the ice, their wings tucked into diving position.

But I'm surprised to see this female – identifiable by her orangey-red lower mandible – hunting so far upstream. Parish records indicate that eels, brown trout, sticklebacks, freshwater shrimps and miller's thumb (European bullhead, *Cottus gobio*) were once abundant here; I pass this section of the stream several times a week and only once have I spied a shoal of small, silvery fish – possibly minnows (*Phoxinus phoxinus*) – schooling in the shadow of the A27 underpass.

I watch as the kingfisher's beady eyes scan for prey. The usually clear water is clouded brown with sediment and urban runoff, and there is no sign of the telltale ripples of fish rising to the surface, but the mere presence of this jewel of a bird is a glimmer of hope in this unpromising suburban landscape.

Claire Stares, 2019

Out on the marshes, a lifetime of cuts

HADDISCOE ISLAND, NORFOLK

Wally Mason may well be the only person in Britain still harvesting thatching reed the traditional way

It's easy to lose your bearings among the vast horizons of Haddiscoe Island. This triangular grazing marsh on the borders of Norfolk and Suffolk, enclosed by the rivers Waveney and Yare, feels far bigger than its 2,000 acres, and more remote than its position just off the A413 to Great Yarmouth should allow.

In this stark, late-March landscape of mudflats and drainage dykes, a small figure is cutting water reed. Wally Mason, wearing rigger boots and home-made gaiters fashioned from plastic sacks and baler twine, is the last person to cut thatching reed by hand in Norfolk. He reckons he might be the last in Britain too. 'The work's too hard for most people,' he explains, offering up a clay-caked palm as proof. Most reed-cutters, including his sons, now use ride-on machines, but seventy-two-year-old Wally has used a hook since the age of five and won't change now.

The reed towers a foot above him as he gathers a fistful of stems in one hand and draws a razor-sharp hook through them with the other. It is a smooth, unhurried action, honed by many thousands of repetitions, though a lifetime of this work has left agonising splits along his fingers. After a dozen or so swipes the reed is tied into a bundle, stomped and stacked, ready to sell directly from the bank.

Mason cuts between thirty and forty of these bundles a day, working from December until the 'colts' – new reed shoots – appear in April. For thatching, the stems must be from a single season's growth and as uniform as possible. Local thatcher Nick Walker, here to inspect this year's crop, believes the winds on Haddiscoe produce stronger, more durable stems. For Mason, however, the cutting easterlies are a constant foe, though there are joys to be found in the marshes too. He has short-eared owls and marsh harriers for company, and loves watching grebes while he works: 'Can't they dive and swim!'

Purple clouds are moving silently towards us over the marshes. 'Best get on,' says Mason, blowing on his hands, 'the cold's getting into me now.' He returns to his cutting, and as I head off the island, car heater on full, the hail comes down like pellets.

Tom Allan, 2019

Traditional Lakeland shepherding at its best

HELM CRAG, LAKE DISTRICT

*A flock of pregnant Herdwick ewes is expertly herded
along the rocky fellside by collies and their masters*

Not a solitary sheep tumbles to its death on Helm Crag or Steel
Fell as I watch, though hundreds of them are picking their way
down fellsides bristling with crags and along precipitous trods no
wider than a single bootprint, and they are all pregnant.

The last time shepherds gathered this flock was in December.
After becoming pregnant, the ewes were returned to the fells, finding their way as if by sixth sense back to their native heafs (pastures).
Now they're being collected again, this time for ultrasound scanning to check how many twins might be anticipated come spring.

Usually, the presence of yapping, chivvying dogs might be expected to induce panic in a flock of three hundred or so white-
faced Herdwick sheep and send them falling over crags. But not
these collies. Quick to respond to their master's whistles and hol-
lers, they demonstrate traditional Lakeland shepherding at its best,
always knowing when to bide their time and steady up the flocks
as they move them inexorably downwards. By a mixture of scolding ('Lie down!' to a dog giving over-enthusiastic chase) and praise
('Good lad/lass!' when a command is obeyed), the sheepmen con-
trol their dogs as if by Bluetooth.

The motorists driving along the A591 over Dunmail Raise, the
mountain pass that links the northern and southern sides of the
Lake District, see nothing of this drama – it is only obvious if you
stop and gaze uphill. But from this direction, you can see on the
skyline boulders where no boulders should be. Through my pocket
binoculars it becomes clear that these are not rocks but sheep. As

one moves downwards and further into view, so another takes its place. Finally, like lookouts silhouetted on the summit, three shepherds appear, bringing up the rear to marshal the dogs while the fleecy river becomes a flood.

As the bleating ewes are safely gathered into the farm's sheepfolds, steam rises from their woolly backs like recent mists lifted over Grasmere's icy lake.

Tony Greenbank, 2018

A final sting in winter's tail (we hope)

COMINS COCH, ABERYSTWYTH, CEREDIGION

We were unusually exposed to this particular storm, and I nearly succumbed to a flying piece of chimney

Our house, tucked under the shoulder of the hill, is well sheltered from the usual winter winds that roar out of the south-west. However, the wide, open view of the hills to the east comes at a price – while we missed the worst of the recent bout of snow (the storm labelled the 'Beast from the East'), it still had a significant impact.

The sudden ice-laden squall drove me outside to salvage some tumbling plant pots. When the steel cowl was wrenched from the top of the chimney, it missed me by fewer feet than I would have liked. It then bounded off down the frozen garden, sounding like a galvanised bucket being dropped down stone stairs.

In the aftermath, as we surveyed the damage to plants and property, the wind dropped almost to nothing, leaving a heavy mist. A few days later, the hillsides emerged into muted sunshine; all but the highest peaks had begun to thaw, leaving lines of white where snow had been heaped against hedgerows by the storm.

As the temperature and light intensity grew, birds that had maintained a discreet profile during the strong winds returned to feed. Groups of starlings noisily occupied and explored the newly exposed fields, sunlight bringing out the vivid iridescence of their plumage. Tempted outdoors, I trudged up the hill and looked north towards Snowdonia. The dull murk of previous days had been replaced by banks of cumulus cloud and a brilliantly blue sky, the ice-patched profile of Cadair Idris starkly outlined against it.

Dropping down into the valley of the Rheidol, signs of the freeze were all but gone. Trees dotted along the floodplain showed the slight bright mistiness that colours them just before the leaves finally emerge. Lodged under a hawthorn hedge, in so protected a position that at first I took it for a lamb, I came across a final patch of snow. Hopefully this tired, slumped remnant of winter will be the last I see before the year's end.

John Gilbey, 2018

Dust hazes the barn where the 'red tyrant' sits

CHIDEOCK, DORSET

*This thresher – or 'thrasher', in the county accent –
is nearly a hundred years old and requires
six thatchers to serve it*

The smell strikes you first. A mealy odour, dry and tickly, of clean straw and grain. Beneath it, a hint of juiciness, from bruised ears of wheat beaten to release their kernels. Seeds shaken free leap and bounce into the waiting trailer. Some will be sown for next year's crop; the rest will go for cattle feed.

Dust hazes the barn, where six thatchers serve a clanking 'red tyrant' not unlike the one in Thomas Hardy's *Tess of the d'Urbervilles*. The thresher – or 'thrasher', in the Dorset accent – is scabby and faded red, like Hardy's 130 years earlier, and was manufactured in the 1930s in Lincoln. On top of it is the comber, which is Edwardian and came from Devon. At the back is a trussler, which binds the combed and thrashed straw into 14-pound bundles of combed wheat reed, ready for thatching. A baler rumbles at the side, compacting broken and short straw into rectangular blocks.

Combed wheat reed used to be unique to the south-west. Grown from heritage varieties of wheat with long, strong, hollow stems, it produces plain, plump, rounded roofs finished with distinctive peaked ends like a ship's prow. It takes five workers eight hours to thrash 3 acres' worth. That's enough to thatch the average 30-foot cottage. In good conditions, it might last forty years.

Dave and Scott Symonds and their crew are thrashing Maris Widgeon wheat they grew themselves. They use old machinery not from sentiment but because there is no modern alternative. It's hard work. Sheaves have to be hoisted up to the platform, the twine cut and the stems spread in the comber. The finished trusses are lifted, trimmed and stacked by hand.

Time for a coffee break. Scott turns off the tractor that powers the thrasher and they stump out. I'm left behind in silence. Giant banks of grey-gold sheaves muffle the outside noise as effectively as snow. There's an occasional tick and rustle as the bundles ease themselves or rodents scritch. The thatch has already begun its long career providing shelter.

Sara Hudston, 2018

Searching for saxifrage, remembering Bill

CADAIR IDRIS, GWYNEDD

My last visit to this mountain was with the friend
and mentor from whom I inherited this diary

On foot from the town of Dolgellau, then up Cader Road, the wind biting my cheek cold. '*Gwynt y dwyrain, gwynt o draed y meirwon*' (East wind, wind from the feet of the dead)! I flinch and turn for the Foxes' Path, which climbs a great slope of red scree to the east summit of Cadair Idris.

Thanks to that scree, this is one of the most unpleasant ascents on any British mountain, fraught and unstable even in descent. I remember running down it once and turning a complete somersault as the block I'd landed on chose to career off downhill. No harm done when you're young, but at the age of worn knees and torn ligaments, it's best avoided.

My last visit here was in 1992, with the friend and mentor from whom I inherited this diary. On a fitfully bright January day, Bill Condry lured me down to Cadair, with a scheme to be the earliest that year to record the flowering of purple saxifrage. He taught me to use my eyes and brain; told me he'd not been all the way up this path since 1923. He confided that our mutual friend, Dewi Jones of Penygroes, had recorded purple saxifrage flowering on Snowdon on 26 January. He wanted to beat him. I suggested that his tribe of botanists were every bit as competitive as my rock-climbing clan. We circled to bluffs beyond. Among tangles of thyme, purple saxifrage was in profusion – but not yet in flower. His hands, like a lover's, caressed the leaves and parted them to view.

Today is St David's Day, the centenary of Bill's birth. I recall his ecstatic expression; recite examples of his informed, unadorned style; remember his wryness, humour, self-effacement, his immersion in contemplation of the object.

Snow flurries past, obscuring all. Once more, the saxifrage is not in flower. I turn back into the bitter wind.

Jim Perrin, 2018

APRIL

Private Archibald Browne is remembered

INGATESTONE, ESSEX

Most First World War 'deserters' are not
commemorated with their name in stone. This
remote churchyard contains an exception

A troop of starlings rummage in a patch of dog violets, battling for grubs. There's a skirmish before some retreat to an ivy-shrouded crypt, while a robin flits between gravestones calling a bugle-esque song, declaring territory won.

St Edmund and St Mary's church sits in the centre of the rural village of Ingatestone. Tucked down the side of the churchyard is a First World War memorial. The obelisk itself is nothing unusual, but one name, tucked into the roll call, sets it apart. Pte Archibald Browne, who lived locally, was twenty-six when he was tied to a post, blindfolded and shot, at 4.30 a.m. on 19 December 1914.

Browne was one of 306 men who were executed during the war for the supposed crimes of desertion, cowardice, falling asleep at post and throwing down arms. Browne went missing on duty and was caught. But while most like Browne were given reduced sentences, a brigadier recommended that he be executed to make a 'serious example' of him.

Some of the 306 were suffering from shellshock (what we know now to be post-traumatic stress disorder); doctors understood the condition, but it wasn't enough to garner sympathy. Others were young. Herbert Burden was only seventeen when he was branded a coward and shot.

Often, men from the prisoner's own battalion – who had fought alongside him just days before – had to carry out the punishment.

Some were sick, others cried, many claimed to point their gun away, not wanting to deliver the fatal shot.

The 306 were collectively pardoned in 2006, and a few, like Browne, have their names etched alongside those who fell in battle. Most have yet to be given the same honour.

In this tranquil springtime scene, blossom falls from the nearby cherry trees on to the path. I spy among it a white feather, and place it on the memorial. These soldiers would likely have found the gesture offensive, an accusation of cowardice. But I intend it as an offering of peace, to all those who gave their lives in the First World War. Every single one.

Alexandra Pearce-Broomhead, 2023

To Ukrainians, the storks' return is a glimmer of hope

LVIV, UKRAINE

Forty of them are gliding above my head – our national bird, back for a spring that is like no other

My name is Oleksandr Ruchko and I am a birdwatcher. Because I am fifty-nine years old, I still have another few months when I can be called into action by the military recruitment office, to fight in the war against Russia. Lately, I have been providing bird-watching tours around the parks in Lviv, my home. The tours are with refugees who have come here from cities around Ukraine, including Kyiv and Kharkiv. They've lost their homes, and some have lost family members. I'm trying to help them to be calm and to take a break from thinking about what is happening.

In springtime here you can hear flycatchers, wrens, black red-starts and yellowhammers, and the migrants are coming back to breed, including swifts, chiffchaffs, golden orioles and cuckoos. The most famous is the white stork – Ukraine's national bird. The stork is sacred to Ukrainians, a symbol of spring, of babies, of peace. They're believed to be a kind of amulet and to protect your house against evil. Nobody here kills storks to eat, not even in the worst times like the Holodomor or the Holocaust.

At the moment, it is a problem to watch birds with binoculars or telescopes. Nobody wants to look like a spy. But sometimes you only need your ears and eyes. My wife and I were driving back from the Carpathian Mountains last week, where we had gone for a few days to escape the air-raid sirens. Near to the village of Rozvadiv, we saw above us a group of storks, gliding in the sky. They looked like aristocrats, calm and sure of themselves. The area is attractive for storks because of the Dniester river – its valley has swamps and small ponds that have the right food.

This was a good sign, I thought. It meant that despite the snow in the fields, spring had finally arrived. Maybe they'll bring us peace soon too. The flying bird is the ultimate symbol of freedom. They don't know borders, they need no visas or permissions to spend winter in Egypt, then come back to Ukraine. And we are all happy that they are back safely, giving us hope for better times.

Oleksandr Ruchko, 2022

I follow a cuckoo into the mist

WEST DARTMOOR, DEVON

*These eccentric annual visitors feel increasingly
precious, so they're worth an early start*

A dense early-morning fog blankets the moorland valley. From my garden I can just make out the submerged shapes of scattered stone buildings, soft silhouettes of trees skirting the hillside, the pale disc of the rising sun like a pill dissolving in the mist. I wait, listening hard for the sound that brought me outside.

Then it comes, cutting through the damp air, two notes repeated like a heartbeat: *Cuck-oo. Cuck-oo. Cuck-oo.*

It must have arrived in the night. Now, at dawn, it is proclaiming its arrival on Dartmoor with such stridency it all but silences the chorus of smaller birds. I hope that other early risers in the village are listening too – it feels too important to miss.

Its clear and simple song sounds as if it might carry for miles. I like to imagine it drifting far and wide across the county, the country, that I might share such a precious sign of spring.

We are fortunate to get cuckoos every year along this western fringe of Dartmoor, but as numbers dwindle nationally it is a relief when they return. Fewer and fewer people will get to welcome back this annual visitor. And that is particularly sad for such an eccentric spring celebrity, with its comical clock connections and dump-and-run attitude to parenting.

The cuckoo is also one of a handful of bird species that even non-experts can recognise by song alone – a connection with nature that is gradually being lost.

I get into my car and drive the short distance to the moor. Windows wound down, stopping every so often, I follow its voice in the mist. There is little sense in getting out and trying to close the gap on foot, given the lack of visibility. It hardly matters. It is the sound, rather than sight, of a cuckoo that is so distinctive.

I sit in a lay-by with the engine off, savouring the notes, until the bird moves on unseen. Gradually its call grows fainter, a fading pulse in the fog.

Charlie Elder, 2022

I am deep in a wood that should be ours to roam

YORKSHIRE WOLDS

I follow a stoat down to a gushing spring, and doze off watching a brimstone. This corner of our homeland should be enjoyed by all

Crossing from road to wood is both easy and hard. Easy because the boundary is a single strand of barbed wire, hard because I'm stepping outside the law, again.

The transgression pays off in minutes, though, as three wood-wraiths rise and drift ahead of me through the trees – brown hares, unhurried, seemingly unafraid. I pocket plastic as I go – cartridge cases, baler twine, a foil balloon – but can do nothing about the feed sacks embedded in the soil or decades-old tree guards, brittle and disintegrating.

When I emerge from the wood at the break of the slope, the landscape unrolls at my feet and I understand why the people who interred their dead in the long barrow at the top of the dale chose this place. The chalky turf is spangled with daisies, violets and celandines, and I see my first bee-fly of the year, my first orange tip.

I doze off watching the flame-flicker of a brimstone, and wake to the black-hole stare of a stoat standing 10 feet away. When it finally moves, it is red as a fox, lithe as a ribbon. I follow downhill to a cluster of tumbledown hawthorns and find rushes teeming with little black spiders, and a gushing spring with the signature clarity of chalk water. I drink. It's good, but there's a different thirst that pulls me to places like this.

It's now ninety years since the mass trespass of Kinder Scout in the Peak District highlighted the burning need for a right to roam, and twenty-two years since the Countryside and Rights of Way Act 2000 gaslit us into believing that the 8 per cent of England to which we have free access is some kind of wondrous benevolence. Fine if you live near one. Elsewhere, public foot-paths and bridleways only hint at what we're missing as we cross private land, often hemmed in by wire, or barracked by signage that forbids us from being led by hares, or stoats, or butterflies or old ways.

When I slipped under that wire into the full breadth of my homeland, something glowed in my animal brain. I'm both adrift and connected: fully *out* and wholly *in*. If I had to put one name to that sensation, it is simply freedom.

Amy-Jane Beer, 2022

A push, a pull . . . and the first calf of spring

LONG DEAN, COTSWOLDS

*It's always a happy occasion, but this little heifer in
particular carries great significance for our farm*

It is calving season. By my estimation, having tracked her cycle
from when she ran with the bull last summer, this beast is overdue.
That's not unusual, but she is a heifer – a first-time mother – so I
have been monitoring closely.

She behaved normally at feeding, giving no reason to suspect
change, but later on, as I pass through the woods with the dogs,
I see her down. By habit, I inspect. She seems uncomfortable, her
breath pulses shallow and quick, though she has been doing this
intermittently for days.

As I look, there is a sudden expulsion of fluid at my feet. She
stands abruptly, just as surprised as me, and sniffs the ground.
Then she makes the tenderest of sounds, instinctively communi-
cating with her unborn calf.

There is a primitive power in this moment when a life is about to
be made living, but additionally so in this instance. The mother of
this heifer was our original matriarch, a cow we relied on. In 2019,
she was condemned with TB, along with almost half our small
herd. We wondered if the farm could continue after such a big loss,
but the orphaned calf – her only surviving progeny – felt reason
enough to try.

Progress is steady. She alternates between lying and standing.
When she goes down, I make sure the calf is presenting correctly –
two blanched hooves, pointing down; inside her, I feel a nose. But
steady becomes slow; she is losing momentum. At the next wave of
contractions, I go to help. With both of us straining – she pushing,

me pulling – we inch it out until the calf fully emerges, a warm, slithering mass.

It is momentarily lifeless, its tongue blueish and swollen. I prop it upright and clear her airways. Mum licks, I rub, we both urge encouragement. Then it blinks and gives a slight shake of its head. It is alive – and it's a heifer.

Opinion is mixed on the naming of livestock, but sometimes the case is clear-cut. Given her provenance and her future potential, we call this new calf Faith.

Sarah Laughton, 2022

A pregnant pause as the ewes return for lambing

TEBAY, CUMBRIA

We rest on the brow of the hill. Even with the uncertainty for small family farms like ours, there is much to be thankful for

It is three and a half miles from one end of the farm to the other, and shortly before lambing we must walk the pregnant sheep home. Since December, the ewes have been grazing down in the lush green pastures surrounding Low Park Farm, which was abandoned fifty years ago when the previous occupants emigrated.

The field systems and the walled garden still survive, but the farmhouse has collapsed. Now only rough fell sheep live there, among the ruins. My son lets out a long cry of 'Come on', and the sheep slowly turn to face north and head for home – Low Borrowbridge Farm. Most have been here all their lives. They know the routine. They are heavy and will tire on the walk, just one week out from lambing. So we walk slowly.

The fields around our farmhouse have been rested for several months and the grass is growing. This grass will enable the yows to make enough milk for the first week of the lambs' lives, before the return journey.

For the first half of the walk, we cannot see home. But there's a moment when the horizon creeps above the yows' heads and the farmstead appears, nearly two miles away. As we approach the brow, the farm spreads beneath us. There is a gate that used to mark the boundary between the farms. We pause there. I call this gate 'Rest and Be Thankful', after the Scottish beauty spot.

I am thankful that despite the political uncertainty about the future of small family farms, we are still here lambing this year. I am thankful that my son is here, taking on the farm for the next generation. But above all, I am thankful that the sheep look well and the weather looks settled before they lamb.

We set off again: two people, one dog and several hundred sheep moving slowly across the landscape.

Andrea Meanwell, 2021

There's a ruckus in the rookery now school has returned

HUNGERFORD, WEST BERKSHIRE

When the bell goes and the pupils move inside, the rooks fall quiet and descend to the playing field

The rookery by the old priory seems strangely subdued – until I remember it is a Saturday. Situated near to farmland, between the common and the secondary school, it is a circus on school days.

Then, the rooks sway on their piratical treetop masts, cawing with a forward bow as the tree dips, as if they were surfing a wave. They cheer me in to work and barrack me out again, just as they do the school buses from the villages and other rookeries.

At breaktime, the students are just as raucous, as the gruff voices mingle with the sharp ones. But when the bell goes, and the classrooms fill and fall quiet, the rooks quieten too. They descend, boldly, their blue-black wings flapping like blazer tails in the breeze. I watch them through the library windows. They arrive with a confident bounce, and swagger across the grass to pick up sandwich corners or pull shiny crisp packets out of the bins, littering the field – something the students will be admonished for the next day.

They're magnificent birds, their bare faces and bone-grey bills reminiscent of Shakespearean plague masks, their feathers glossy with good, greasy living. In the light, their blue hue is like the sheen from a broken ballpoint pen. They lope among the blue-eyed neatness of the smaller jackdaws, shaggy-throated year 11s to the jackdaws' more awkward year 7s.

I wonder what they made of the last lockdown, when four hundred children and their snacks became thirty. For the birds, perhaps it was a kind of extended, unseasonal summer holiday, when they would be catered for instead by the picnics and cows on the hot common, pecking at drying cowpats and riding on the backs of heifers, picking at ticks. Although none of those things would have been there. It's hard not to think that the ruckus, now that the buses are rolling in again, is as appreciative as a round of applause.

Nicola Chester, 2021

All of life lies in the planted seed

STOKE-ON-TRENT, STAFFORDSHIRE

I plant French marigold, calendula and nasturtium.
This is the first hopeful step to turning my yard
into a small wilderness

My countryside is a small terraced yard, bricked in by peeling houses and crumbling walls. It is the only countryside I've had access to for a long time, but it has all the important parts: good earth, things that grow, things that sing, crawl and buzz. My physical disability keeps me contained here, but despite me, it is a place of endless life and movement.

Every year, seeds become good companions in constraint, teaching me what restriction is and what it isn't, showing me when to wait and when to move. However long and cold the winter, eventually I get to take my first unsteady steps down the path to the potting shed – the old outhouse, in fact, piled high with seed trays and flowerpots – to begin anew. No matter what grew or failed last year, I get to fill the trays, start again.

The wonder of it. French marigold seeds like fairy arrows, the dried-up caterpillars of calendula, shrivelled brains of nasturtium. Seeds like stories. Seeds like dust. It takes me forever to sow because I can't help but pore over them. They are young like me, but look tired, dry and useless, much like me too, and yet, and yet . . . I hold these tiny, still specks and I know that, with enough of them, I could leave this place and turn this town into countryside. Sometimes I imagine throwing them in fistfuls from my mobility scooter, slowly watching flowers take over every overlooked crack.

For now, I scatter my seeds neatly, restrained, into my waiting trays, satisfied that the small wilderness I can make in my yard is enough. But I like knowing that I could. Perhaps all seeds dream of spreading.

Josie George, 2021

The ospreys are back – this is the ultimate spring thrill

BADENOCH, CAIRNGORMS NATIONAL PARK

*The sight of the male taking up his proud perch
and the sound of his high-pitched call mark
the climax of the season*

The ospreys are back! All the way from west Africa, more than 4,000 kilometres away, these powerful birds of prey have returned to the Scottish Highlands to breed. There is a nest near me, a twiggy crater the size of a truck tyre balanced precariously at the top of a tree on an island in my local loch. Part of the floodplain of the upper Spey, this area is called Badenoch – 'the drowned lands' in Gaelic – and is cradled by the Cairngorm mountains to the northeast and the Monadhliaths to the south-west.

Ospreys pair for life, and the male comes first to prepare the nest, usually returning in the first week of April. For me, the sight of him taking up his proud perch and the sound of his high-pitched call ringing across this amphitheatre mark the climax of spring. This arrival is not just a sign of the eternal cycle of seasons and renewal of life, but of the possibility of recovery. Persecuted to extinction in Scotland from 1916, ospreys began recolonising naturally in 1954, and there are now 158 breeding pairs who can hatch up to three chicks each year.

Just a week after the male returned, spring was overthrown by winter again, with snow and bitter cold winds. I wondered if he was cursing his northern home. If so, he will be joining the local shepherds muttering darkly at the 'lambing snows' of April.

Today I crunch down to the lochside over a sparkling white crust, and stare through my binoculars, the sun cresting the hills behind the loch. The osprey silhouette takes off, and there, like a cutout copy behind, is a second one. The female has arrived. The male comes and goes, once presenting a fish – the mainstay of their diet. On another return, he hovers in a display of wing-beating and wild cries, light caught in his feathers.

He must woo his mate every year, as a competing male may arrive. The delivery of fish, nest-building and sky-dancing are all proof of his prowess. I think his efforts are succeeding, as when he settles down, he is rewarded by a look and a touching of beaks.

Merryn Glover, 2021

Lessons from the birds on self-isolating

BELFAST, COUNTY ANTRIM

With the flight path above my home fallen silent, I hear
the birds clearer now. And their message is all the same

Working from home, I'm heeding the counsel of master self-isolators. Every spring, male songbirds emerge and turn this street into a racket of announcements and warnings.

It begins with the robin's plaintive heralding of first light. If I shook off the duvet's warmth and peeped through the curtains, I'd see him on his regular streetlight song-post. But I tell myself the movement will disturb him, so I lie on to listen for the dunnock. He's due any minute. I tense with waiting, praying that his predilection for the garden's low bushes has not meant that he has succumbed to a cat overnight. Ah! There's his cheery warble. I can get up.

Breakfast is both strangely quiet and startlingly noisy. I live under an airport flight path that's weirdly muted. But the absence of planes magnifies the birdsong. The chaffinch, with his individual take on the terminal flourish of his species' song. Two wrens rattle sabres across a no-go zone that includes our back garden. Eventually, my neighbour's wren falls silent. I settle to my laptop.

Throughout the day, I get more reminders of the importance of social distancing: the song thrush in the canopy that fringes the River Lagan, his flutings clearly audible against the traffic's lowered growl; the cosy house sparrow chatter that accompanies lunch; the slurred exhortations of a collared dove; the thin exasperation of a goldcrest. The tunes vary, but the message is the same. In the afternoon, the nearby pedestrian crossing beeps, and a great tit responds with furious monosyllables. I wonder who has provoked it, for when I check the window there's no one to be seen.

Evening: our blackbird has assumed his usual position on the chimney opposite. I stop to listen to his gorgeous baritone. And further away, another. And another. The chain of song reminds me of 'all the birds' of Edward Thomas's poem 'Adlestrop'. 'Farther and farther.' All heeding, all reminding each other: 'Keep your distance, keep your distance.'

Mary Montague, 2020

Lockdown silence is big and strange

WHARFEDALE, YORKSHIRE DALES

*With human interactions suddenly fraught, I'm
grateful for it all: the mewing buzzard, the chirping
dipper, the gentle encounter with a stranger*

In Lower Wharfedale, there are new kinds of silences everywhere. Around Beacon Hill, on the Chevin, the seismic roar of aircraft booming off to Edinburgh or Alicante has given way to the white noise of a sunny heath in April; a silence textured with the bee-charged buzz of a goat willow, the delicate song of a dunnock or the soft gloops of mating frogs in a pond. Along the verdant stretch of the Wharfe near Otley Mills, where peace is usually eclipsed by the rush of the A660, birdsong glitters in the fresh green trees like sun in a stream, and a dipper alerts me to its presence with the tiniest of chirps.

Today, in the high pastures north of Otley, the Harrogate road is so empty I could nap on it, and the silence up here is big and breezy, with buzzards mewing and curlew calls bubbling up from the hazy fields below. You can hear these things usually, of course, but in this strange world of light traffic and unblemished skies, the clarity of it all feels like hearing with new ears; the lockdown has brought a wild quiet to populated places.

I don't mean to suggest this horrible coronavirus situation has done us a favour by turning the countryside into a prelapsarian paradise. The silence can also be eerie and strange, or mask an underlying hostility. Huge construction fencing has been put across the right of way that runs alongside Lindley Wood reservoir, not far from Otley. Residents in nearby Clifton have put up 'locals only' signs around the public road running through the village and have berated passing exercisers.

A little later, the path goes close to an elderly farmer working in a field. I approach tentatively, but my caution is misplaced: we chat amiably about the weather, and she laughs at my careful, fretful use of the gate. It is an ordinary, gentle encounter with a stranger, and I am excessively grateful for it.

Carey Davies, 2020

Trapped in our garden with a gang of outlaws

WENLOCK EDGE, SHROPSHIRE

*The robin, bee-fly and other anarchic creatures
enact their Wild West dramas of the soil*

Billy the Kid rises from the grave in our back garden. Scuffing the soil in the shadow of a flowering currant, my daughter's eye is caught by a tiny human shape. She picks it up and rubs the subterranean years off to discover a little brass figurine, an inch or so tall, of Billy the Kid. His rifle is broken but his cocky pose and battered sugar-loaf hat are as distinctive as the 1880s photograph taken not long before he was shot dead aged twenty-one. How he got here goodness knows, but Billy shines in bright spring sunshine.

He's not the only outlaw in this garden. Watching from the hedge is Robin Redbreast. As quixotic a mix of charm and violence as Billy, Robin is a mythic creature loved by the people, too. He cocks his head to watch everything we do. He has no fear of us. We are, after all, only substitutes for wild pigs rooting through the earth; he waits for a fork to turn up the real treasure in the soil – worms. 'Who killed Cock Robin?' asks the eighteenth-century murder rhyme. 'Who saw him die? / I, said the Fly / with my little eye.'

A ginger dot on whirring wings bounces over the surface of the soil in a curious flight behaviour called 'yawing'. This is *Bombylius major*, the large or dark-edged bee-fly. She is searching for the tunnel entrances to the underground nests of the solitary bees that she mimics. The bee-fly is a true fly and a parasite of bees; she will flick her eggs down their tunnels, and when they hatch they will wriggle into the bees' nest to feed on the larvae. In the meantime, the bee-fly's yawing helps pollinate spring flowers.

Anarchic creatures enact their dramas in the Wild West of the soil. Buried secrets and the dirt under our fingernails connect us back to growing and the source of life.

Paul Evans, 2020

Fishing teamwork between heron and goosander

LLANDECWYN, GWYNEDD

I watch in wonder, and am left in no doubt that there is communication between the two birds

After descending from the Rhinogydd, I rested against an outcrop that juts into the exquisite water-lily lake of Llyn Tecwyn Isaf, and watched.

A grey heron soon came stalking round the shallow margins, aware of my presence, his suspicion allayed by my stillness. I wondered if he might be one of the nestlings I visited each day five years ago, in the heronry among the larches of Harlech Castle. To see (and hear – herons are very vocal birds) the whole process of their rearing at close quarters over several months was enthralling. Those fledglings' parents would surely have fished in this teeming pool, before labouring back against the wind to disgorge the contents of their crops into the ramshackle, stinking nest, while the young birds kept up their bizarre, cacophonous repertoire.

That cycle is beginning again now, the heron fiercely intent on fishing to feed his sitting mate. As I watch, he strikes, comes up with a flash of silver in his beak and juggles it down – a small trout, perhaps, or a gudgeon. A splash behind him momentarily distracts. He peers round. A drake goosander has alighted on the lake and is swimming rapidly towards him. I focus my glass, see the dark green of his crown, the faint early-spring flush of pink across his ivory flanks, the teddy-boy greased-down head plumage. He scuds across to the heron, dives in the deeper water a few metres away, and also comes up holding a silver fish.

The heron returns to his task – another stab, another fish. And for the goosander, too, another brief but fruitful dive. I have the clear impression that there is communication between the two birds. The goosander dips under again, resurfacing seconds later 10 metres away. Luckless this time, he sails across the pond. The heron watches, then breaks into an awkward, splashy run through the shallows to the goosander's new fishing place, where both birds again strike lucky. Teamwork? I think so.

Jim Perrin, 2019

That Darth Vader soundalike is one ungrateful beaver

CROPTON FOREST, NORTH YORKSHIRE

Beavers are being reintroduced to maintain flood defences, but some seem happier about it than others

We make a strange procession as we descend the steep trail in single file, like a scene painted centuries ago on a Chinese silk scroll. We wind between tall pines and rhododendrons, crossing tiny watercourses and cascades. In the midst of the group, two large wooden crates are carried, slung from stout branches.

This is Cropton Forest, a part of Yorkshire that, thanks to a Forestry England flood management project, is about to regain something of its primeval identity. Earlier in the day, a huge and deeply disgruntled female European beaver hurtled into one of the crates from her temporary lodgings at a local zoo, 25 kilos of rage. Through the mesh door I glimpsed lustrous fur, two bright eyes and a flat black nose, before she turned and slapped a tyre-tread tail against the mesh, an emphatic gesture of rejection.

Her mate in the second crate is smaller, younger and silent, but the female keeps up a mixture of Darth Vader mouth-breathing and dinosaur growls all the way to our destination: a large pool, pea-green with duckweed, fringed with alder, goat willow and birch, flag iris and wild daffodils.

The crates are lowered, and we step back. The air is warm, heady with birdsong. New leaves are pushing the last old brown ones off the alders. Daffodils bob and quiver. The growling stops.

Quietly, the mesh doors are opened. The female is first out and makes for the pool, hauling through the shallows like a hippo. As soon as water depth allows, she starts swimming, directly out into the middle, and on without a backward glance, disappearing into the carr on the far side. We don't see her again.

The male, however, takes his time. He potters to the water's edge, then spends the next hour gliding back and forth, leaving a slow, swirling wake in the weed and pausing often to peer around. He nibbles some leaves from an overhanging dog rose, then clambers on to a mossy, sun-dappled log and begins grooming with dexterous, careful paws.

Amy-Jane Beer, 2019

This spring belongs to the red dead-nettle

CLAXTON, NORFOLK

The unexpected super-abundance of one particular plant at this time of year is always a welcome surprise

I'm often struck by the extreme seasonality of many parts of nature. A recent example here was a colony of Clark's mining bees, which occupies a wood bank on the way to the marsh.

On 20 March it had an almost metropolitan sense of busyness, with hundreds, if not thousands, of insects. The whole stretch was pitted with holes and small mounds of 'mine tailings' composed of the crumbly soil where the bees had dug out egg chambers, to which they trafficked leg-loads of sallow pollen as food for their young. Yet when I went to check on 5 April, it was not only deserted, but the vegetation had so smothered the earthworks that soon you wouldn't know the bees had ever been there.

Another example of this seasonal brevity is the recent blooming of common whitlow grass. Everyone has seen it, if only in their dreams, since it best registers at a subliminal level. It is the ground-hugging crucifer that loves kerbs, concrete, cracks and construction sites. The 2-millimetre flowers create that white pointillist flush in early April, which brings a strange delicacy to the crash barrier on a motorway's central reservation. The flowers come and go over a two-week period, adding a ha'p'orth of re-assurance that the world is turning truly.

Then there is another kind of seasonality, one that is less regu-lar but more dramatic. It's the unexpected super-abundance of one particular plant. Sometimes it's buttercups, and 2010 was one of their last big years. Spring 2019, however, belongs to the red dead-nettle. I've never noticed such a flowering, but would love to understand what causes this change of behaviour in a plant that's already widespread and highly adaptable.

Red dead-nettle is a total misnomer. The flowers are magenta, and in Claxton nothing could be more vibrant and quick-growing. To fulfil someone's obsessive notions of tidiness, our village green suffers an all-too-frequent mow that wastes both carbon and money. Mercifully, within days, red dead-nettle, daisies and dande-lions have practised the forgiveness of nature and restored colour, bees and butterflies to a shorn, lifeless space.

Mark Cocker, 2019

Spring arrives on many wings

FERRY MEADOWS, PETERBOROUGH

Bumblebees, mining bees, honeybees and green furrow bees – they've all awoken from their slumbers and taken to the skies

Spring arrives on many small wings. During the winter the insects retreated to the undergrowth, but the freezing easterlies have now passed, and the gentle warmth of the sun has released the bees and flies from their deep slumbers.

Ferry Meadows is busy with families enjoying the open air, the meadows and flooded gravel pits. A young girl and boy, engrossed in play, pick daffodil heads and marsh marigold flowers and cast them on to the surface of a pond. The spring flowers are as attractive to us as they have been to pollinators for 80 million years – although some of the less conspicuous flowers are the most appealing to the emerging bees. The bumblebees – the common carder bees (*Bombus pascuorum*) in their golden fleeces and the big bumbling buff-tails (*Bombus terrestris*) – favour the dead-nettles and sallow blossom, while the various fluffy brown mining bees (*Andrena* spp.) frequent dandelions and blackthorn blossom.

The mining bees could be mistaken for small, hairy honeybees, but the green furrow bee (*Lasioglossum morio*) could not be confused with a honeybee. She is less than 6 millimetres long, not at all furry and glistens metallic green. Despite being common, furrow bees are rarely observed, and most people are surprised at how small a bee can be. This lack of familiarity is a pity, as they exhibit plenty of endearing beeish behaviour. This one allows me to watch up close as she ferrets about in a daisy.

Nearby there must be an area of bare ground where she and her kin will soon start to dig their nesting burrows. Although each female furrow bee builds her own nest, the bees nest close together and co-operate, sharing foraging and nest protection duties. Her first offspring will all be female, which enables a deepening of their egalitarian society when her daughters then help their mother to provision their next brood.

Matt Shardlow, 2018

On the trail of elusive wood anemones

ABBEYDALE, SOUTH YORKSHIRE

Years ago, I stumbled across a patch of bone-white flowers that I've treasured ever since. Could I find it again?

When our children were young, we'd take them on voyages of exploration to an extensive patch near our home of what is sometimes called the unofficial countryside, and by 'unofficial' I mean, of course, forbidden. Trespassing wasn't mentioned, but children know when parents are being shifty. The subterfuge only added to their excitement, and having to ford a river to reach this lost Eden was very heaven.

One April we stumbled across a large patch of wood anemones that hardly anyone would ever see, treasure that could never be moved. So when this past winter suddenly gave way to blazing sunshine, I wondered: could I find it again?

Despite the sun, the moors were still heavy with rain, so the water flowed deep and fast. I threw my boots to the far bank and teetered across, immediately rewarded with a thick spread of ramsons, still fresh with dew. This is a plant almost designed to please children. It stinks and you can make up stories about the bears that grub for the bulbs (wild garlic's Latin name being *Allium ursinum*). I stepped carefully, toes pushing into warm earth.

On top of this sensuous richness was a wall of sound, a depth of birdsong increasingly hard to find on these fringes of the Peak District: chiffchaffs and blackcaps, wrens and nuthatches, wagtails zipping down the river and trees full of jays. A woodpecker chattered to its mate on a neighbouring oak before both fled at my approach: so elongated against a tree, so stubby-tailed and compact in flight.

But of the anemones there was no sign. Was I in the wrong place? Ahead of me was an expanse of brambles so thick that I put my boots back on. As I stepped cautiously, the thorny mass finally cleared to reveal a patch of bone-white flowers turned towards the warm sunshine. It was much as I remembered, certainly no bigger. Wood anemones spread so slowly, rhizomes creeping through the soil, that their presence is a drift of time deeper than the oldest trees around me.

Ed Douglas, 2018

A predatory fish out of water

SANDY, BEDFORDSHIRE

There was something terrible about this pike, so strong and adept, as it broke loose from its watery domain

The inflatable banana caught my eye again, drawing my attention from a stretch of riverside towpath that had been mined and undermined by rabbits, tunnelled by moles and pummelled into unevenness by the hooves of the Travellers' horses that were once left loose to run here.

The day before, on the same walk, I first saw the metre-long, primrose-yellow plastic banana lodged in bankside vegetation, as clean and bright as the moment it had been laughed down a weir or launched on the water to see how fast this bent canoe would go. Did they wonder if their joke would carry to the sea, the open ocean? Did they think the river was a sink that would wash it down the plug hole? Had they even heard of microplastics?

Unable to retrieve it, I walked on, still simmering, only to be distracted by a snatch of movement on the surface of the river. My brain was computing the possibility of a rat or water vole, when up it burst out of the water, the head of a giant pike, the length of my hand. It opened its long jaws in a great yawn, to display a mean row of jagged teeth. It fell back into the river, then up it came once more, baring the insides of its pale, membranous mouth. I looked into the big, black, blank dead eye of a fish that was very much alive. There was something terrible about this predatory fish out of water, so strong and adept in open air, breaking loose from its watery domain.

The pike sank one last time, then rose to leave the rim of its jaw glowering on the surface. A fish expert told me later that this might have been a male engaged in some ritual of breeding activity – a show of strength, perhaps? And then I thought of this animal's descendants decades hence, opening wide to swallow small fry, the little fish that would themselves have gobbled down bits of water-weed, mixed in with a fruit salad of plastic banana.

Derek Niemann, 2018

MAY

A bog is only quiet at human height

FLOW COUNTRY, CAITHNESS AND SUTHERLAND

*Lower yourself to peat-bog level, and you'll
find a burst of pops and gurgles*

The white flowers of the bogbean shake, sprinkling starlight over
the bog. They stand unsteadily in the pools, moving with the slightest wind. As the first colour of the morning fills in, it comes not just
from above but below, where red mosses glint from the dark peat.
Sphagnum capillifolium – acute-leaved or red bog moss – forms
dense hummocks, rising from the ground like an outward pulse of
blood: a fleshy, silent circuitry.

Stretch upon stretch of red courses through the heather and bog
myrtle, while the dim mountains beyond are hugged by cloud.
Shadows move in. Rain begins. Small circles form on the top of the
bog pools as the sweet scent of myrtle washes through. The only
sound is the rain hitting my coat and the surface of the pools. The
only movement is the drop of the water and the cool brush of leaf
into leaf, stem against stem.

I lower myself and listen. Here, by the bog, there is a squelch
and a gurgle and a pop. Here, by the moss, is a sink and a suck and
a thirst. Known hoarders, some sphagnum mosses can hold around
twenty times their own weight in water.

Most peatlands, above the water table, receive their only water
from rainfall. And there is an urgency now to the drumming fall
and its eager recipients. The water's volume increases with each
passing minute. Tiny springtails leap between the leaves, their
crashing bodies finding their feet in rhythmic miracles of landing.
This close to the sphagnum is a sounding of what is often hidden,
a burst of microscopic living. The bog is only quiet at human

height. The moss is only silent from our distance.

I pull myself back up, following the trails of red bog moss through the heather. Its silent circuitry is now one of pops and tremors. Its exposed veins are flaming tributaries flashing by the rising pools. The bogbean quakes in the rippling rain. The mosses soak, filled with light again. Day breaks. Rain slakes the yearning ground.

Elizabeth-Jane Burnett, 2023

There are blue tits in the bird box, repeat, blue tits in the bird box

WEST NORWOOD, SOUTH LONDON

After four years of sitting empty, the bird box is the centre of the universe – for the blue tits and us

They have a routine. Swoop into the hazel. *Chhrrrrrrrrrr-chidik*. Check for danger. Look left, right, left again. Alert, always alert. Up to the feeder. Flick tail, peck food, turn, peck, turn, flick, back to the bush. Whizz, whirr, flurry.

Busy birds, blue tits. But today their routine changes. From the feeder, not back to the hazel, but up to the box on the whitewashed wall near the kitchen. We installed it four years ago. It's been a monument of neglect ever since. Too near the house, we thought. Apparently not.

I monitor it. Household chores go unchored, emails unwritten. Work? Pah. This is important. She comes back, holding something in her mouth. A bit of moss – just the kind of thing you might use if you were a nest-building blue tit.

So now we're condemned to six weeks of daily stress. Are they laying? Have they hatched? Will they fledge? Then what? Parenthood was never this bad.

Some people have nest-box cameras. They can monitor the birds' every move, thrilling to the emergence of the hatchlings, cheering them on as they grow. Upstretched beaks begging for caterpillars. Then the first exploratory wing flaps, followed by the inevitable: out into the wide world of adventure, excitement and – this is suburban London, after all – cats. No camera for us, though. The box is a world of mystery. What's going on in there?

With any luck, this: the female builds the nest. It'll take her a week or more. Then the laying – between eight and twelve eggs, one a day. Obviously, that's her job too. As is incubation – two weeks of it. You see the pattern.

In the male's defence, he might chip in by bringing food during incubation. And in the three weeks before fledging, they're both run off their feet. One chick can eat a hundred caterpillars a day, and they are demanding diners. Bring me food. Now.

One day, maybe in early June, they'll be gone. Fewer than half, on average, will survive. Good job they lay so many – a sensible evolutionary strategy. But that's all in the future. For now, we wait.

It's the stress that kills you.

Lev Parikian, 2022

The fresh, almost fluorescent green of early spring

COMINS COCH, ABERYSTWYTH, CEREDIGION

The woodland is coming alive after the dourness
of winter. But one young inhabitant must learn
fast if it is to survive

It is well after midnight when the tawny owl begins to call. With no wind, the sound seems unreasonably loud and close; it is probably perched in the large beech tree in the corner of the garden. Minutes pass before the calls are returned by another, more distant, owl.

I step outside, trying to locate the second participant, but can gain only the vaguest impression of direction and distance – placing this owl somewhere across the hill. With the moon below the horizon and a continuous covering of cloud, the darkness is profound – apart from a solitary light in the hamlet across the valley. It's several minutes before I can make out the outline of the trees and the distant profile of the hills against the clouds.

When morning comes it brings a still, overcast sky that drains and flattens the colours of the landscape. The deeply shadowed lane below the beech wood is deserted and almost silent. A short stretch of the road hosts mature trees on both sides, the upper boughs crossing over like the vaulting of a Gothic cathedral. From beneath this canopy of branches, the vivid – almost fluorescent – green of the spring leaves stands out against the grey blur of the sky. The vibrant colour will quickly lose its lustre, though; the interval between brilliant emergence and full, sombre maturity is only a few days.

The steep slope of the wood is covered with a mass of bluebells. These blooms are short-lived, becoming pinched and faded as they pass their peak, but for now they are a welcome block of colour after the dour shades of winter.

A scuffling sound in the hedge bank makes me look down – a young rabbit, barely bigger than my hand, caught between the competing choices of curiosity and flight. Breaking my stride breaks the spell, and it heads off into the undergrowth. It will need to improve its reactions if it hopes to reach adulthood in a landscape rife with dangers.

John Gilbey, 2022

A safe place for slow worms to breed

ALLENDALE, NORTHUMBERLAND

With three wooden compost bins in my garden, there's always one with just the right temperature for them

When I was a child, I witnessed my parents' gardener killing a snake. It was a beautiful, large grass snake. He brought a spade down sharply behind its head as it rippled across the lawn. At the age of five I knew this was wrong. Instead of making me afraid of snakes, this has given me a lifelong affinity for them.

The grass snake, *Natrix helvetica*, is harmless, but I like to think that the gardener didn't know this. In Northumberland they are extremely rare, though on the moors above this valley, I might spot a shy adder – *Vipera berus*, the UK's only venomous snake – as it slithers away to safety.

So there are no snakes in my garden – but there are slow worms. Snake-like, these are legless lizards. Look in their eyes and you can see the difference: instead of the snake's vertically split pupil, theirs are rounded, with eyelids that blink. This garden, with its dense borders, meadows and mulches, is a place where slow worms breed each year.

I lift the carpet that covers the compost and feel heat emanating from the rot. With three wooden bins – one being filled, one cooking and one cooling – there's always a spot with just the right temperature for *Anguis fragilis*. And there, locked in an embrace in the luxurious warmth, are two sleek slow worms. The male has his jaws clamped behind the female's head; they can stay like that for up to ten hours.

The female is pale bronze with a dark stripe. The male is smaller. Ovoviviparous, she will incubate her eggs internally before the young hatch. She'll then give birth to up to fifteen tiny wormlings. The compost heap is full of the invertebrates they'll feed on: spiders, earthworms, beetles and slugs.

I've laid sheets of tin as refugia for the slow worms to take cover, though if attacked they can self-amputate, the shed tail writhing as a distraction. With luck they can live for twenty years. I quickly replace the carpet, leaving the pair in peace.

Susie White, 2022

Goldfinches one, two, three, lift into the boughs of the pear tree

CREEDY VALLEY, DEVON

Their irresistible colour and song nearly proved their ultimate downfall. How lucky we are to still be witness to their charms

The free tumble of yellow and red as the goldfinches swerve in the spread of colour is infectious. Like throwing a pack of cards up and seeing the court faces fall, there is a regal brightness, and such thrall in their deft abandonment to air. These distinctive finches, with striking red, white and black heads and yellow wing bars, are uncommonly vivacious. They shimmer and swoop in rampages of energetic flight.

In his 'Cook's Tale', Chaucer describes his apprentice protagonist as 'lively . . . as goldfinch in the glade'. This liveliness has also been translated as boldness, flamboyant dress, even joy. While we may not be able to tell if these birds feel happiness, we know that goldfinches have long evoked pleasure in their human observers. Their arresting colours and song made them popular as caged birds in the nineteenth century, with large numbers taken from the wild to the brink of extinction in Britain.

While their population has now recovered significantly, more than doubling since the 1970s, this caged history makes their buoyancy seem even more celebratory. Chaucer found his goldfinch-like apprentice 'full of love . . . as is a beehive full of honey sweet'.

Now the apple blossom is out, I step into the scented drip of shaking white and pink where the goldfinches have shot up from the petals. I'm sprinkled in spring perfume as the flowers stir then settle back into the branches. High, the flashing bodies twist: one, two, three, entwined as they lift into the boughs of the pear, making a theatre of the air; it is difficult not to get swept up in the action. Theirs is an irresistible attraction, a sweeping rush of momentum that longs to take you with it.

Highly sociable, a generous spirit of raucous play follows these birds through their beaming display. Could it really be said that they are full of love? It is not our privilege to know. But their residue of sweetness runs thick and full and slow, pouring through the lengthening light, a trail of spring's ebullient life.

Elizabeth-Jane Burnett, 2022

In the dawn chorus, everyone must be heard

LAGAN MEADOWS, BELFAST, COUNTY ANTRIM

For these early birds, it's all about doing
whatever it takes to stand out

First light. I emerge from the gloom of the woods to a stain of sunrise above the far trees. The meadow is encircled by a bower of song. Thrush species dominate: a blackbird's languidly phrased minor notes; rival song thrushes brandishing what the poet Katharine Towers aptly described as 'tried-and-tested triplets'; and distantly, the urgent strains of a mistle thrush. Against this musical canvas, a nearby robin skirls plaintively. From the foliage behind him, my ear catches a whispering crescendo – its squeaky tone and rolling delivery make the goldcrest a cinch.

The woods are a battlefield, and not just between opposing males of the same species. The dawn chorus may sound like an orchestra but is really a sonic ecosystem where the competition to be heard has driven every species into its own acoustic niche. So each one – here's the shivering flourish of a blackcap – can be sifted from layers of sound.

Spectrograms show that the songs of close relatives – for example, thrushes, such as the song thrush and blackbird – are structurally very similar: distinct voices evolved thanks to changes in pitch and tempo. This is convenient for me. Walking at this time in this popular area has shifted my bird-watching to bird-listening.

Beyond the trees, there's a growing hum from the A55, the city's outer ring road. As if on cue, a great tit saws his repeated chimes into the chorus. The great tit was the first species to reveal how, confronted by the urban racket, birds can tweak the pitch of their songs to a higher register. This means, like the wheedle of a goldcrest that's audible through robin song, they are a rung above the background din. They also sing more loudly. And they may adjust the timing of their singing by avoiding the worst of the morning rush hour, and by singing more briefly during its rumble. Whatever it takes.

But if this great tit fledged last year, he learned how to sing in another world. When he was a nestling listening to his elders and, over the winter, while he was practising his juvenile verses, this was a quieter city. Now it's resuming its former noisy ways. My fingers are crossed that his song is fit for it.

Mary Montague, 2021

We are down to our last nightingale

BILLINGSHURST, WEST SUSSEX

Last year, the nightingales were a lockdown highlight.
Now, there is just a solitary, defiant song

The wind is subsiding and the sun is beginning to set, lighting up the edges of the clouds. I follow the worn footpath across the fields on the outskirts of the town, and almost immediately hear the nightingale, its pure voice carrying through the cold evening air.

This time last year, I found three singing males holding territory around these fields, hidden in the dense trees, hedges and brambles. There was a fourth singing near the railway line, too. Those birds were my highlight of last spring's lockdown – their virtuosic songs lifted my spirits. But all I can find now is this single bird. Ten years ago we had even more, but a combination of building and 'tidiness' reduced their numbers to just the occasional nightingale – except for last year.

It's been a cold spring and many summer migrants seem to have been late arriving, but there are certainly fewer around than last year. Have the cold northerly winds held them back or is there more disturbance this time? In February, many of the bushes and young trees were removed and the hedges cut back, so the wild rose, juniper and bramble that fed birds in winter and gave cover to whitethroats last spring are mostly gone, apart from this island of impenetrable, untidy growth.

I try to get closer to the nightingale, peer into the voids between the bramble twigs. I can just glimpse movement, an obscured brown bird, its body vibrating as it sings.

I record its position on my phone and head for home, across the open fields, silvered dandelion globes shining on the dark grass. I can still hear the nightingale behind me, singing from its untouched stronghold of twisted branches – a lonely, beautiful song of defiance.

Rob Yarham, 2021

Nothing beats the thrill of having whales on your doorstep

STROMNESS, ORKNEY

Via a WhatsApp group, fishermen inform us
landlubbers of any interesting sightings –
then off we dash to the coast

Orkney has an amphibious quality to its daily life. The passage of the day can be marked by the movements of the ferry – that sci-fi mammoth that powers over the horizon – or the merry little creel boats that come and go, blue and green, stacked with lobster pots and strung with bright buoy baubles.

Beneath the waves, the waters are busy too, with a changing cast of marine mammals. It can be difficult to keep track of our seagoing neighbours: a dorsal fin here, a tail slap there, and that's all that might alert you to a passing pod.

Last year, I joined a WhatsApp group run by the Orkney Marine Mammal Research Initiative, a charity that records sightings of whales, dolphins and porpoises in local waters. The group has more than two hundred members, who report their sightings in real time. The most prolific contributors tend to be the fishermen and ferrymen, who send terse dispatches from offshore locations: 'Common dolphins SE of Graemsay'; 'Possible fin whale off Orphir, heading towards Scapa buoys'. The buzzing of the messages forms a backdrop to my days, like radio chatter.

Mostly I lurk. I just like to know they're out there, somewhere in the deep, working to their own agenda. But every so often, there's a sighting so tantalisingly close that I have to jump in the car. We'll dash to the coast with cyclists and camper vans in a game of Wacky Races. Often the whales are then nowhere to be seen. No matter.

Then, on Sunday, another buzz. Orcas moving fast through the Scapa Flow! We trailed them for an hour, always one step behind, until finally we caught them in the Clestrain Sound, 500 yards offshore. Four of them, at least. Just staggering to see those lacquered black backs, those white-flashing eye patches, those dagger-like dorsals stabbing through the water. Unmistakable. Powerful. Totally alien. So close that we could hear the air through their blowholes.

They dived; twenty strangers held their breath on shore. And then they rose again. It was worth the wait.

Cal Flyn, 2021

My eyes do not deceive me –
this is a black squirrel

LETCHWORTH GARDEN CITY, HERTFORDSHIRE

*There are about 25,000 of this melanistic form
of the grey squirrel in the UK, and here
they are local celebrities*

Above my head, two squirrels race through the sycamores. They are not the same colour. The pursuer is a flash of grizzled pewter, russet stains around its flanks and eyes; the other, a streak of inky darkness. Pewter – black – pewter – black. My eyes struggle to follow their acrobatics, until they call a truce. For a moment they're both visible, shelling acorns in the crook of a thick ivy stem. Then the black squirrel pauses and winks out of existence, its dark fur swallowed by the shadows.

I'm not surprised to see a black squirrel on Norton Common this morning, but it was a different story twenty years ago, when I looked up from digging the veg beds to find a jet-black apparition eyeing me from a neighbour's fence. As a newcomer to the county, I was dumbfounded. Was this a figment of my imagination? And where was the nearest optician?

I found out that black squirrels – a melanistic form of the grey squirrel – had been in the area for decades. Thought to have escaped from a private menagerie in the early twentieth century, the UK population is now estimated at 25,000, based mainly in Hertfordshire, Cambridgeshire and Bedfordshire.

Letchworth Garden City, with its broad tree-lined streets and green parks, has become a stronghold for these charismatic rodents. Over the years, they have acquired a quirky celebrity status, lending their name to a dark ale, a credit union and the first pub to serve alcohol in this Quaker-influenced town.

I rarely walk on Norton Common without learning a little more about squirrel business. Last week it was a lesson in design, when what I thought was a burr on an oak uncurled a long black tail. Black on back, legs and head, the squirrel had a ginger belly and a mossy green beard that turned out to be a mouthful of lining for its drey.

Often, like today, the squirrels are engaged in a mating chase, or perhaps they are establishing dominance. Whatever their purpose, for these two, snack time is over. With a shiver in the shadows, the black squirrel reappears, and they're off once more, racing into the sycamore canopy in a spiralling game of follow-my-leader.

Nic Wilson, 2021

The queen bee is a ray of sunshine in a gloomy May

WENLOCK EDGE, SHROPSHIRE

This spring has been hard on the insects, but the garden bumblebee is here, piloted by an ancient impulse

The queen makes a solar landing. During the briefest moment of shine in the wash cycle of our local low-pressure area, a queen garden bumblebee, *Bombus hortorum*, settles on a dandelion. The flower's brilliance draws insects to its gravitational field and the promise of mining the flaring florets for nectar and pollen.

But this burning sun of a flower is cold comfort. May has been hard, with blossom battered by hail, frosts, rain, rain and more rain. The gardens the bumblebee gets her name from have saturated, 'can't get on it' soil, struggling seedlings and soggy blooms. Birdsong is muted, wildflowers thin. The fields are sodden, the rivers close to flood. I suppose we're lucky we haven't had a drought and the hills aren't on fire, but we have made insect life hard enough without a washout spring.

Apart from a defiant common blue butterfly, and gnats that catch the fleeting beams to dance between the downpours, the air is quiet. After anxious days of waiting, the swifts scream their arrival around the church tower – but where do they go in the rain and what aerial plankton is there to trawl up there when all is drowned down here? Perhaps, at night, they fly into the moon's halo, where they are changed and one day may not return.

There are other signs of misfortune down here, too: new fences to block old ways around fields, verges of cow parsley mowed down, magpies caught in Larsen traps, gunfire. There are harsh changes afoot in this landscape, and a resentful cynicism gaining confidence. Still, to walk from our claggy enclosures into the woods, to sigh that mean-spirited humour out and begin a forest breath full of green light under leafy ceilings fresh with rain, is to thank our lucky stars.

The queen is making up for lost time. As if piloted by some ancient entity inside a protective space suit of bumblebee anatomy, with sensory devices attuned to a world behind the rain, on wings that set the frequency for spring, she finds the fire to which we are all drawn.

Paul Evans, 2021

An agitated scene upon the pond

MARSHWOOD VALE, DORSET

*A pair of mallards were paddling in flustered
circles. Something wasn't right*

My dog slunk across the lawn, crunching guiltily. She had been sniffing around the garden pond and found something tasty. I shut her in the house and went to investigate.

Hidden beneath a clump of pendulous sedge, I discovered an untidy heap of broken reeds containing nine large eggs. Five were pale blue, three were greeny-brown and one was an indeterminate light colour – duck eggs, from a wild mallard. The blue ones were slightly bigger and grubby, indicating perhaps that they were laid first and had been rolled around more.

Mallards lay once every couple of days and do not start incubating until the clutch is complete, usually at around twelve eggs. With ten eggs in total, including the one the dog filched, the female and occasionally her mate must have been active outside my kitchen window for about two weeks. My pride in being an observant country diarist was bruised. How could I have missed them?

With the dog banned from that part of the garden, I went back later to check if the duck had returned. She was there, sitting tight, neck snaked flat, astonishingly well camouflaged. Her brown and buff-striped plumage mimicked the vegetation; only an eye stood out, unblinking orange ringed with black.

She laid one more egg and then began to brood. The drake was absent during the day but roosted near her every night, flying in at dusk, punctuating the melodious evening songs with loud, repetitive quacks.

A week into incubation she rearranged her nest, adding feathers pulled from her breast and rags of moss. When she was away feeding, I noticed there were now only eight eggs, all blue. There had to be a nocturnal predator, possibly rats but most likely a fox.

One morning, about ten days before hatching was due, I found the duck and drake together on the water, paddling in agitated circles. The nest was scuffled out and the whole clutch gone. I think a vixen took the eggs, carrying them off to feed her cubs. The ducks flew away and have not returned.

Sara Hudston, 2021

The strangeness of wildlife was there all along

AIREDALE, WEST YORKSHIRE

*Lockdown is opening our eyes to that
which we take for granted*

Things seem askew. In the ash trees of a Bradford park, the chew-toy squeals of rose-ringed parakeets rise above the songbird natter. A friend sends pictures of a goshawk seen, improbably, in a suburban Airedale woodland. High on the mill chimney, framed by lightning conductors, a peregrine falcon watches over my lockdown coffee on the back step. None of this, surely, is normal. Might it be the new normal I've heard so much about?

What is normal? The chiffchaff's tireless two-step sounds all morning long from the allotments at the bottom of the street. From adjacent birches in that parakeet-ridden Bradford park, two cock blackcaps spit breakneck territorial song at one another. These tiny birds have just come tumbling in as part of a 15-million-strong contingent of spring migrants from Africa and southern Europe. How is that normal? It wouldn't be, if we weren't so used to it – it would be jaw-dropping if it didn't happen every year.

The parakeets are not so strange as they seem either. They have long been old news in trendsetting London, but it turns out that Bradford is not so far from the leading edge as may have been supposed: our park's population has been here for years (about as long as I have). The peregrine, too, is only as fantastical as you want it to be. We've all seen the webcam footage of chicks hatching on cathedral spires, or seen the adults pitching head-long off high-rises – but to a birdwatcher who grew up knowing the peregrine as a creature of remote wilderness and a species on the brink, it's still hard not to feel a sharp rattle of dissonance. The goshawk, meanwhile, proves to be an escaper, from a breed-ing centre somewhere to the south. People complicating things again.

The only real constant in nature is change. I like to be reminded of this – I like to remind myself that if I step outside and don't see something new, something weird, it's only because I've not paid enough attention. Until last week, I'd somehow never noticed the extraordinary skylarking display flights of the starlings over the streets here. But this isn't lockdown wildlife. It's just wildlife. Turns out nature was weird all along.

Richard Smyth, 2020

The atmosphere in the hawthorn hedge is electric

OTLEY, WEST YORKSHIRE

*The lavish blossom smells of sex and death, and the
bees are positively charging towards it*

The hawthorn blossom by the River Wharfe is white and bright
and overflowing from the tree like a foaming mug of beer. Amid all
the new life of spring, it smells subversively of sex and death at the
same time; an undeniably bawdy sweetness underlain by the repel-
lent odour of trimethylamine, a compound that is also produced
by rotting flesh. It is a strange, discomfiting smell, mingling desire
and depravity in a way that doesn't belong in polite company, but
the hawthorn has no such inhibitions, wafting its profanity across
the path in the hot sun.

The smell may be ambivalent, but the sight of hawthorn blossom
is thrilling, so celebratory, like a wedding in a hedgerow. I look
closely at the snowy bouquets of pearl-like buds and cupped flowers hanging from the branches; like May itself, there is too much
beauty to comprehend. But the sight is not made for me – and what
I see is only part of what is here.

The flowers have evolved over millennia to attract pollinators.
I watch honeybees and bumblebees flitting between the pink stamens, immersed in the work of gathering nectar and pollen. While
I see pretty off-white petals with blushes of pink, the bees see
ultraviolet colours, markings and patterns that are invisible to me.

Bees build up a positive electrical charge through friction in
flight, which means the negatively charged pollen grains 'fly' to
them when they alight. There is even evidence that bees can sense
the strength of the electrical field surrounding flowers, helping
them choose which ones to land on.

It seems absurd to wonder if the bees have anything as human as an aesthetic reaction to the flowers. But the evolution of flowering plants, so much of which is aimed at appealing to pollinators, pre-dates us by about 70 million years. The unfathomable beauty of the flowering world is, in a sense, a by-product of insect consciousness, shaped by their minds. No wonder we struggle to comprehend it.

Carey Davies, 2019

Cool weather has prolonged flowering in the orchard

KIT HILL AND METHERELL, TAMAR VALLEY, CORNWALL

May brings a morris dance celebration, the first cuckoo of the year, and thick clusters of blossom

At dawn, birdsong floats up from shrubby undergrowth towards the cold summit of Kit Hill. Mist lies in the lowest valleys and, much like the scattered enclaves of yellow oilseed rape and plastic-covered maize plantings, appears luminous among the patchwork of fields and woods.

The first cuckoo call of the season impels a brief runabout – a family tradition to ensure another year of liveliness – although my predecessors would have had no need to come uphill from the valley to hear this bird. The sound of melodeon, trombone, drum and bells echoes around the monumental mine stack as the Cornish Wreckers dance morris in celebration of May and of 'winter gone away'.

Later, 750 feet lower down, we look back up to that landmark from the blossoming orchard, propagated, cared for and documented by Mary and James (my sister and brother-in-law). The varieties here are mostly local. Close to the sheltering hedge and deer fence, cherry specimens are over 40 feet tall – a Fice originating from Boetheric, Mazzard from Tutwell, Bullions from Latchley and Beals Mill. Burcombes feature the thickest clusters of blossom, and cool weather has prolonged the flowering.

A small horticultural tunnel, to be netted later, contains cherries on dwarfing rootstock, but if there is a good set of fruit on the full-sized trees there should be enough for us and the birds. Pear trees are overgrown with blossom, and Mary is painting what she and James call 'Mrs Bomford's tree' (its variety is not yet formally identified), which is spectacular with creamy blossom on wide-spreading branches, different from the more vertical forms of the Harvest, Green Sweats and Chisel pears.

Now sweet-scented apple blossom emerges from pink buds on Ben's Red, Mrs Bull's, Listener, Hockings Green, Lizzy and Tregonna King. Overhead, a swallow twitters and swoops, in need – like the flowery canopy – of warmth and more insects.

Virginia Spiers, 2018

A milky way of bird life – is this not 'civilisation'?

TITCHWELL MARSH, NORFOLK

*Godwits and plovers, curlews and spring's first
swallow, ruff in summer plumage all feeding in
sewing-machine mode*

It was wonderful as well as instructive to sit with my younger daughter at the edge of the wetland scrape that is the showcase of the Titchwell Marsh RSPB reserve.

Here before us, in lines that were as clear and true as the grating calls of the 1,000 breeding gulls, were godwits and plovers, curlews and spring's first swallow. Here were the sounds of shelduck and Cetti's warblers, avocets and redshank. Here were ruff in summer plumage, heads up and down, all feeding in sewing-machine mode, while teal with shoveler dabbled in the shallows. All intermittently fed and flew, buzzed by a sparrowhawk or passing harrier, when a spreading arc of wings would swirl into the air, and then, all of a sudden, they would plump back down as one and appear again as they had begun. It was the typical exhilarating stuff of spring at this spot – a perpetually renewed milky way of birds stretched across a marsh.

As we watched, we also pondered the recent BBC television series *Civilisations*. Great, we said, that they had added to the dead white European men who were the only constituents of Kenneth Clark's original series, *Civilisation*. The presenters, Mary Beard and David Olusoga, add diversity to the mix – yet the essential fixture is still apparent. We seem unable to escape or rise above the idea that civilisation is *things* – paintings, sculptures, buildings, art. The Canadian ecologist John Livingston once lamented that 'our sundry aesthetic models' have no place for living processes and that 'our culture is essentially abiotic' – i.e. lifeless.

We recalled the programme's images of Simon Schama amid the ecstatic powers of Chartres Cathedral and wondered whether Titchwell too – here, now – wasn't also a kind of cathedral, an endlessly renewed scene of biodiversity and beauty made by sunlight and fashioned from stardust.

In the same spring that we saw the last male northern white rhinoceros, that giraffes were declared at risk of extinction, and one in eight of the world's 10,000 bird species are judged to be similarly imperilled, do we not need to visit the whole idea of civilisation once more?

Mark Cocker, 2018

The adders have been waiting for this warmth

AIGAS, SCOTTISH HIGHLANDS

*Emerging from hibernation, they seek out a warming
rock to energise themselves for the hunting ahead*

Warmth is what it takes, that's all. Every spring, that first burst of sun in clear skies brings our adders back to life. In common with most other reptiles the world over, *Vipera berus* has to warm up. They are cold-blooded and have been hibernating underground for more than six months. Their metabolism needs to be fired up again.

I once found one inside a dry-stone wall I was repairing – cold, curled and comatose. I carefully put it to one side before returning it to the depths of the wall to complete its hibernation.

With the warming soil, adders wake up and very slowly slither out. They must be hungry, but hunting for mice or voles takes action – which requires a warm-up to get the cold blood flowing. So they head for a rock in full sun. They wait until the stone has absorbed some heat, then out they come into full view, each basking reptile gloriously happy to be warm.

So out I went one afternoon a couple of weeks ago, a day of full sun to a cheering 19°C. Up on to the moor, to a large exposed rock where I have seen adders many times over many years. I knelt to feel the stone. Perfect: a deep warmth issuing to my palm. But not a snake to be seen. I walked on, keeping my Jack Russells, Nip and Tuck, obediently to heel. Ten minutes later, Tuck growled.

There, on a rock just a few feet away, neatly coiled like a braided rope, head resting on the fattest coil, black eyes gleaming and bifid tongue flicking, was the most exquisite male adder I have ever seen. His long dorsal zig of pure jet black zagged against a ground of pale lemon. He was magnificent. I stepped back and hauled the dogs in to my feet. He had seen us, no doubt about it, but wasn't budging. This was his moment, his warm-up. He had waited a long time for that day.

John Lister-Kaye, 2018

Bogbean adventures

NEW FOREST

Janet Elizabeth Case braved treacherous sinkholes and snagging briars to see these enchanting flowers eighty years ago

Fascinated by JEC's account of her search for the bogbean (*Menyanthes trifoliata*) in a Country Diary dated 5 June 1933 (I'd come across it in the slim grey selection of her diaries published posthumously in 1939), we tried to relive the adventure.

When Case – a classics scholar who had taught Virginia Woolf – was writing, the forest retained a sense of wilderness that is hard to find now. Cars were around but did not infest it as they do now, and car parks were virtually unknown. She describes leaping from clump to clump of sweet gale (bog myrtle) to get a footing as she and a friend named only as 'E' crossed ground that was sticky and treacherous, even on a hot day. Persistence was rewarded when they came across 'a great stretch of its shining triple leaves and – best of all – spike on spike of its amazingly lovely white-fringed flowers and rosy buds'.

Today there are several bogbean sites that can be reached easily from car parks. We visited some we thought fitted her description, but there was no trace of the plants.

It's said that the bogbean gets its name from the triple cluster of leaves that are reminiscent of the broad bean, but its enchanting flowers are unlike anything else. This spring, the plants are coming into flower somewhat later than in recent years – we have seen them here in late April – but, because of the drenching we have had over past weeks, the forest is very wet, the ground indeed sticky and treacherous. As we found out, keeping a sure footing requires good balance.

Perhaps, though, the real adventure belongs to the modern age. Getting into position to frame a good picture from a low perspective is a challenge. The forest's boggy areas often conceal sinkholes, just where bogbeans thrive, often in shallow water with a glutinous muddy bottom.

Graham Long, 2018

JUNE

We live in hope of rain – a normal amount of rain

WELLINGTON, SOMERSET

*Our fragile forest garden just needs some help from
above, anything that won't bake it to dust or wash
away the topsoil*

It's another beautiful day. This sentence doesn't usually elicit a collective groan of despair, but after three arid weeks, the gardeners of south-west England are entitled to sigh a bit. In the nearby Fox's Field, volunteers from Wellington's Transition Town group are hauling water from the stream up the slope to carefully rehydrate the herbs in their newly planted forest garden.

The ground is covered with a layer of woodchip, hay and municipal soil improver. It has been so toasted by the sun that you can crumble it in your fingers like granola. At intervals, tufts of green poke up through the mulch: oregano and lemon balm, bergamot and sweet cicely, chamomile and clary sage.

The last rain fell in biblical proportions. On 9 May, the air turned beige, lightning crackled and thunder rolled from the Blackdowns to the Quantocks and back again like a timpani section gone mad. The rain, when it finally fell, hammered the freshly ploughed fields, blasting away the topsoil like a pressure washer. Roads turned into rivers, carrying away whatever nutrients farmers had applied. Half the average month's rain fell in the space of twenty-four hours.

It's not so much the quantity as the quality of the rain that's the issue: a 'wet' month isn't much use if it all falls at once. Quite the opposite, in fact. And, after the flood, the run of bone-dry days and chilly nights have made the usually soggy south-west feel like the high sierras. No wonder the plants are struggling.

The 'no dig' method can give the soil half a chance. Here, the team has spent eighteen months suppressing the grass with cardboard, hay and woodchip, and in one section a sheet of black plastic. This not only helps retain the soil structure and avoids releasing carbon, it also provides the soil with a protective layer. It is less likely to dry out, is more stable and absorbent, and is therefore richer in nutrients and microbial activity.

But if the current conditions prevail, without the intervention of these water-bearing humans, even these lucky plants will eventually die. We walk back to the river in evening's golden light, our empty watering cans swinging.

Anita Roy, 2023

Birdsong fills the farm – and suddenly I know what it all is

TEBAY, CUMBRIA

My experience of doing the daily tasks has been transformed by an app. I'm amazed at what I have around me

It's been five years since we entered into a Countryside Stewardship environmental agreement on the farm and fenced off a wide riparian strip alongside the River Lune. There were already quite a few trees in this patch – mainly oak, sycamore and rowan – but the livestock exclusion has allowed some to self-seed and regenerate. One of the rowans is now taller than me.

The farmhouse looks out over part of the strip, and we can hear a variety of birdsong coming from it. The game-changer has been the Merlin Bird ID app. I downloaded it last week and since then have been making recordings as I do my work on the farm.

This morning, I recorded the birdsong as I walked across the field to let out the hens. I recognised the cuckoo and robin, but other songs I didn't know. The app told me they were greenfinch, spotted flycatcher and hawfinch. I did another recording to make sure – the same species came up again. Across the day it picked up calls by willow warbler, blackcap, song thrush, peregrine, snipe, short-eared owl . . . All the while I've been trying to get my 'ear in', and can now recognise a wren, having heard it so many times this week.

I googled the species and was amazed to find that many of them are red-listed birds, meaning they are of the highest conservation concern in the UK. I knew that the tree sparrows that inhabit our barn are red-listed, but I had no idea there were so many others. The app isn't always right, I'm sure, but it is making my summer mornings more interesting, and it's heartening to know that, with our wilded strip, we're doing our bit.

Otherwise, the cows are now out of the barns where they have been living for the winter. Every couple of days we move them to fresh grass. It is hot, so we all walk slowly, oystercatchers peeping overhead. That's one bird call I don't need the app for – it's the sound of summer here.

Andrea Meanwell, 2023

The closest I have ever been to a buzzard

EGGLESTON, TEESDALE

*In all my years of nature-watching they have been
distant apparitions, until today*

Buzzards were uncommon here when I first became a Country
Diarist, thirty-five years ago. To watch them then, I would need to
cross the North Pennines into Cumbria. Now there are few days
when I don't hear their mewing calls in the Durham dales, almost
always soaring high above, on the lookout for carrion.

Once, on a memorably hot summer afternoon, I watched eight of
them, soaring in languid, effortless circles on rising thermals, with
hardly a single wing stroke, stacked one above the other like airliners
in a holding pattern. Sometimes, encounters have been more dramatic. This spring I watched as one turned on its back and displayed
its talons to another flying alongside. A courting pair, or rival males?
I don't know; the sexes are indistinguishable at that distance.

Most often, they are targets of harassment by other birds, with
crows the commonest aggressors. There is something very satisfying about the way a buzzard easily dodges and out-turns its tor-
mentors, unflappable unless they become too persistent. Then it
wearily drops a wing, turns tail and glides away in a serene, shallow
dive, a mile in a minute, while the hapless crows wonder where it
went. But in all these years, buzzards have always been distant apparitions; I've never been close to one, until today.

Sunlight streamed between gaps in the foliage of riverbank trees.
Through one, I caught sight of scaly yellow legs and talons gripping a branch, just above head height, about 10 metres away. The
breeze shifted the branches, revealing beautifully patterned chest
feathers, a yellow and black hooked bill and the raptor's ferocious

gaze. Neither of us blinked, for perhaps twenty seconds. Finally, it stretched its wings, turned, released its grip and allowed itself to be carried away on its element, the air; disdainfully, as if I had been another tiresome crow.

I doubt I'll ever be this close to a wild, live buzzard again. Later I wondered, did it really happen? Undoubtedly – I had taken a photograph. But that was unnecessary: moments like this are once-in-a-lifetime gifts, indelibly etched in the memory.

Phil Gates, 2022

Thatching reed is on the rise again

TOTSCORE, ISLE OF SKYE

I'm here to thatch a restored blackhouse, with material that grew from the embers of a devastating fire

Just sometimes, thatch needs fire. Controlled winter burning is an important tool in managing reed beds for thatching, to clear tangled vegetation and encourage the growth of straight, uniform stems. When not kept in check, the effect on wildlife can be devastating – as it was with the wildfire of April 2020 that destroyed a 3-kilometre stretch of reed by the River Tay. But from those charred beds something miraculous emerged: a vintage harvest of thatching reed.

Here on the Isle of Skye, I am using some of it to thatch a restored blackhouse on the north-west coast of the island. Across the Little Minch, the mountains of Harris keep watch. In the next field, a pair of stonechats flick through a ruined building, surrounded by tufts of rushes (*Juncus effusus*). This plant was once used by Highlanders to thatch their roofs; today it has mostly been replaced with water reed (*Phragmites australis*), a more durable material that is mostly imported from abroad.

Reed is shipped here from as far afield as China, and is now harvested in just two parts of the UK: the Norfolk Broads and the Tay. Perthshire holds Britain's largest continuous reed beds, and at its peak the Tayreed Company cut 40,000 bundles a year. The arrival of cheaper reed from eastern Europe in the 1990s drove prices down, and Tayreed ceased operations in 2005. Since then, only a small amount of reed has been harvested, but the fire in 2020 has produced the best crop for years.

The air is full of skylarks as I dress the final bundles into place on the roof, using some of the last of the harvest gathered after the wildfire. This winter's crop will mostly be used to rethatch the Crannog Centre on Loch Tay, which – in another conflagrant twist – burned down last summer. After all, thatch and fire do not usually mix well. The owners of the Skye blackhouse have taken no chances and have stopped up its two squat chimneys with concrete.

Tom Allan, 2022

Chalk hills glowing in the near-night light

INKPEN, NORTH WESSEX DOWNS, BERKSHIRE

*At this time of year the landscape is dreamlike
and monochrome, with Earth and moon
beaming back at each other*

The water has been off again in the village. In these dry chalk hills, the pipes crack, letting the water leak away to nothing. The kitchen tap judders and spits with such reluctant violence that I am soaked. I fill half a glass to drink. It swirls, cloudy with calcium.

At dusk, I walk up the track to the down. In June, the night glow that comes off the high chalk is at its most pronounced and dreamlike. The old lane from here to Prosperous Farm looks laid with concrete, but in fact it's chalk – long-worn, hoof-hammered and wheel-hardened, harder than tarmac and slick with the faint watercolour sheen of algae. The soil is so very thin here that the white bones of the earth gleam through its green skin.

Field margins and headlands glow with the light of moon daisies (called oxeye daisies in the daytime, or ockser daisies in our westernmost Berkshire dialect). All is a grainy, cinematic monochrome in the still-light dark of midsummer. Along the track, the dog roses have been leached of their pink blush, and the fragrant tips of wild privet and ringlets of honeysuckle intensify their scent. At intervals, elder trees hold their flat, creamy flower plates out to passing moths, like silver-service waitresses.

After the rain, the air seems as infused with chalk as my glass of water. The moon, a half-tipped cereal bowl, hauls everything towards it, so that even the glow is drawn upwards, pulling the moon daisies, hogweed, the elder-waitresses and the new-eared barley stalks up, straight and quivering.

I am back home in time to see the gauzy barn owl leave its box silently, like one of those elderflower plates, sheared off and lobbed like a Frisbee across the dark paddock.

The white track is undimmed. Land and moon beam back at one another in a silent exchange of percolated light, water it won't hold on to and chalk. The moon, like a micraster – an echinoid fossil or 'shepherd's crown' – is half buried in the flint bed of the night.

Nicola Chester, 2022

Avian flu is devastating the seabirds here

BIRSAY, ORKNEY

*This catastrophe has global significance – at this
time of year, Scotland has 46 per cent of the world's
northern gannets*

Walking the Orkney shoreline, usually such a peaceful and calming activity, has been disturbing of late. Along the strand, a succession of small, bedraggled forms lie prone, victims of the avian flu ripping through the seabird populations of the Northern Isles and up the east coast of Britain.

Crossing over to the Brough of Birsay (a tidal island) via a narrow causeway, I stumble across the first gannet. Its long, streamlined body is immediately recognisable: spectre white, misted with gold at its crown. Its eyes, staring blindly, have that piercing, icy quality of a husky, while its beak is the palest powder blue lined in black, as if designed with a felt-tip pen. It is unusual to be able to admire such a creature at close quarters, but I keep my distance. Best not to touch it. There's a second bird just a few metres further on, this one sprawled across the strand, wings outstretched. A pitiful sight.

It's the same story all up the coast, affecting many species at once. Last year it was the geese. This year: the gannets, guillemots, great skuas and more. A catastrophe in our midst, and one with global significance: at this time of year, Scotland is home to 46 per cent of the world's northern gannets and 60 per cent of all great skuas.

There is horrifying footage from the famous gannet colonies at Hermaness in Shetland, where more than a thousand dead birds have been recorded in the waters, and the Bass Rock off East

Lothian – the largest such colony in the world – where there are similar scenes of devastation. Birds slide from their rocky perches, hang lodged in the crags while their close neighbours continue to feed and fledge amid the corpses. This annual gathering, where birds feed and fledge their young collectively and in close proximity, is what we now call a superspreader event.

Thought to be the UK's worst ever outbreak of avian flu, much of the drama is unfolding offshore; the true toll in those remote colonies, where birds crowd tightly together, is not yet fully known.

Cal Flyn, 2022

There's no other bird quite like a swift

WEST NORWOOD, SOUTH LONDON

Enjoy these golden few months when the masters of the sky are here

Other birds are great. Of course they are. From goldcrest to eagle, they all have their allure. But they're not swifts.

Swifts are magical. It's their otherness, the impression they give of coming to us through a portal from an alien world – a world in which the air is the natural medium, the ground to be abhorred. Why walk when you can fly, and especially if you can fly like a swift?

The year's first appeared one evening in early May, during a filthy hailstorm – the antithesis of swift weather. Some instinct made me look up, and there it was, darting around, dodging hailstones. Within seconds it was gone, back through its portal. We didn't see another one for a week, but then the weather changed and there they were – eight, ten, fifteen and more – wriggling around high in the sky like excitable parentheses.

We are blessed in our corner of south London. They nest in the eaves of the house to our left; they nest in the eaves of the house to our right; they nest – and this feels like a deliberate snub – in the eaves of two more houses down the road. We could take umbrage at the rejection of our bijou swift box, erected a few years ago in an effort to keep up with the neighbours. But we still get the benefit: the kind of aerobatic displays that would set you back £50 in the West End.

And over the course of their three-month stay, they illuminate our lives on a daily basis. Some mornings they scream past my office window in tight formation, writhing in and out of each other's slipstreams, squealing with the thrill of it all. Dart, swoop, sweep, glide; round, up, whizz, gone.

The speed is one thing, but it's the manoeuvrability that has me gawping. To earthbound humans, flight is freedom, and the swifts' flight is its embodiment.

Relish them now. Because soon, one day in late July maybe, they'll slip back through that portal and head south, leaving a sickle-shaped hole in our lives for nine long months. While they're gone, I'll content myself with watching other birds.

Other birds are great. But they're not swifts.

Lev Parikian, 2021

A pair of pygmy shrews, fighting in fast forward

LANGSTONE, HAMPSHIRE

*Two velvety balls of fury came tumbling down the
slope and landed at our feet, locked in battle*

Walking along the hollow way – a sunken, tree-lined path that cuts through the coastal grazing – we were stopped in our tracks by a high-pitched chittering, reminiscent of bat echolocation or cricket stridulation.

Our eyes roamed over the bank in search of the source. Even though there were several rodent burrows among the oak and field maple roots, there was no movement at any of the tunnel entrances. We heard a scuffle of paws in the leaf litter, but our vision was obscured by the lush overlying vegetation – brambles, holly, ivy, rosettes of dock, the arrow-shaped leaves of lords-and-ladies, and a froth of cow parsley.

Suddenly, two velvet-coated shrews came tumbling down the slope and landed at our feet. The creatures were locked in battle, rolling and writhing, both combatants jockeying for a throat-hold.

As one animal momentarily pinned its adversary to the ground, I was able to identify them as pygmy shrews – they have a smaller, more streamlined body, pointier snout and proportionately longer tail than the common shrew. Both species have grey-brown fur, but the pygmy shrew's is two-toned, with a dark back and pale underbelly, whereas the common shrew has a tricoloured pelage.

Pygmy shrews are widespread and common, with the British population estimated to be around 8.6 million, but it's rare to encounter these secretive creatures (unless, of course, you own a free-roaming cat). Foul-smelling and -tasting secretions from scent glands on their flanks make shrews unpalatable to predators, so they are often killed, then the carcass abandoned.

These tiny mammals are aggressively assertive, defending territorial boundaries and fighting for mating rights. The mating season occurs between April and August, so these were almost certainly competing males.

The tussle was so frenetic, it felt as though we were watching the action on fast forward. Slipping from its rival's grasp, one shrew uttered a single shrill note and turned tail, skittering into the labyrinth of runways through the undergrowth. Tail swiping from side to side, the other gave chase.

Claire Stares, 2021

The world looks different to a long-eared owl

GOYT VALLEY, DERBYSHIRE

Pity the vole caught in its formidable sight beam.
Capture is a mere formality

If you want a lesson in how little you notice about the world, I recommend an hour watching parent long-eared owls gather food for their chicks.

Recently, I saw the adults detect, pinpoint, catch and return to their brood five voles in one twenty-minute period. Witnessing this feat, you could assume that the place was hooching with vole flesh. Not at all. I walked through the vegetation where they were hunting. It was a dense, tangled, knee-high world of heather, bilberry and grass thickets. Had I spent a month on my hands and knees, I may conceivably have found some old sign of where voles had once camped, but I doubt I'd ever have clapped eyes on the mammals themselves.

The owls do it by having laser-like acuity of hearing and a flight mode softer than the warm breeze. But it is watching them watch that I find most incredible. Long-eared owls have flame-coloured eyes on a neck that can rotate through 270 degrees. The mechanism swivels sweetly, like a telescope on its mount. Yet none of this conveys the intensity of the sight beam, the way the bird, perched on a wall, scans and probes the realm of light photons, recoils the head to flame-throw its vision deeper into a spot.

If an organism could physically manipulate the world by sight, owls would evolve it first. You realise that once the search image has been fixed, the capture is mere formality. Clamping eight razor talons into vole fur is just dotting the owl's contractual Is.

As we come out of lockdown, environmentalists are falling over themselves to tell one another and anyone who'll listen about how good nature is for us. I want to rebel and to ask, paraphrasing President Kennedy, not what nature can do for us, but what the hell can we do for nature? If I must add to the eco-chorus on wildlife's instrumental purposes for us, I'd say this: owls help me see that I see so little, that we are party to something vaster than we know. Owls make the world richer, wider and deeper for us all.

Mark Cocker, 2021

Tuning in to the summer soundtrack

ABERNETHY, SCOTTISH HIGHLANDS

*Resident birdsong mingles now with the
sound of seasonal visitors*

In mid-April, I noticed shifts in sound that aligned with changes in colour. Soon I was in surround sound. Thrush song began earlier, at times of the day that, two months before, would have been the middle of the night. Greater spotted woodpeckers pecked and drummed, wrens scolded me from the junipers. One day, just once, I heard the falling cadence of a willow warbler, gone before I quite registered what I'd heard. The next day, a couple more, then more still.

When the bird cherries blossomed, they were encompassed with a thick drone of bees. Now the bees range more widely, buzzing low among the vetches and trefoils, lingering in the red and white clover that abounds. Slowly, cuckoo song dotted itself around the pinewoods, and for weeks they were more heard than seen. Then a moment arrived when three or four of them were restless presences on the wires outside the house.

As we head beyond the solstice, the strath has its summer soundtrack – resident birdsong mingles with the songs of the summer visitors, including the now omnipresent willow warblers, the tree pipits that parachute down to the treetops, and the twitter of martins and swallows. Summer's going on and I've seen two broods of peewit chicks. I realise I've not heard a cuckoo in a couple of days, and I suspect the adults are already on their way south.

Meanwhile, below, a patch of twinflowers has emerged. Their thready leaves intermingle with new blaeberry growth and now we see tiny stems forking to form a Y. These rare and delicate flowers are so small it's hard to tell whether they're white or pink, but they're always a summer joy.

Above them we hear a familiar giggle, a soft titter: a crested tit, black and white with a flick at the back of its head, flitting among the pines. It flies to a hole in another Scots pine, and into its nest.

Amanda Thomson, 2021

The dusty colours and frayed textures of full summer

COMINS COCH, ABERYSTWYTH, CEREDIGION

After a dry May, the grasses are high and the foxgloves busy with bees

Across the valley, the hills have slowly adopted the dusty colours and frayed textures of full summer. Widening patches of pale green meadow stand out across the landscape as the silage is cut, wilted and gathered in the sunshine.

The lack of significant rainfall during May has reduced the flow of the stream to a trickle, altering the soundscape of the lane and bringing into focus the background patterns of wind and birdsong. The last of the bluebells, nearly hidden by tall grasses, top the bank, while the seedheads of dandelions – perfectly mature – wait for a liberating gust of wind.

At the top of the track, beyond a field of rushes tall enough to conceal a fox, I take the path across the hill towards the quarry. As I pause to look through a gap in the hedge, one of the grazing horses wanders over to check my pockets for snacks, leaning its head over my shoulder as if to share the view of the Cambrian Mountains.

The tunnel of branches over the track brings cool, dappled shade, but just down the hillside the canopy is more open than last year. The savage gales of February partly toppled two of the shallow-rooted oaks, which now rest uncertainly on their neighbours. In the open arena of the disused quarry, the turf overlying the thin soil is crisp and yellow from drought. The emerging flower spikes of the foxgloves that dot the ground have matured in the days since my last visit, and wild bees swerve urgently between the newly opened blooms.

At the end of the old coach road, a right turn would take me down to the coast. The temptation is strong, but it has been many weeks since I could justify a walk on the narrow cliff path, and I settle for a view of the sea glint on the horizon. With regret I turn left and, clambering over the stile, take the footpath across the top field towards home.

John Gilbey, 2020

A brimstone? Here in the north?

ALLENDALE, NORTHUMBERLAND

*It's a good year if the county sees more
than two of these dazzling insects*

I grew up in Berkshire, and the butterflies of my childhood were the red admirals and commas that I'd gaze at on Michaelmas daisies way above my head. Orange tips danced in spring meadows of cow parsley and hedge garlic, small tortoiseshells overwintered on dusty shed beams, and white admirals fed on bramble flowers by a local ford. The commas followed me north when I moved to

Northumberland, a species extending its range, but not the brimstones that were a zing of lime yellow in the rambling garden. I haven't seen those for many years.

So it was with a bolt of recognition that I spotted a large yellow butterfly as I was putting away my gardening tools in the late afternoon heat. I chased it excitedly with my phone for ten minutes, as it jerked and kinked over the vegetables, pausing on some woody cranesbill, where I got a distant shot as an initial record. With a strong, determined flight, it favoured the red campion in my wildflower meadow and, with careful stalking, I managed a closer photograph. The acid yellow of its wings looked dazzling next to the vivid pink flower. A male brimstone butterfly, here in Allendale!

It was still around a day later, again on the campion. *Gonepteryx rhamni*'s ridged veins resemble those of a leaf; together with its angular wing shape, this protects it when roosting in foliage. Some believe that it is the male brimstone's yellow colouring that inspired the word 'butterfly' – the females are pale green.

The longest-lived of our British butterflies, adult brimstones can be a year old, often overwintering among ivy or holly leaves. Though they mainly feed on thistles, their spring nectar sources are the plants that are now in flower in my garden: bugle, cowslip and red campion. Their caterpillar food plants, though, are leaves of buckthorn and alder buckthorn, neither of which are known to grow in this area, which explains why there are so few recorded here.

On average, there are just two brimstones a year in this county. As I garden, I turn to look at every passing flickering of wings, but with neither a mate nor a larval food plant, it will probably remain a solitary record.

Susie White, 2020

Last dance for the mayfly

ABBEYDALE, SHEFFIELD

The clock is always ticking for this short-lived creature, but this really is crunch time for the male to find a mate

Where nature is concerned, expect the unexpected. One day I was listening for cuckoos on the moors above my home, the next I was having surgery on a part of my body I didn't know existed. After a week in hospital, I was returned to my garden, quietly grateful and as weak as an infant, to lie on the grass in a daze and watch insects busying themselves among the flowers. I had never properly stopped to notice how many and what kinds our little patch supports: bumblebees, among them common carders, mining bees, butterflies, solitary wasps, ants marching over my legs, beetles muscling through the wild strawberries.

One small drama in particular held my attention: a single male mayfly, pulsing up into the air and drifting back down. As it floated towards my feet, the mayfly's elongated front legs, used for grasping the female during mating, and its even longer tail appendages, called cerci, bent into an arc – an improbable contraption for flight. Yet when it pushed itself back into the air, it did so almost without effort on slender, transparent wings.

As a young fly-fisherman, I spent hours tying March brown mayflies to catch trout; the life cycle of these insects became a fascination to me. This one was another species, even more common, *Ephemera danica*, one clue being those immensely long front legs, a particular feature of the mature adult. Mayflies go through four stages, from egg to nymph (the longest portion of its life, spent in or near rivers and ponds), to a brief intermediary stage, the subimago (known to anglers as a dun, a sexually immature adult that emerges on the surface of the water). When its new wings are dry, it flies somewhere sheltered to shed one more exoskeleton. Then it becomes an imago, or spinner, a fully reproductive mayfly that will live, at most, a few days.

In these final hours, the mayfly has no functioning mouthparts because it doesn't need to eat. It has but one compulsion: to mate, then die. Perhaps the whole convoluted business had been in vain for this fellow. There were no females nearby to impress. But the possibility kept lifting him back into the summer sky.

Ed Douglas, 2020

The lanes are rampant with green growth

ST DOMINIC, TAMAR VALLEY, CORNWALL

A much-needed wet spell has stimulated everything,
with pennywort growing inches and honeysuckle
shooting above the hedgerows

Substantial rain has at last soaked into the dry earth. Gangs of jackdaws flock and peck over cut silage fields and, in the vacated pasture opposite home, swallows wheel low behind the tractor-drawn topper that is cutting off ungrazed thistle and dock plants.

Throughout the summer grazing season, the pedigree South Devon suckler herd will rotate from field to field. The cows and their offspring were brought from their winter quarters in mid-April, joined by the new bull a month later. He arrived by truck, strolled down the ramp and sauntered between the alert and attentive cows and calves, who then followed as he patrolled his new territory. An inquisitive calf touched noses with him and since then the bull has been in charge.

Grassland thrives in this parish, where shallow, free-draining soils are usually watered by regular doses of rainfall. There are no longer any dairy herds, and grass is used for beef and lamb production; farmers aim to become self-sufficient in winter fodder, concentrating on home-grown silage instead of cereals that need ever-dearer pesticides and artificial fertilisers.

To make most efficient use of the grass, cattle and sheep are sometimes grazed together in the same small field for just three or four days, before moving on to verdant fresh pasture. In one such field, recently shorn sheep appear strangely pale and long-legged beside their still-woolly lambs, accompanied by black and white yearling bullocks (born last year).

Landmark clumps of beech trees are laden with mast and, out in the lanes, rampant growth of greenery smothers faded bluebells and campions. Flower spikes of pennywort have grown inches higher in this rainy spell; bryony coils around ferns and invasive bracken stalks; dog rose and honeysuckle shoot above the dense leaves of hedgerow shrubs, and magenta foxgloves relieve the prevailing green.

Down the hill, by Halton Quay, tendrils of traveller's joy envelop bushes beside the old lime kilns; warblers churr in the greening reed beds, and sun emerges through clouds to sparkle on the ebbing tide, flowing downriver towards the wooded bend beneath Pentillie Castle.

Virginia Spiers, 2019

Feeding frenzy at the drowned town

DUNWICH, SUFFOLK

*In the unpromising drizzle, we walk past anglers
huddled in tents – then we're stopped in our tracks*

The fourteenth-century Gough Map of Great Britain, drawn with east at the top and north to the left, looks like a pantomime dame's shoe. Scotland is the long toe, Wales and Cornwall form an ornate block heel, and East Anglia and Kent a sort of ankle cuff.

I've travelled from Yorkshire to Suffolk – cartographic left to right – to a place marked on the map by a cluster of red roofs and a spire, indicating one of England's largest towns. But the port of Dunwich is long gone, its bustling harbour obliterated by storm surges, and its affluent streets, guildhall and fine churches lost to tide after insatiable tide. What remains is a row of well-tended cottages, a pub, a shingle beach and a still-hungry latte-coloured sea, sucking noisily at the pebbles.

This high-summer excursion with fellow writer Matt Gaw was intended to be one of sultry air, dragonflies, a swim maybe. Instead, we're buffeted past anglers huddled in tents, backed to the wind, each in thrall to his own tiny arc of horizon. Out there, wraiths of drizzle dither, harried and tarried by the wind – not yet part of the sea, nor still part of the sky.

The beach seems to be scattered with dung, but the dark clods are peat from marshes inundated long ago, coughed up for a final feel of sunlight on their ancient fibres. The marshes that remain are protected by the shingle bank, their pools still fresh for now and sentried with little egrets. Crossing them towards the woods and rounding a bend in the track, we're brought up short.

Against a backdrop of heavy green, a swarm of midday bats is flickering. Blink. Not bats, but swifts. Oh God, in this year of so few, *so many* swifts. An aerial feeding frenzy. They're gorging on insects kettled by wet and wind in this one sheltered acre. Hawking, swerving, flick-flacking, turning almost upside down to flash with paler brown, and circuiting so fast it seems impossible that they do not collide. It takes them only a couple of minutes to clean up – the feathered tornado rises and expands, a few crossbow silhouettes slingshotting over our jaw-dropped heads. Seconds later, they're gone.

Amy-Jane Beer, 2019

Curious jewels on the lavender

STAMFORD, LINCOLNSHIRE

*Cuckoo spit – a white foam – is a sign of
summer and an unlikely home to an insect*

The light catches something in the lavender, something snared on the stems, something bright, like a fistful of little jewels. Balls of white foam, bright in the brilliant after-rain light. A seasonal signal: cuckoo spit.

This folk name came about because its appearance is said to coincide with the first calls of the cuckoo, though for many of us the latter is becoming rarer and more unpredictable; I haven't heard one this year. Another name connected with this phenomenon is 'spittlebug' – though this refers to the creator rather than the product. *Philaenus spumarius* is the common version of the ambiguously named froghopper. Does it hop over frogs, or hop like one?

These white blobs are made by the nymph froghoppers, which in their vulnerable youth push air through a sticky secretion that coats their abdomen, rather like a child blowing bubbles. This foam eventually covers their bodies and protects them from desiccation while they feed on the sap of, in this case, lavender. Eggs are laid in November in the nooks and crooks of stems; each spring hatchling makes its own foam-ball.

I look more closely at the 'spit', the smell of the plant pleasantly overpowering as I approach it. The intricacy and density is impressive. The spittle cocoon is the size of a thumbnail, the bug the size of a linseed. If I touch it, apparently, it will leap. I don't.

What I do is search the internet, and all of a sudden there is negativity: 'How to get rid of . . .', 'remedy', 'pest'. *P. spumarius* is unwelcome to gardeners because it can sicken a plant. Apparently.

But here's something else: people are being asked to report spittlebug – that's the name they use – to map a potential infection zone of *Xylella*, a tree-killing bacterium rampant in Europe. Britain has escaped the disease so far, but if it arrives it would start where the spittlebugs are. Dutifully, I file a report online. Then I marvel at how an eye caught on a lavender bush grew to worry so quickly.

Simon Ingram, 2019

Perhaps the loneliest house in all of Wales

MIGNEINT, SNOWDONIA

*Decades ago, old Mr Roberts, who shepherded
on horseback, departed his remote home,
leaving it to the wild*

There are places among the Welsh hills where you may 'grow rich /
With looking'. In my copy of R. S. Thomas's *Collected Poems*, the
verse from which that's taken is marked with a curlew's feather,
picked up by Cefn Garw, perhaps the loneliest house in Wales. I've
often followed the 4-mile climbing track to it alongside the Serw
river.

Decades ago, old Mr Roberts, who shepherded on horseback,
departed his remote *tyddyn* (farm holding), leaving it to be used by
shearers who gather the moorland flock each year, or by occasional
hill-wanderers, or fishermen who cast a fly to lure the small brown
trout. With the shepherd gone, the moor was left to fox, raven,
pipit-hunting merlin, mewing buzzard. Nature eventually set to
reclaiming his house. Frost jagged cracks into the gables. Wind
rattled slates free from rusting nails. At some stravaigers' baccha-
nal, the beam supporting the chimney breast charred through. For
years, barn owls nested here. They too are gone.

I walk back there on a glorious early-summer day. Breezes rif-
fle the tawny grasses; curlew and cuckoo call distantly, merlin and
kestrel drop silently into tussocks to rise again with vole or shrew.
It is so lovely, so expansive, this moor with its 'clean colours / That
brought a moistening of the eye'. Sphagnum; bog cotton; heather's
umber soon to bloom purple.

Inside the *tyddyn*, the mural of a ram is faded, though still distinct. The roof has been repaired, the burnt beam replaced. Graffiti

is scrawled on flaking plaster: '*Jac Fedw, Dewi Garmon, yn hela llwynog 10/2/80*'. Do Jac and Dewi still 'hunt the fox' hereabouts? Is what brings them here the 'depth of silence, its being outside time and the chiming of a clock, the awesome quality of such a vast landscape with nobody in it'? That's Ian Niall, the Galloway writer, who came here often and first told me about it.

I leave with regret. A gibbous moon illuminates me down-valley. By the footbridge over the River Conwy, an owl hushes down as I cross the gorge to quit his pristine territory.

Jim Perrin, 2018

JULY

The hay harvest has begun, and the air is vanilla-sweet

CAISTOR ST EDMUND, NORFOLK

We badly need rain on the farm, just
not for the next five days

Three red kites slowly stir in the sky like sentinels. My eyes trace downwards to a cloud of dust swirling up from the ground. A neighbouring farm has started cutting the long grass to make hay. As the habitat is razed, wildlife will be scattering – voles, mice, deer, hares.

Back at High Ash farm, my brother consults the forecast. Should he too be cutting the hay? It's a high-risk crop. Most harvests are removed the second it is cut, safely into the barn. But hay must be left on the ground, at the mercy of the weather, requiring five sunny days before it is fully dry.

Overnight, the dismal grey cloud that has been shrouding Norfolk vanishes. The decision is made to cut a few fields, and the machinery roars into action. Wildlife here takes precedence. All the wildflower 'pollen and nectar' mixes will be left untouched until late August. Early cutting of hay is not ideal from a wildlife perspective, but nature-friendly mowing practices help reduce the impact. This includes cutting the field from the centre outwards, and having other uncut fields where animals can flee to. By contrast, in my dad's boyhood, terriers and lurchers would have been on hand to catch escaping creatures.

Later, as I stroll across the freshly mown field, I inhale that distinctive sweet, almost vanilla hay aroma that epitomises summer. The scent is known as 'coumarin' and is found in sweet vernal grass. It becomes more aromatic as it dries, and has even been synthesised for use in best-selling designer fragrances.

Going back a century or so, half this farm was hay crop, grown to fuel the working horses that laboured on the land. Today it is needed for leisure horses. The irony is that many owners will need to soak the hay to remove sugars and prevent horses becoming overweight.

This summer, we're heading into drought conditions, with young trees already dead or showing signs of stress. But just for a few days, we stop hoping for rain. This year's harvest is under way, and there's no turning back.

Kate Blincoe, 2023

The absurdity of being human in this unbearable heat

WELBURN, NORTH YORKSHIRE

I'm trying to escape it, but am thwarted at every turn by the impenetrable vegetation

On the hottest day England has known, I try to follow one of the springs to its source in the woods, thinking the shade and cool water will be soothing.

I'm wrong. The humidity under the canopy is almost unbearable, the saturated ground sucky, the vegetation impenetrable. We spend so much of our lives in spaces designed for humans, it's instructive to be reminded how easily nature can keep us out, turn us back. Despite our felling and our fences, our concrete and cultivation, despite parcels of data relayed to our pockets by satellite, we're not really in charge. I squirm and scramble and sweat, am scratched, stung, mired. I lose my sunglasses, am lucky to find them again. The wood swallows me effortlessly.

My feet find trails made by non-human strides. Along a deer passage, through spires of hedge woundwort, willowherb and figwort, I reach for a handful of raspberries, but hesitate when I find the canes are interwoven with woody nightshades. In an area where ailing ash trees have been clear-felled, dog's mercury – an ancient woodland indicator – is wilting badly. Looking spring-fresh, though, are dense stands of horsetail, those living fossils with far more archaic ideas of green. What year is it again?

The deer trail leads to a badger track lined with more toxic bonbons – the luscious-looking berries of lords-and-ladies. I have to duck and weave and climb to negotiate the low branches that badgers barrel under with ease, but it's still easier than forging my own path, so I go where it leads: to a disused sett, surrounded by half a tennis court of packed earth. It would make a good camp, and I wonder how many human settlements owe their location to the simple fact that badgers chose them first.

I reach a break of the slope from which I can look down on my house – it's only 100 metres away, but looks small and distant, like a cottage in a fairy tale or a horror story, wildwood pressing in on every side. And despite the heat, I feel a chill premonition of how easily we will be forgotten by this implacable wild, as the walls crumble, engineered angles soften to curves and green comes again where for a short while there was grey.

Amy-Jane Beer, 2022

The quiet horror of our picturesque views

THE MARCHES, SHROPSHIRE

When the 40°C heatwave passes, we'll go back to admiring our country vistas. But our plants will be changed forever

Thistles stand against the western view from the top of Lyth Hill. Armed against the changing weathers of history, the plumes of thistly defiance feel as indomitable as the far hills, as if whatever climate or human ambition sets against them will never dent their delinquent glory.

Increasingly, all these signs of permanence and reliability come closer to going up in flames. The day we moved house it was 40°C. It was crazy that this was happening here, and it felt as if everything was going to burn. In many other places, it did. Now that the rain returns, it's easy to fall into that convenient amnesia – what happened was just a weird episode that we'll forget, until the next time.

But plants can't forget. Back in the drought and heatwave of 1976, I was a gardener at Powis Castle and watched many old trees defoliate. Their annual rings bear the record. Some never fully recovered; many were weakened by the stress of heat and lack of water that opened them to attack by pathogens. Some died years later; others are still affected by that incident, compounded by more recent events.

Many of the trees I know and admire are declining, a visual illustration of a more pernicious reality. A post-traumatic stress has set into the vegetation of these islands and, as these so-called extreme events occur more frequently, we will watch as the trees and the fungi on which they depend change forever.

Looking west from the hill, the picturesque view to the Marches is not of an idyll but a con we construct in photos, paintings or writings of timeless hills, foregrounding the rude and rugged thistles as character actors in a historic drama, as if they have some kind of truth.

Perhaps this retreat into the picturesque is a reaction to the cycle of creation and destruction we think of as nature, but now that wheel's on fire and we are responsible. The picturesque is a sedative like the healing rain: it only works until the next time nature terrifies us. Maybe *Cirsium vulgare* thistles are tough enough to outlast the woods, to outlast us.

Paul Evans, 2022

A simple picnic in a miniature jungle

AUCKLAND PARK, BISHOP AUCKLAND, COUNTY DURHAM

*All around me the grassland is teeming with life,
from busy spiders to chocolate butterflies*

A geometrid moth caterpillar undulates through the grass. Grip with front legs. Cast off astern. Loop the body, drawing in the tail, and grip. Let go for'ard. Stretch to measure its length, with geometric precision, along the leaf. Grip again for'ard. And repeat. I tap the grass and the caterpillar freezes, relying on its resemblance to a dead twig to keep itself safe.

Dappled shade cast by a hawthorn makes this a perfect spot to sit and rest on a sultry summer afternoon. Nothing fancy for a picnic, just a cheese and chutney roll, a pear and a carton of orange juice, but the company is endlessly fascinating. The calcareous grassland of this ancient wood pasture is teeming with invertebrate life.

It's the season for plain-chocolate-coloured ringlet butterflies and meadow browns with milk-chocolate wings and a flash of orange. They pass through, rarely at rest. But the chimney sweepers – geometrid moths with sooty wings tipped with white – settle to lay eggs on flowers of pignut, a short, lacy umbellifer growing among grasses, clover and hawkweeds.

A couple of metres away, down the slope, lie hummocks of meadow-ant nests, smothered in tiny flowers of white heath bedstraw and pale-blue heath speedwell. The ants are rarely seen on the surface but are, even now, in subterranean tunnels beneath me, farming honeydew secreted by aphids that feed on grass-root sap.

The tallest grass around me is crested dog's tail. Its stiff straw, once used for weaving lightweight straw hats for days such as this, makes it unpalatable to sheep. It provides scaffolding for webs spun by spiders that abseil between its culms on near-invisible threads, apparently walking on air.

What will be the highlight of this summer? There was a time when it might have been finding rare species in grander locations. But perhaps it will be this, watching hoverflies investigate my pear core, or the spider spinning a silken thread from the grass on to my knee. It seems like a kind of acceptance into the world of myriad species whose brief lives are going on all around me.

Phil Gates, 2022

These wild grasses whisk me back to childhood

WELLINGTON, SOMERSET

*There are a bewildering number of species bursting
forth, conjuring memories of summers past*

We're a month beyond midsummer and have hit peak grass. The
narrow lanes that wind through the countryside round here are
narrowed further with the overspill of hedgerows on either side.
The hedges have lost the shocked, raw look after the springtime
flail and are bursting and frothy with life. Bracken tumbles on to
the tarmac, an unruly pitch invasion. The umbellifers lift their lacy
white parasols to the blazing sky, and 12-foot-high nettles lean in,
hoping to skim some passing skin.

I've been nettled so often this year, I'm beginning to quite like it.
There's a stimulating bite to the sensation that makes you feel extra
alive. The female flowers have ripened to seed, and each plant is
festooned with strings of densely clustered green seeds. Up close,
they look like *payals* – the anklet-bells worn by Indian dancers –
and it feels like, if your ears were sharp enough, you might hear
their tiny jingle.

It's not just the hedgerows that are zinging with life; the verges,
roundabouts and lawns are too. And once you get beyond the
clumpy cock's-foot grass, and the neat spikes of rye with its prim-
ly alternating chevrons, there is a bewildering number of grass
species – all those fescues, oat grasses and bents. Rather like moths,
listing the names produces a kind of poetry: smooth finger grass,
marsh foxtail, cock's-foot, Yorkshire fog, false oat grass, quaking
grass, colonial bent.

I often walk down a particular lane near my house just for the
wood melick that grows along one bank. This little grass loves

shady lanes and woodland edges, its tiny pale flower heads suspended on filaments so fine as to be almost invisible. They float like bubbles trapped in the amber of a dark-dappled lane at the drowsy, drunken height of the season.

Summer would not be summer without pinching a head of dry grass seed between finger and thumb and sliding your hand up the stem till you are left with a floret of beige seeds that smell like biscuits and summer holidays and all the long-lost dizzy days of childhood. Perhaps, down among the wild grass amid all this effervescent inflorescence, we are finally coming to our senses.

Anita Roy, 2021

Thank you to Norwich Cathedral for delivering this local specialist

CAISTOR ST EDMUND, NORFOLK

The hoary mullein may not be a beauty,
but its roots in this area go deep

Hoary Mullein. She sounds like the bawdy character in a medieval play. And certainly, there is nothing couth or overly refined about her – a statuesque candelabra of a plant, taller than me, with fluffy greyish leaves and often dishevelled yellow flowers.

I stroke its downy leaf, remembering that mulleins are known as 'Andrex plants', presenting as they do the ideal soft wipe for those caught short al fresco. The name 'hoary' – meaning greyish white, as if with age or from the ice of a hoar frost – is a reference to its pale fluff. Wriggling motion catches my attention. A large caterpillar marked yellow and black munches away on a leaf. It can only be the larva of the mullein moth. A bee gathers pollen, the pollen sacs on its legs turning bright orange-red like painful growths.

The plant has a wasteland, murder-drama vibe. Like a forensic pathologist, it often favours soil that has been disturbed, such as railway embankments, old quarries and gravel pits. It arrived here, at our farm, in soil excavated from beside Norwich Cathedral. The seeds had probably lain dormant for decades, just waiting for the right circumstances.

Blackstone's *Specimen Botanicum*, published in 1746, states that hoary mullein was first recorded in 1745 in a typically unglamorous location, 'about the ditch on the outside of the city walls at Norwich'. But a quick internet check indicates that there are records dating back to 1670. While the great mullein is widespread, hoary is not. It is a Norfolk and Suffolk specialist, although increasingly found elsewhere. As a fellow Norfolk girl, I feel bonded.

Hoary mullein is just a plant. An easily overlooked, not particularly attractive specimen found in some not particularly attractive spots. I want to make it enough. Enough for us to care about as a small link in an ecosystem, with local history growing through its veins. Maybe by recording its presence, connecting Blackstone's record to mine, it will somehow matter. So here we go: 'Hoary mullein, on rough ground by farm track, July 2022.'

Kate Blincoe, 2022

It's clipping day on the farm, but the wool is worthless

TEBAY, CUMBRIA

Sheep are clipped because of the heat. This year's mountain of wool will join last year's in the hay barn

Around 6 p.m. the wind drops, and we feel the full force of the sun on the clipping trailer. We started gathering the sheep at 9 a.m. and have been clipping ever since. My job is to move the waiting sheep through a series of pens, up a ramp and on to the trailer to be clipped.

Most of the sheep follow on up the ramp, but some are reluctant, so I must encourage them, or push. The sheep weigh about 70 kilos and push back with great force. My knees and thighs are very bruised.

The clipping shears buzz constantly, and every couple of minutes there is a bang as a new sheep comes through the gate. Once they're on their bottoms, though, the sheep do not struggle. They go into a sort of trance and allow themselves to be moved gently from left to right by the clipper as their fleece is removed. It must be a tremendous relief in this heat.

The lambs were separated from their mothers this morning, and they hang around the trailer waiting, some bleating constantly. As the day wears on, the noise from the lambs dies down as ewes and lambs are reunited. The dogs lie sleeping under the trailer in the shade, and we all long for the last sheep to be clipped so we can jump in the river to cool off.

The wool is shoved roughly into the wool bag. It is virtually valueless. Once, rough fell wool like this was used in mattresses or carpets, but now it's only worth about 5p per kilo – less than it would cost to transport. We still have last year's wool in bags in the hay barn, and this year's mountain will join it.

Clipping is done out of necessity: no sheep would want to wear a full fleece in this heat. But it is no longer a money-making activity for the farm. Manufactured synthetic materials and plastics have wrecked the value of this sustainable, renewable fibre.

Andrea Meanwell, 2021

A grasshopper in the sun shows me the way

WARDLOW, DERBYSHIRE

It's the colour of limes with chocolate stripes, a well-hidden gem – though not the one I was searching for

If you're given a treasure map, you feel some obligation to follow it – especially when the treasure is a rare flower and the map's clues are so beguiling. That's how I found myself in the fresh early morning, following a dry valley uphill, ignoring a cart track as advised, stepping across a broken fence and passing through a thick stand of hawthorn, where I paused and looked for an unlikely detail: a wooden step in a dry-stone wall.

Beyond that was a cliff, and in between me and the void, a rich bank of flowers: St John's wort and sweetbriar roses, knapweed and spear thistle, pink-tinged yarrow and the deeper pink of oregano. A treasure chest, but not the jewel I was looking for. There were larks singing at my back and song thrushes below, their bubble of music rising up from woods still in shadow at the base of the crag. I eased closer to the edge, since that's where so much of the world seems to be these days, and scanned the ground: nothing.

Except, not nothing. True, I'd trapped myself into seeking a goal and chided myself a little for that. But while I was hunting, my concentration had sharpened and I'd become unusually attentive. That's how I spotted the grasshopper crouching in a clump of heath bedstraw at my feet.

The low sunlight had picked out its head and the pronotum, the plate-like structure just behind the head. It was the colour of limes, fringed with a paler border along its keel where it curved around the body, but with chocolate stripes running vertically either side towards the rear. The whole arrangement was faceted, like a gem. I saw one beaded wing sticking out at right angles, which seemed odd. Grasshoppers are cold-blooded, so perhaps this one was warming up.

Then it was gone, and I stood up to stretch. At which point, from the corner of my eye, I saw what I'd come for: a low plant with unmistakable flowers caught in the sun on the edge of the abyss.

Ed Douglas, 2021

A prickly love affair in my garden

LANGSTONE, HAMPSHIRE

Britain's hedgehog population has declined by a third in urban areas – but it's not too late to take action

For the past decade, my garden has been enclosed to provide a home for non-releasable blind and amputee hedgehogs. A six-foot perimeter fence kept them safely contained and presented an impenetrable barrier to their wild kin; so when my last resident, Poppet, passed away at the grand old age of ten (a hedgehog's average life expectancy in the wild is two to three years), I signed up to participate in Hedgehog Street, a nationwide conservation initiative empowering people to improve their neighbourhood for these much-loved mammals.

Since the millennium, Britain's hedgehog population has declined by a third in urban areas, but the appearance on my driveway of glistening black droppings packed full of invertebrate exoskeletons gave me hope that I wasn't too late to take action. A foraging hedgehog can roam up to a mile a night, so ensuring they can travel freely between gardens is vital to reduce habitat loss and fragmentation.

I pulled the bottom slat off a fence panel (alternatively, a hole measuring 13 centimetres square is sufficient for an adult to squeeze through) and, as dusk fell, I scattered a trail of hedgehog food on either side of the 'hedgehog highway' and settled down to wait. Before long, I heard the crunch of footsteps on the gravel drive and the pig-like grunts and snuffles that give hedgehogs their name. In the shadows, not one but two pointed snouts appeared beneath the fence. The first scuttled past me. The second, larger animal trundled behind, pausing to sniff my bare feet, its moist nose dabbing my ankles.

They were a courting couple, the male pursuing the female across the lawn, round the pond and through the flower borders. Cornering her, he began to circle, the female pivoting to face him. Round and round they spun, like Viennese waltzers, the female jerking her body and chuffing like a steam locomotive.

This courtship ritual can last for hours, but just as I was about to turn in, the female stilled and pressed her belly to the ground. As she flattened her spines, the male mounted her, biting the prickles on her shoulders to steady himself.

Claire Stares, 2020

Gripped by a grayling's disappearing act

DARTMOOR, DEVON

*I pinpoint the butterfly's position and approach
carefully, but still it eludes me*

The path ahead runs like a threadbare strip of carpet between low-lying vegetation. Scuffed by walkers, eroded by the elements and frayed by sheep, its worn matting of coarse grass scarcely covers the stony ground.

As I follow it up the slope of this west Dartmoor hill, I can hear on all sides the pistol-crack of gorse pods popping in the heat, firing their seeds around them, and sunshine has set grasshoppers on the trail, chirping in bursts that sound like tiny pneumatic drills.

Small heath butterflies flush in front of me, thumbnails of orange that settle nearby, and there's the occasional meadow brown. Then a larger butterfly takes me by surprise, rising suddenly and racing away on dark wings, twisting above the path before landing abruptly on dry grass.

I pinpoint its position and approach carefully, but somehow can't locate it. Only when it flies do I see that it was right where I was looking. Then once again it deceives me, touching down on the track ahead and seemingly vanishing.

This master of camouflage is the grayling (*Hipparchia semele*), a species of open terrain that hides in plain sight. It collapses itself in two movements, like a foldaway table on an aircraft, closing its brown-and-orange wings and sliding away the front half. With its prominent eye spots and concealed colouring, all that remains visible is the muddy grey underside of its hind wings. Their marbled and mottled patterning blends perfectly with pebbles, bark and bare ground in the places it inhabits, and wings are often tilted to catch the warmth of the sun, reducing the shadow it casts.

The grayling is a butterfly for the holiday season – a late-summer, hot-weather-loving species found in Britain's coastal areas and southern heathland sites. However, it is a disappearing act in more ways than one, having declined in many areas over recent decades.

I spot only a couple of graylings on my walk, and it feels like a triumph to eventually get close-up views – though who knows how many others I missed along the way. When it comes to a game of hide-and-seek, don't expect to beat the grayling.

Charlie Elder, 2020

Spectacular moths, dark stars of the forest

WYTHERSTON, DORSET

A night of moth-trapping in ancient woodland reveals some stunning species, including Britain's largest

'What's that stealth bomber?' Anna points to a charcoal and black moth the length of her little finger. It perches motionless, velvet abdomen curved upwards as if ready to sting, scalloped wings tilted, silver antennae stowed tight along its chunky thorax. It's an eyed hawk-moth (*Smerinthus ocellata*).

We've been moth trapping on the edge of Powerstock Forest, an ancient woodland. Overnight, the lightbox has attracted a baffling range of insects. A burnished brass moth (*Diachrysia chrysitis*) gleams in a cranny near the lid, its metallic wings winking penny-bright in the morning sun. Several buff-tips (*Phalera bucephala*) pretend to be chipped birch twigs. A tiny orchard ermine (*Yponomeuta padella*), white wings peppered with black flecks, rests on an eggbox.

The hawk-moths are spectacular. The drab khaki and dusty-pink striped elephant hawk-moth (*Deilephila elpenor*) is the most familiar. Elephant refers not to its size but to its caterpillars, which supposedly resemble elephants' trunks. It looks small beside the privet hawk-moth (*Sphinx ligustri*), which, with a wingspan of up to 12 centimetres, is Britain's largest resident species. This specimen must be nearly that big. Its huge, elongated, furry abdomen is banded rose carmine and black like some carnival hornet.

Sphinx ligustri is often found in Dorset woods and gardens, where it feeds on nectar from night-scented flowers. July is the month its massive caterpillars will be hatching. Lime green with white and lilac side flashes, their soft, yoghurt-gum bodies culminate in a black and yellow tail horn.

But the true dark star is the eyed hawk-moth. We gently coax it on to a hand, where it slowly wakes, unfurls long antenna lined with bristly filaments and starts to vibrate its wings to warm up its flight muscles. As it revs up, its hind wings open fully, revealing a startling pair of blue 'eyes'.

It doesn't let us admire them for long. With a flip of its abdomen, it suddenly defecates thick blobs of yellow, before taking off into a shadowy bay tree.

Sara Hudston, 2019

How much life can there be in one square metre?

CLAXTON, NORFOLK

An experiment in my back garden highlights how disgraceful it is that our greens and verges are incessantly mowed

This spring, Rotherham borough council received deserved praise for the banks of native flowers it now allows to flourish on its verges. During this period, I noted how most main roadsides across Norfolk had been turned brown with herbicide spray, although presently the dual carriageway around Norwich has slopes awash with the colours of wild perennials.

In our parish, the small green, barely 15 metres by 100 metres, is mown according to the unthinking orthodoxy that prevails across much of civic Britain. It's a waste of money, fuel and resources, but does it really matter to wildlife that the patch is reduced every fortnight to shorn turf?

I set up a one-hour experimental watch on a garden spot where we have abandoned all but a single annual cut. It supports about twenty self-willed plant species, especially yellow rattle, marjoram, oxeye daisy and a sun-specked horizon of common cat's-ear.

In sixty minutes, I recorded on one square metre – featuring, it must be said, a triffid-like hogweed spike – a Congo-like delta of black ant trails; a common carder bumblebee; two unknown solitary bees; one meadow brown butterfly; two solitary wasp species (new for the parish); swollen-thighed, pollen and varied carpet beetles; a soldier beetle (*Rhagonycha limbata*); variable damselfly; harlequin ladybird; common green capsid bugs; a greenbottle; as well as common banded, marmalade, long and bumblebee hoverflies. Pride of place among the named – and there were too many unnamed or unknown insects – were a gorgeous pink form of meadow grasshopper and a flake of scintillating bronze soldered to a lozenge-shaped emerald that entomology has chosen to name the 'broad centurion' soldier fly.

The hogweed was subsequently visited by aphid-feasting blue tits, while the seed-setting cat's-ear, before it could parachute away, drew in a charm of feeding goldfinches. Overhead, the village swifts have screamed blue murder every daylight hour.

Assailed with thoughts of the sixth extinction and the Anthropocene, people often ask how they can feel hopeful. Perhaps we should note that a patch the width of a single pace gives home to fifty species or more, and hope grows with each small step we take.

Mark Cocker, 2019

Harassed by the jackdaws, impressed by the gannets

ST NON'S, ST DAVIDS, PEMBROKESHIRE

*The intelligence of crows never fails
to make itself evident*

On a fine summer's morning, there were more jackdaws than pilgrims at St Non's, the birthplace of Saint David, the patron saint of Wales. The spiritual accountants deemed that two journeys to this shrine were worth a pilgrimage to Rome. Medieval hagiography describes Non giving birth outdoors in a tempest so violent that not a soul set foot outside to help.

Jackdaws ushered me away from well and chapel. They hurried me along the coastal path with querulous calls, cocking their heads, fixing bright eyes on a rucksack that, to corvid consciousness, clearly proclaimed food. The intelligence of crows never fails to make itself evident.

Once I'd reached a favourite rock seat, they were bouncing up and down and coming close with their rollicking walk. Such neat and beautiful birds. They charmed the greater part of my picnic from me, made off with chunks of home-baked rye bread with rosemary and walnuts, squabbled over slivers of cheese, snatched after biscuits and noisily bade me farewell when all was gone.

It was in the ensuing silence that percussive reports from below registered. I peered over the cliff edge. A squadron of gannets had raced in from the guano-painted rock of Grassholm. They plunged down in 45-degree dives, sending up plumes of spray, emerging with mackerel from the shoal they'd followed here.

I focused my glass on these majestic birds, their heads pollen-yellow, the white cross of their narrow wings, which they fold as they crash into the water, tipped with black. I remembered visiting the world's second-largest gannetry (the largest is on the Bass Rock in the Firth of Forth, from which comes the gannet's scientific name *Morus bassanus*) in Canada's Gulf of St Lawrence twenty years ago. The stench of 100,000 nesting, jostling birds lives with me still.

'Yarra, yarra, yarra,' they scream, filling the air, swirling above the sea, their skulls equipped with air-pocket shock absorbers, protecting their brains against the impact of those spectacular dives.

Jim Perrin, 2019

The soft sounds of sparrow seduction

SANDY, BEDFORDSHIRE

The house sparrows are busy caring for their young,
but still find time to mate dozens of times a day

Lolling in the shade under a hazel bush, I had become the inadvertent eavesdropper on a private conversation. Out of the canopy came a whispered 'brrr' whirr of wings, then the soft sounds of sparrow seduction, a love song of tenderness that is scarcely imaginable from a bird known for its strident chirps.

Gentle, soothing, piteous peeps drifted down, an intimate dialogue that was both charming and disarming. I caught a glimpse through the sparrows' bower and saw the female, mouth agape, wings a-flutter. The male rode her for a second or two only. House sparrows may mate up to forty times a day, but it's always a quickie.

For the female, coitus interrupted something far more pressing. The instant he dismounted, she flew back to her chick-packed nest box, clawed against the rim of the hole and tipped inside.

For a full fortnight, I have shared outdoor mealtimes with the sparrows. I knew the eggs had hatched when the pair started making frequent sorties to a row of nearby lime trees. They were probably bringing back baby food, their beaks stuffed full of soft-bodied aphids. Days later, the female took in bigger, hard-bodied prey – I saw the tangle of legs and wings of a cranefly, and a giant baguette of a broad-bodied chaser dragonfly, only just fitting through the aperture. By now, the male had vanished, and feeding was done by the female alone.

Each arrival at the nest set off a thin, piping chorus. She would habitually fly from the nest hole with a cream-coloured faecal sac in her beak. The peeps grew louder and more chirp-like, the chick 'nappies' got bigger.

On one of the last days, I counted the times between her leaving and returning to the nest – thirty-two seconds, twenty-seven, thirty-five. She had found a source of fast food – a ground feeder in a neighbouring garden – but the switch to a seed-packed diet was exactly what her nearly grown chicks needed.

The chicks have now fledged, and the female and her new beau were at it again just now up on the gutter. I listened hard and caught the quiet hum, the murmur of sweet sparrow nothings.

Derek Niemann, 2018

We can't blame the heatwave for this desiccated landscape

ROMBALDS MOOR, WEST YORKSHIRE

Peatland habitats are vital and precious, yet we've spent decades deliberately drying them out

It's early morning; the day hasn't yet been fully cranked up, and the broken sky is a messy palette of blues and greys. The moors, though, are a tinderbox. Parched and crisped by weeks of dry summer heat, the heather is a burnt brown-to-burgundy, the moorland grass yellowed. The bracken is still a deep pea-green (it takes a lot to bother bracken), but finger-wide cracks have opened in the colourless peat of the footpath.

Rombalds Moor covers the hump of upland separating Airedale in the south from Wharfedale in the north. Walking the sun-baked flanks of the Wharfe catchment, we'd found that Barden Moor and Barden Fell had been closed due to the risk of fire. Those are grouse moors, and so is this; every so often I frighten a bird up out of the bents, and I can hear them burping and clucking around the feeding stations set up by the gamekeepers.

A dry peatland is a man-made phenomenon. 'Peatland habitats form over thousands of years,' Dr Tim Thom, peat programme manager at Yorkshire Wildlife Trust, tells me. 'As a society, we've spent decades drying them out.'

A healthy peatland should be wet; a cool, dark blanket of deep peat and saturated sphagnum moss. Breeding waders like it that way, so do raptors, lizards, cotton-grasses and carnivorous sun-dew plants. But years of 'reclamation' – ditch-digging and burning, mainly – mean it's now a threatened habitat in the UK.

Some peatlands amount to historical ruins: landscapes that were millennia in the making (a metre of peat represents a thousand years of steady mulching) reduced to bare dirt and ragged peat hags. A few, thanks to back-breaking work by conservation and restoration groups, like the Yorkshire Peat Partnership, thrive. Most are somewhere in between – their fate still hangs in the balance.

From Ilkley Moor, to the north, a curlew whinnies. A short-eared owl flaps heavily along the near horizon. The sun is beginning to break through.

Richard Smyth, 2018

AUGUST

The murderous wails of polecats in high summer

INKPEN, NORTH WESSEX DOWNS, BERKSHIRE

*Their hysterical yikkering even cuts through the drone
of a distant night-time combine harvester*

Nothing seems to be sleeping in the heat. Our neighbour's bedroom TV plays a loop of old films, sending clipped, forthright phrases drifting into the night. In the eaves between us, sparrows flutter uncomfortably. Even the lullaby drone of the field-away combine harvester isn't soothing. Flint lies on our fields like broken crockery, and there have already been combine-sparked flint fires. We are all a bit jittery.

A sudden hysterical yikkering outside makes me sit up. The polecats are back! I go first to the window and then outside, grabbing the big lamp on my way, keeping it switched off. In high summer, jill polecats and their kits can be vocal for several nights, play-hunt-fighting in the arable.

The barley shifts and crackles right up to the garden gate like a dry, restless sea. I stand and watch. There are more murderous wails, yips and squabbling. These whirling dervishes must be just feet away. Subconsciously, I curl my toes in and tuck my nightdress between my knees.

The sound becomes a crescendo. In a moment of doubt, I switch on the lamp – perhaps it is cats after all, or fox cubs – and am presented with a face. It's the briefest snapshot: bright eyes in a Lone Ranger bandit mask; fierce, ferrety features; a teddy bear's ears and nose. It vanishes after the ripple of barley ahead, flowing its luxuriant stole of black-and-cream fur behind it.

The former gamekeeper sometimes used to call them by their old names: 'fitch' or 'foulmart'. They have returned to southern

England from a wild population in Wales on their own terms. These ones are on the edge of my hearing when the combine reaches a gap in the hedge. It raises its wide header on the turn with a roar and a flash of headlights, illuminating a plume of chalk dust.

I think of the glimpse of sable fur, a smouldering coat of fury, ash and white-hot embers. A thrilling fire starter of an animal. From behind me, canned laughter peals from next door's upstairs window.

Nicola Chester, 2022

Choughs patrol the cliffs, cawing at everything

THE CHASMS, ISLE OF MAN

The island is a stronghold for these boisterous corvids, thanks to our tightly grazed farmland

I sit as close to the edge as I dare. Below me, great hulks of former cliff sit below the surface. Rising up among them is the Sugarloaf. Just a few weeks ago it was festooned with thousands of seabirds. Now, only three kittiwake chicks remain unfledged among the guano. But today I'm not here to see the seabirds, I am here to see a crow.

Chiarr! It takes just two minutes to hear one. These birds want their presence known. Soon it is not just one bird I hear, but four – no, five birds patrolling the clifftops. I have found some choughs.

They approach noisily, flying into the steady breeze, scolding as they draw near. Their flight is erratic, travelling in one direction yet many others at once. Like a gang of bullies, they caw at everything and anything, including me. They pass over my head, then tuck in their wings and plummet, demonstrating their unique, undulating flight reminiscent of a roller coaster. Once across the bay, they alight on a steep grassy bank, where they feast on what are presumably flying ants.

The Isle of Man is a stronghold for the birds, with around one pair for every kilometre of rocky coast, about 130 pairs in all – an incredible one-third of the British and Manx total. On the southern coast of our small island nation, you can regularly see flocks of fifty to sixty birds, sometimes more.

The reason for such abundance is simple. In summer, being insectivorous, choughs gather in our tightly grazed farmland, where there is dung. In winter, when the fields are bereft of tasty morsels, they take to the seaweed-strewn beaches and dine on sandhoppers. Come the spring, they seek out the caves, abandoned buildings and (increasingly) farm barns for nesting. Nowhere do they thrive as they do here in Ellan Vannin – the Manx name for the Isle of Man – with its green hills by the sea.

Back on my spot, 100 metres above the sparkling sea, I see in quick succession a family of peregrines, a male hen harrier, two ravens and a basking shark. But none to me are as captivating as the feisty, red-legged king of the crows.

David Bellamy, 2022

A quiet stretch of river where the dragonflies and trout thrive

ABERAERON, CEREDIGION

It's a hot day for a walk, so I pause by the Afon Aeron. Even for late summer, its levels are low

The worst of the heat has slipped away into the east, and a wind from the sea is starting to cool the stone of the harbour walls. It is just after low water, and the streamers of seaweed below me are beginning to turn upstream with the flow of the tide.

I follow their lead, crossing the harbour on the wooden foot-bridge and taking the path inland on the southern side of the Afon Aeron. New, bright thistle flowers erupt from the old stone wall that guards the stream, the stems describing narrow arcs in the breeze. The tidal limit is quickly reached, and even for high summer the level of the river is low.

As I continue east, the trees in full, dark summer leaf block out much of the remaining glare, shading the banks where black-birds perch to drink. Further on, grey wagtails make short, erratic flights over the water, taking flies on the wing before landing on water-rounded stones to rest and demonstrate robustly how they got their name. My walk has a welcome interruption when I meet an old friend on the path and get introduced to their young and very enthusiastic spaniel, who looks down at the cool water with obvious longing.

Above a quiet bridge, the river pools idly between overgrown margins. Barely conspicuous over the pebbled bed, small brown trout – hardly more than fingerlings – ease their way against the gentle current. On the smooth surface of the water, growing rings appear like the marks of raindrops, but these plot the floundering impact of newly hatched flies. The trout approach and strike, taking the insects with a barely audible plop, while large dragonflies halt and dash in an ancient pattern above the water.

I have paused too long, and dark heavy clouds are starting to build in the humid late afternoon. Taking the lane to the north of the river I head onwards once more, leaning into my stride in an attempt to make up time.

John Gilbey, 2022

Cherishing the true-blue skies, free of 'aerostratus'

TEMPSFORD, BEDFORDSHIRE

This time last year, the planes stopped. By rising early on a summer's morning, you can, briefly, recreate that pristine moment

If only we choose to raise our eyes, so many of us can look up to an unmarked sky. How long will this last, the second truly blue summer of our lives, and will I live to see another?

A surreal moment from the first – when the world stopped last year – will stay with me. I'd stepped outside, phone in hand, and pointed it above my head to record the pristine blue over the rooftops, over the limes, the sycamores, willows and cherry. No raggedy off-white ribbons, messy cross-hatching or blurred bands of a false front. Heaven had healed the scars, scores and slashes of aircraft vapour trails. Week after week we were blessed with the sunniest, bluest, purest skies we had ever known.

A year later, it's early morning and I'm standing on the high footbridge over the river, girdled by water meadows full of ruminating cows. I want to mark this precious period before the low rumble of high thunder begins again, the human traffic that lifts off from Stansted or Luton. I want to at least half remember a time I wish never to forget.

To the north, purple clouds are carrying away the unwept remains of that pre-daylight shower. Low on the eastern horizon, a narrow cloudless bank of pink glows, the remainder of a dawn passed. Shafts of god rays break through a chink, maybe 100 metres above. To the left, a ripple effect, like tide marks left on shale sand. And swivelling right, more shaping: a herringbone pattern that half fills the southern sky. Unusually, it is from the west that puffy optimism comes, billowing white clouds edging closer with grey wisps and backed by the lightest sky blue.

I have read the minutes in nimbus, cumulus and cirrus, untainted by 'aerostratus' – the residual trails of planes. And then comes the air traffic: a skein of six Canada geese passing overhead. They leave nothing in their wake.

Derek Niemann, 2021

Fill your nose with a cornucopia of August scents

WOLSINGHAM, WEARDALE, NORTH PENNINES

Smell can be so specific – the fragrance of meadowsweet blossom reminds me of my late aunt Pat

The hottest day of summer so far, in an exceptionally fine week for haymaking. Long windrows of mown grass pattern the meadow, shimmering in the heat haze, and the still, humid air is saturated with the fragrance of drying hay. A day to celebrate one's sense of smell – especially now, when its loss is recognised as an early symptom of Covid. We take deep, reassuring breaths.

Fifty years ago, when I was a botany undergraduate, a lecturer taught me that a nose well attuned to the odours of plant species could be a valuable asset. Compare crushed hedge woundwort (nauseating) with marsh woundwort (pleasantly fruity), he advised, and their identity will never be in doubt again.

But the language for describing the subtlety of plant scents to others, with broad-brush adjectives such as fetid, pungent or aromatic, is too vague. Often, conveying perceptions relies on comparisons with something unrelated, from shared common experience. The stench of flowers of alexanders – a widely naturalised pot herb – was once memorably likened to that of an overflowing public urinal on a hot summer day.

Sometimes these experiences can be very personal, even generation-specific. Crushed tansy leaves remind me of a long-discontinued brand of floor polish used by my grandmother. The wintergreen-oil scent of meadowsweet leaf sap is reminiscent of the green healing ointment applied by a kind primary-school teacher to a bleeding knee grazed in the playground. The fragrance of meadowsweet blossom, perfuming the air on the edge of the meadow here today, connects me with the face powder used by my late aunt Pat.

Each month in the countryside has its own bouquet of scents. This afternoon, the base fragrance of drying grass was lifted by citrusy notes of oil released by ripening hogweed seeds when I rubbed them between finger and thumb. And in the shade of trees along the riverbank, the cool, reviving tang of aniseed from crushed sweet cicely seeds and foliage put a spring back in our step, just when our energy was flagging.

Maybe Covid anxiety, with its threat of olfactory loss, might make perfumers of us all.

Phil Gates, 2021

Making hay on a family farm

MORCOMBELAKE, DORSET

Under livestock farmer Tom Sneath's chemical-free management, plants are starting to reappear in the fields

This has been an exceptional year for haymaking, with some fields producing double the usual amount. A wet growing season and then a sustained hot spell have provided near perfect conditions.

Hay is livestock farmer Tom Sneath's most important crop. It provides winter fodder for his sheep and black-and-white belted Galloway beef cattle. Last year, they ate 700 of the big round bales and 1,000 small rectangular ones.

Tom is the fourth generation of his family to farm the damp, hilly pastures around Morcombelake. He rents nearly 200 acres, almost half of it from the National Trust. The land includes several protected Sites of Special Scientific Interest, some noted for brilliant autumn displays of coloured waxcap fungi. A few of the fields were once part of a conventional dairy farm. Under this previous regime, they were ploughed, reseeded, fertilised and sprayed with herbicide, reducing the variety of plants in favour of fast-growing 'improved' grass species.

After five years of Tom's chemical-free management, the fine-laced, creamy umbels of corky-fruited water dropwort sway beside branching sprays of yellow cat's-ear and clumps of purple knapweed. Tall marsh thistles with deep roots bring up minerals from far below the reach of a ploughshare.

Haymaking has helped the plants reappear. When Tom's stock are overwintering in these particular fields, he feeds them bales made on 'unimproved' pastures nearby. The animals spread their fodder all over the ground, shaking free the seed and trampling it into the mud. In spring, the seed grows and flowers before being mown, and the cycle begins again.

Tom has finished haymaking for this season. The brown shorn fields are already greening, and the autumn flush of grass will soon be here. Tom plans to run some sheep there before the cattle return. Then it will be time to feed them hay again. Breaking open the bales will release the fragrance of summer past, and the potential of summers to come.

Sara Hudston, 2021

Flying ant day is here, there and everywhere

LANGSTONE, HAMPSHIRE

Flying en masse means safety in numbers, though thousands are still picked off by an avian onslaught

I awoke to the raucous screeching of black-headed and herring gulls, punctuated by the exclamatory yelps of Mediterranean gulls. Pulling back the curtains, I saw they were swooping and swirling above the garden in a feeding frenzy, bills snapping as they snatched insects on the wing.

There had been a heavy downpour overnight, and the subsequent combination of bright sunshine, high humidity and low wind speed had triggered the mass emergence of black garden ants (*Lasius niger*). Outside, I found fertile winged adults – known as alates – erupting from a crack in the paving slabs, while more streamed out from a second nest beneath the bird bath.

'Flying ant day' tends to be spoken about as a nationwide event. Certainly, if conditions are consistent, the spectacle can be witnessed across a wide area – social media alerted me to concurrent emergences all along the south coast. However, it often takes place over several days and can occur anytime between June and August, depending on local conditions.

The ants took to the air and scattered, the larger virgin queens wafting pheromone trails to lure drones from other colonies. The fastest, most robust suitors coupled with the queens in nuptial flight. As well as increasing the probability of finding a mate, flying en masse means safety in numbers, though thousands of individuals were still being picked off.

The feasting continued for almost two hours, the gulls joined by a flock of swifts, scything through clouds of ants on crescent wings. Swallows and house martins followed, hawking over the trees and chimney stacks, where the insects were gathering in dense swarms – a behaviour known as 'hilltopping'. These aggregations sometimes grow dense enough to be picked up on the Met Office's radar.

After mating, males die within a few days. Surviving fertilised queens have an average lifespan of fifteen years, but the remainder of their existence will be earthbound, as they strike out on their own to establish new colonies. That evening, I found their chewed-off wings littering the patio like iridescent scraps of cellophane.

Claire Stares, 2021

All around the Bone Caves, the stillness is spectacular

ASSYNT, SUTHERLAND

Here lay the bones of bears, wolves and humans,
the past looming heavy on the present

The signs at the start of the glen tell me that a mile and a half beyond lie caves that held the bones of reindeer and brown bears, horses, Arctic foxes, lemmings, wolves and lynx. It's a dreich day with a heavy sky as we walk up to the Bone Caves. The path is fringed with bracken and heather, and populated by midges that are thriving in the stillness.

Last time I was here, an early July a couple of years ago, the bracken was alive with magpie moths, black and white with just a touch of orange. Today there's only the clack of a stonechat and, once, a flurry of grey wagtails. There are flowers too in this glorious limestone glen – occasional sunbursts of yellow mountain saxifrage, and near the caves the remnants of beautiful mountain avens, the back of their leaves extraordinarily silver in hue. This place always feels like the domain of ravens, but the sky is birdless, and in the glen no animals can be seen.

The caves themselves are up a steep path, and I can't help but wonder whether anyone would attempt to climb up and peer in if they were not pathed and signposted. They're tucked into the bottom of a smooth cliff, easy to miss, and don't look particularly impressive. And yet here we are. This glen, these caves, forged by glaciers and water over millennia, and populated by birds and animals that in some cases are no longer found in this country and are globally scarce. Where human remains have been found, they have been radiocarbon dated to over 4,500 years old.

We walk beyond the caves and follow the circular route back down the glen just as the rain starts. We look down towards Loch Assynt and the mountains beyond. I've a line of a Norman MacCaig poem in my head – 'As in the long ago, as in forever' – and as we look west we see a brightness to the sky that has not yet reached us, but will reach us soon.

Amanda Thomson, 2021

A giant of the Alps has appeared over the Peak District

CROWDEN, DERBYSHIRE

Glamorous and calm, the bearded vulture soars above us with barely a flap, making buzzards look like jackdaws

A vulture in the middle of England? A wild, free-flying 9-foot-winged bird of the Alps and Pyrenees, a bone-eating, tortoise-dropping inhabitant of wolf-haunted montane crags – here, over the Derbyshire moors, with their grouse and their sadly piping pipits? The very idea seemed momentous.

Even as we watched the creature – a second-year, probably female, bearded vulture (*Gypaetus barbatus*) – sail along Shining Clough Moss, it was hard to credit something so expressive of European wilderness. Yet there it floated with barely a flap – massive, glamorous, completely calm – and wheeling away from aggressive buzzards that mithered after it. These lesser predators, which are themselves no mean aerial masters, looked by the side of the giant no bigger than jackdaws. Each one in its entirety was less than one wing's length of the vulture.

Yet there have been precedents and predictions of just such a visitation to Derbyshire. On 4 June 1927, two griffon vultures were seen in the skies over Ashbourne. Sadly, the record has since been rejected, but there are some who still believe in those birds of nearly a century ago.

Reintroduction programmes in Switzerland, Austria and Italy have seen bearded vulture numbers treble in recent years. There have also been numerous modern records of wild birds wandering across northern Europe. In 2000, when several griffon vultures were seen in the Netherlands, it was pointed out that at 22,000 feet, a vulture could look across the North Sea and actually see, on a clear day, all the way to the Peak District.

The more troubling reflection concerns the bird's safe return. The Peak District National Park holds several grouse moors that are among the worst British localities for the illegal killing of raptors. So far, the bird has managed to avoid any mishap and has survived on sheep carcasses (its old German name, *Lämmergeier*, means 'lamb vulture'). To return to the mountains of its birth, however, this bearded vulture must fly back over the heads of roughly 90 million people. One can only pray it completes the homeward leg of its adventure just as safely.

Mark Cocker, 2020

A prickle of excitement among the purple thistles

EMPINGHAM, RUTLAND

These emblematic plants may be under-appreciated south
of Scotland, but they do attract the odd rare butterfly

Empingham Marshy Meadows has transformed since April. The spring flora has been succeeded by clouds of fragrant meadowsweet along the damp, sedgy bottom of the valley, and on the slopes by bird's-foot trefoil and buttercups.

Although they are the national flower of Scotland, south of the border we under-celebrate thistles, their subtle shades and spiky architectures. Here, in addition to mauve-flowered spear thistles and shiny-leaved lavender creeping thistles, there are at least two less ubiquitous species present. Marsh thistles dominate along the edge of the damper soils; their extra-prickly stems shoot up 2 metres and curve over at the apex, where exceptionally nectar-rich clusters are frequented by a stream of bumblebees.

The second specialist is the almost stemless dwarf thistle; with a touch of cerise in its flowers, this is the most vivid in colour. Sheep fields west of the village host a fifth species: the magnificent musk thistle, with its drooping, satsuma-like, royal purple blooms.

Seven young white-and-black dappled Friesians have arrived and are lazing in the meadow. There is plenty of sward for them to consume, and doing so will ensure that the flowering herbs don't get crowded out by grass and shrubs.

One thing guaranteed to set a flutter in my chest is the moment a butterfly's wings unlock and reveal an unexpected picture; the instant when the routine becomes the exceptional. I spy a whiteish butterfly on a yarrow umbel; as I approach, its wings snap open, revealing the chequerboard patterning of a marbled white. Like the dwarf thistle, it is primarily a denizen of chalky grasslands in the south-east and a rare sight in the east Midlands.

As we depart, a couple pass in the opposite direction. 'I don't even know what a painted lady butterfly looks like,' the woman says. I hope she finds out, and in a moment as satisfactory as the one I have just had. Perhaps she will spot one drinking nectar from a purple vessel and laying its eggs on the stem – the caterpillar of this international migrant consumes thistles.

Matt Shardlow, 2020

Beguiled by the chalk hill blues

ISLE OF PORTLAND, DORSET

I'm supposed to be down in the cove, but the dance
of this powdery pair is leading me astray

I've climbed higher than I intended, lured up the cliff path by flurries of chalk hill blue butterflies: skittish pied pipers with an infuriating habit of dipping as though they're about to land, only to rise again and disappear over the next ridge. Below me, I can hear faint laughter as my children search for ammonites among the rocks in Church Ope Cove.

Stopping to catch my breath, I spot a pair of six-spot burnet moths mating on a small scabious flower. Lizards dart in and out of the limestone crevices and tiny snails dot the vegetation, some resembling miniature cream horns, others more akin to Danish pastry swirls. One has a sheen like freshly glazed ganache that wouldn't look out of place in a French patisserie.

The path leads up to a south-facing slope where the chalk hill blues gather. It is encouraging to see them here in such numbers. Butterfly Conservation is concerned that the range of this chalk and limestone grassland specialist has decreased across Dorset, but they still appear to be thriving around Portland's cliffs and quarries.

Just ahead of me, a pristine male alights on the golden head of a carline thistle and opens its powder-blue wings to bask in the sun. It could have flown straight out of a child's pastel drawing, with an iridescent patina that looks like it would wash clean in the first rain shower – fleeting beauty on an already ephemeral host.

These landslip-prone cliffs seem a fitting place to reflect on transience and the brevity of life, as time is running out for these chalk hill blues to find a mate. So they fly low over salad burnet, bird's-foot trefoil and horseshoe vetch (their sole larval food plant), obeying the urge.

The male on the thistle flicks into the air to join the dance, pairing with a chocolate-brown female in a flighty *pas de deux*. After a moment she retreats to a burnet seedhead, seemingly unimpressed by his antics. I ought to follow her example and return to the cove, but the temptation to keep climbing is too strong. Just another minute, a little higher, a few more chalk hill blues.

Nic Wilson, 2020

Turning back time with a parade of steamships

CALSTOCK, TAMAR VALLEY, CORNWALL

The boats are a reminder of an era when this
waterway bustled with trade

A westerly breeze ruffles the neap tide as it floods upstream, running slow and low between purple-flowering reed beds and shady woods. Dozens of jackdaws swirl high above the viaduct just before the two-carriage train glides across the border from Devon.

At river level, whiffs of coal smoke and the sound of whistles announce the presence of thirteen steamboats. These were launched at Cotehele Quay, towed up the river and moored off the pontoon before leaving for Morwellham – part of a heritage weekend marking an era when the Tamar waterway bustled with trade and excursion vessels.

Around midday, the little boats curve quietly away and upriver. Later, in the distance, near the derelict mine stacks of Okel Tor and Gawton, faint puffs of steam mark the passage of the craft below the dark greenery of Maddacleave and Sheepridge Wood.

Here, on the outskirts of Calstock, hot sun strikes south-facing land where new houses have been built on former market gardens and terraces where once tomatoes were grown in glasshouses. On the quayside, onlookers relax, drinking outside the pub, eating ice cream and admiring shanty singers and jangling morris dancers. In the parish hall, a display of archive material includes photos, cuttings and recorded memories of industrial days, when locally produced bricks, tiles, ores, granite and agricultural goods depended on river barges and market boats for transport towards Plymouth. Trippers came on pleasure steamers and, in 1909, competition between the Millbrook and Saltash fleets allowed the price of the return journey to drop from 1s 6d to one shilling.

Today's enthusiasts steam past former boatbuilding yards; en route to Morwellham, they round the Harewood meander – the site of a racecourse in 1894, and cultivated with runner beans inter-planted with melons as recently as the 1950s. Returning with the ebbing tide, the little boats echo the tradition of steamers like the *Ariel*, which, after turning around at Weir Head and giving passengers the opportunity to 'walk on the Morwell Rocks', called in at Calstock, where disembarking visitors were greeted by locals and taken to 'a place for tea . . . along to where I live'.

Virginia Spiers, 2019

The few swallows we see are already looking to Africa

TRAETH LLIGWY, ANGLESEY

Their migration back through the Mediterranean isn't just long, it's far more perilous than it ever should be

At dusk, the campsite owner popped his head into the washing-up hut and the clatter of tin mugs, and asked me to come outside. He wanted me to see swooping dots in the sky: a flight of swallows, maybe a hundred strong, preparing to roost. There had been more than two thousand swallows here a couple of years ago, he said; he attributed their decline to mist nets around the Mediterranean, particularly in North Africa, where millions of migrant birds are trapped to be eaten.

I thought of Sir Philip Sidney's 1590 poem *The Countess of Pembroke's Arcadia*, when he talks about man's cruelty to animals:

'Worst fell to smallest birds [. . .] At length for glutton taste he did kill them; / At last for sport their silly lives did spill.' Today, the situation is even more desperate for migrating birds.

Chaucer (in *The Parliament of Fowls*) called the swallow a murderer of 'the fowles smale that maken hony of flowres fresshe of hewe', i.e. bees. And there were both swallows and bees flying over the coastal footpath the following day – but not as many as there should be.

Rounding on to the headland, however, revealed a great patch of lilac thistle, pink bramble and purple knapweed, supporting a circus of butterflies: an embarkation of painted ladies, a creaking of gatekeepers, a mowing of meadow browns. I haven't seen a gathering of so many butterflies in one place for decades and, though it couldn't counteract the horror story of migrating birds caught in nets, it caused a joyous flutter of the heart.

That evening, as darkness fell into Traeth Lligwy (Lligwy Bay), so the swallows dropped into the reeds of the Afon Lligwy estuary. Before sleep – if that's what they do, do they dream? – the swallows filled the quietly spoken reed beds with a hushed twittering that, far from expressing 'silly lives', held a language of community wisdom, the swallow story in which each voice speaks as one, and each one is known to the other. Now that Lammas – the first of August – has passed, the birds were talking themselves out of here, making plans for navigation in convoys, the lodestones in their heads swinging south, towards Africa, towards the mist nets.

Paul Evans, 2019

Goodbye midges, hello mozzies

AIGAS, SCOTTISH HIGHLANDS

*The summer's sunlight and wind have dealt a blow
to Highland midges, but now there is the
tropical whine of mosquitoes*

It continues to be an extraordinary summer. While the Highlands haven't seen the extreme temperatures of London and the south, here at Aigas, south-west of Inverness, we have had no significant rain since early May, and many days have been exceptionally hot – to the surprise and delight of visitors – and reliably bright and sunny, with light breezes week after week. Like most of the rest of Britain, our grass stopped growing in June and has been biscuit brown for two months; the burns and rivers are dry or dribbling, and the moorland bogs are firmer underfoot than I can ever recall.

One apparent benefit is the lack of midges. The pinhead-sized females of these aggressive arthropods need blood before they can breed, and the Highland midge's scientific name, *Culicoides impunctatus*, broadly translates as 'little puncturing bastard'.

Throughout the mountains and moorlands – they seem to love boggy ground – in normal years they can plague the mornings and evenings in relentless hordes. On the west coast I've seen people fling themselves into the sea to escape their torment. Here, only a few miles from the more arable Black Isle, we usually get a pestering few – but not this year. Midges do not like direct sunlight or wind, and for many weeks now we have enjoyed both.

The buzz in the glens is that perhaps the weather has dealt them a mortal blow. Alas, not so. The midge larvae bury themselves in peaty mires and damp patches of soil where the sun never reaches –

and there they wait through several instar phases before emerging in favourable overcast and humid conditions.

The midges will be back, I'm certain of that, but a worrying development this summer, and perhaps a sign of climate change, is more mozzies. The exact species of mosquito I'm not sure, but on hot nights the dreaded tropical whine has awoken me many times. While endlessly tolerant of most invertebrates, this naturalist has no compunction in dealing death to mosquitoes. I cannot go back to sleep knowing one is lurking nearby. At the risk of marital disharmony, on goes the light.

John Lister-Kaye, 2018

Face to face with an underwater monster

ST AGNES, ISLES OF SCILLY

Giant gobies are the largest fish of their kind, found only in this far south-western extremity of the British Isles – for now, at least

The directions I've cobbled together read like a treasure quest: a tiny sun-baked island, unlikely-sounding rock formations, a sandy cove, granite pinnacles, a hidden pool.

The turf is crispy with drought, and arrays of desiccated thrift vibrate like the wires of an arcane musical instrument whose bass is too low for me to pick up. Instead, I hear the incessant chirping of house sparrows, gulls crying, a stonechat chipping away in the gorse.

Crossing from turf to beach, I pick my way over seaweed that was dumped during a recent storm – a wreck of wrack, fronds of kelp lying like banners dropped in battle. There are two rock pinnacles: granite stacks with cracks and rakes smoothed by the fingers of wind and wave into forms that feel aboriginally significant. From an elevated shelf on the first, I spot the pool on the next, above high water but beyond a neck of boulders. I calculate that I have an hour to climb there and back before it will be cut off by the tide.

But among the boulders are pools of such wonder they might have been created to waylay me. Candy-pink, viridian and magenta algae, studded with anemones, topshells, limpets, periwinkles, and framed by fanned, feathered and tentacled forms so beautiful I can hardly tear myself away.

I eventually reach the second stack. The pool there is completely different: a lido, with sunlit edges and deep, green-shadowed depths. All is still as I approach, but there's a flicker in my peripheral vision. A swish and a splash lead me to what I came for.

Monsters. Tapering speckled bodies, 8–20 centimetres long, frog faces, topaz eyes and huge but delicate pectoral fins that appear to hug the rock. Giant gobies, *Gobius cobitis*,[*] are the largest fish of their kind, found only in this far south-western extremity of the British Isles – for now, at least. Their pool looks inviting, the water pleasantly cool. But it is their world, not mine, so I lie on my front, my nose almost touching the water, and we gaze at each other across the divide.

Amy-Jane Beer, 2018

---

[*] Giant gobies are protected under Schedule 5 of the Wildlife and Countryside Act 1981, which prohibits their killing or taking by any method.

SEPTEMBER

An all-white hen harrier, ghosting along the cliffs

LAXEY BAY, ISLE OF MAN

These raptors do well here, thanks to a lack of persecution. And this one is so remarkable I can hardly believe my eyes

It's not every day I see something that I'll remember for the rest of my life. My sister and niece are over on holiday, and during an amble along the coast we witnessed what will perhaps be the greatest ornithological sighting I will ever make from home: a ghostly all-white hen harrier.

To see any hen harrier is a sight to behold, even here on the Isle of Man, where we boast some thirty-eight pairs – surely the highest breeding density across all of Britain and Ireland. On a summer walk in the Manx hills, I would be amazed not to see one. But down along the rocky coast by our home, I rarely see them.

All three of us saw the leucistic (unpigmented) bird – a reassuring fact when you can't quite believe your eyes. It flew slowly along the cliffs in a deadly, unnerving silence. Where were the crowds with their long lenses? Aghast, we enjoyed this private yet all-too-brief encounter until the bird flew out of view over Laxey, a village of some 1,800 residents, of whom I bet not a single one noticed.

I have counted hundreds of harriers coming in to roost at nightfall over many a dreary winter's day, a two-hour-long task that makes you question your sanity. Earlier this summer, after induction into the ornithological inner sanctum, I spent many late evenings monitoring their nests on the Manx hills, an area that

BirdLife International has deemed to be of global significance for this species. Despite this, I had never seen a leucistic one.

My young niece lives in Yorkshire, so – regrettably – this was her first hen harrier sighting. She should see them breeding on the moor up behind her house, but it lies empty, largely due to the existence of driven grouse moors; these harriers are Britain's most persecuted raptor. Thankfully, here on our little island, they find refuge among our serene, heather-clad hills, far from the danger of the moors that are just discernible across the sea on a summer's day.

David Bellamy, 2023

On the farm, water is scarce and getting scarcer

TEBAY, CUMBRIA

We are increasingly struggling to get enough for ourselves and the animals, so drastic action is needed

As I work with my sheep in the pens, getting them ready for the autumn sheep sales, there's an unfamiliar sound on the farm – drilling. A huge rig is drilling a borehole, looking for water. This is the second contractor we've asked to try to find us a water supply, given the farm isn't connected to the mains. The first one dug to 50 metres without success; today's rig is currently at 70 metres, and the vibrations echo around the farmstead.

When the Romans built their fort here, they built an aqueduct down the fellside to bring water to the fort. This functioned well until the motorway was built in the late 1960s and a new supply was put in (a spring on Grayrigg Forest, a nearby peak).

During the last few years, we have struggled to get enough water for ourselves and our animals. This may be because of climate change, possibly coupled with the change of land use on the fells above, where more water is now held by the increased vegetation for flood alleviation downstream.

One of the worst times was during the first lockdown, when it was very warm. We had no water for about four weeks. My parents had also just moved in. We were constantly being told by the government to wash our hands, but we were unable to. While you can buy drinking water, it's more difficult to buy water for washing and for the animals. You couldn't even go to a swimming pool or hotel for a wash as everywhere was closed.

This came after a run of very hot, dry springs, so urgent action was needed to enable three generations of our farming family to continue living here. We ended up with an industrial storage tank in the yard full of water, and buckets.

The drilling stops before teatime, and I wonder why the workers have driven off. I get a text message: no words, just a video of a jet of water squirting out of the borehole. Success. Now we need to test the water and install filters and UV zappers to make sure that it's safe. We keep our fingers crossed.

Andrea Meanwell, 2022

I've put this house spider outside
before – several times

*It's the time of year when the males are roaming
in search of a mate. This one seems to have
strong homing instincts*

A silent scuttle seen from the corner of the eye – there it is, a spider, bristle-legged on the cream-coloured carpet. It freezes, then dashes behind the chest of drawers.

It's a male giant house spider of a subspecies (*Eratigena saeva*) common in the West Country. I can tell it's male by the large, club-like palps in front of the head, and by the time of year. In late summer and early autumn, males emerge from their webs and roam in search of a mate.

They're most active at night, climbing stairs, falling into baths and pattering across beds. These are fast runners, capable of sprinting half a metre a second, which adds to their capacity to surprise and unnerve.

This male I think I have seen before. Either that or I've put six identical males outside in the shed. It's possible; anecdotal evidence says these spiders have a homing instinct and will return if removed. Three times now I have found what looks like the same individual determinedly climbing the stairs a day or so after being gently ejected.

But his persistence could lead to a sticky end. There are daddy-longlegs spiders (*Pholcus phalangioides*) occupying several corners of the bedroom ceilings. Large but almost invisible, they build inconspicuous webs and can hang motionless for hours. Disturb one and, rather than running off, it will keep its feet still and whirl its body in a circular motion.

I am frightened of spiders, but I don't mind the *Pholcus*. Their annoying habit of spattering books with pale spots of defecation is outweighed by their usefulness as a predator. As well as catching flies, they eat other spiders.

Pholcus use their long legs to throw silk from their spinnerets, enmeshing their prey from a distance before moving in for a bite. There are a couple of daddy-longlegs above the chest of drawers that harbours the big spider.

When I look the next day, there is no sign of my friend, but one of the *Pholcus* is cradling a bundle with a crumpled brown body inside.

Sara Hudston, 2022

This is surely my last dragonfly of the year

GLENTROOL, DUMFRIES AND GALLOWAY

One by one summer's lights are going out, so
I'm thankful to see this black darter
skulking in the shadows

Black darter dragonflies get darker as they age. This one has an almost blue sheen. Through binoculars I can make out three smudges of dull yellow on the tip and base of the abdomen, two stripes slanting across the thorax, and one bloom of blond down. But these are mere details compared to its crushed-velvet blackness and wings made of wrought iron and glass.

Black is the right word for this one. Darter, not so much. Its flight is too reluctant, too cold-muscled. I first saw it by the path, slipping slowly between the seedheads of ribwort plantain, almost invisible in the shadows. At rest, they're easy to pass over. This one could easily be a fragment of a stem, broken and bent by the rain showers that have washed the light from the afternoon. Today has given us both heather glowing pink and purple in the sun and a glen capped in thick grey. A day for shirt sleeves and waterproofs.

The friend I'm walking with is a trees and wilderness person. Insects don't really do it for him. I think about explaining that the black darter is our smallest dragonfly species; that the black markings aid thermoregulation, useful in this moment; or that it is an acidic habitat specialist, declining in range. Or how it seems to me that dragonflies – so seemingly fussy about what weather they will fly in at the start of their season – cling on at the end of the season, in the unlikeliest weather, eking out each day until they eventually succumb to the cold.

I settle for telling him that I'm pleased to have seen it, that it might be the last dragonfly I see this year. It feels important to recognise this, because one by one the lights of summer go out. First, the swifts leave our skies, then the Scotch argus disappears from these moors, and soon it will be the swallows' turn.

It's easy not to notice it happening until – suddenly – you regret not noticing the last of them. We have to make the most of summer while we can.

Stephen Rutt, 2022

Drought has turned the garden into a wasteland

STOKE-ON-TRENT, STAFFORDSHIRE

The hydrangeas have turned to ghostly brown lace
too soon; piles of viburnum leaves have
dropped early in fright

I try not to make excuses, so I'm just going to tell the truth: everything in my garden is dead. The drought was fierce, and I was sick, distracted. I couldn't bear to look at it, but I'm trying to now.

It feels like sitting in a crypt. I've pulled up a damp chair and I am surrounded by skeletons, the limbs of my perennials dried, bent and snapped. The hydrangea's flowers have turned to ghostly brown lace too soon, drooping leaves turned almost black like prayer flags. There is copper, rust and blood: piles of viburnum leaves dropped early in fright. The penstemon looks as if it has been set alight then frozen, its orange flames still and hellish. When the rains finally came, too late, the parched snails came out of hiding and ate everything that was left.

Dead plants trigger strange feelings. I name them, like a kind of emotional botanist. There is sadness. Grief has wrapped itself around anxiety. That's shame over there, and this tangle is me feeling simultaneously culpable and yet completely powerless. I think about climate change. I think about my own ailing body and how I struggle to take care of things now. Everything is a metaphor for everything else.

It's important to do this, I think. It's important to sit out here and face it because now I'm here, I can see that not everything is dead – far from it. Strawflowers continue to quietly open and close, in among their ruined neighbours. Sunflowers with deep roots tower overhead. *Verbena bonariensis* has thrown its purple fireworks all over the patio and there is still the buzz of bees.

If everything really had been lost, it would be easy to give up and walk back indoors, but a single late rose makes me get up and shuffle over to bury my nose in it.

Josie George, 2022

Relief and triumph as the Weardale agricultural show returns

ST JOHN'S CHAPEL, COUNTY DURHAM

After the cancellation last year of the 150th show, the 151st has been blessed with perfect weather

Days like this, with unbroken blue sky and not even the faintest whisper of wind, are rare on Chapel Fell. It is so quiet: the only sounds we can hear are trickling spring water and our own laboured breath, after the uphill hike along Harthope Burn.

Summer is almost over, yet down in the valley there is no hint of autumn. Meadows surrounding farmsteads in the dale have regained their lush green grass after haymaking, and cattle are grazing on the aftermath.

But up here in the high sheep pasture, on the edge of open moorland, the colours of autumn have truly arrived. Thistle seedheads have burst in the warmth of the early-morning sun, waiting for a breeze to carry the candyfloss of thistledown aloft. They stand among tall, sun-bleached grasses, along with spires of ripe, dark-umber dock seeds. With every footstep, scores of gangly craneflies rise up around our dew-soaked boots.

We are halfway down the stony track to Daddry Shield before we hear the first sounds of human activity: music. 'The Floral

Dance', played by the Stanhope Silver Band, drifts up the fellside. This morning is the opening of the 151st annual Weardale agricultural show, and the organisers must be offering up a prayer of thanksgiving for such perfect weather, especially after last year's Covid-enforced cancellation.

Through a gap in the trees, we look down on the showground and its marquees. The car parks are filling fast. Showjumpers are exercising their horses. There are penned sheep, a line of tethered cattle, vintage tractors and a flock of Indian runner ducks under the gaze of a pair of Border collies.

There will be prizes for baking, art, garden produce, handicraft and horticulture, quoits, pets, bale stacking, dry-stone walling and chainsaw carving, ending with tug-of-war and cross-country running competitions. Families from more remote farms, who may not have met for a year or more, will share tales in the refreshment tent of the highs and lows of hill farming. A day full of promise, a highlight of the year in the dale.

Phil Gates, 2021

A sea eagle sits in the mist, medieval and unreal

HOAR OAK WATER, EXMOOR

*The signs were there that something magical
was about to happen, and it did*

Foggy conditions can be the best time to see wildlife on Exmoor. A kind of twilight descends and the wild creatures become bolder. On the moor above Lynton, 'each hill had a hat, a mist-hackle huge', to borrow from the medieval poem *Sir Gawain and the*

Green Knight. When mist falls in Arthurian quests, it is a sign that something magical is about to happen.

We had been riding for about an hour towards the Chains, a high, remote plateau, accessible only on foot or horseback. Passing through a series of old field enclosures above Hoar Oak Water, four red deer stags materialised in the bracken. Three big males, their magnificent branching antlers still grey with velvet, and a pricket – a teenage stag – whose spikes were shorter than his large ears. They gazed at us before cantering away.

We rode on to where a line of wind-warped beeches clung to a bank of turf and stone. For once, though, the Exmoor ponies sheltering under the trees were not the focus of my attention. There, silhouetted on a low branch, was the unmistakable side-on shape of an eagle. She sat motionless, shoulders hunched against the drizzle, staring away from us down the combe. The profile of her massive beak with its rounded curve and long hook was sharp as a paper cutout. The wild ponies below her snorted and began to trot away, but the eagle didn't move.

White-tailed or 'sea' eagles (*Haliaeetus albicilla*) are the UK's largest birds of prey, with wingspans of up to 2.5 metres. Seen so close, the sheer size and heft is breathtaking. This was a young female, known as G405, released last summer on the Isle of Wight as part of a reintroduction project. White-tailed eagles are nomadic in their first few years and can travel great distances: 405's radio tracker shows she has wandered from southern England to East Lothian.

Our route lay directly beneath her perch. As we walked the horses quietly towards her, she turned to consider us, shifted her weight, raised her huge wings and took off, the fingered tips of her outstretched feathers searching and stroking the air as she disappeared into the mist.

Sara Hudston, 2021

Winter visitors fly in to a mixed reception

STENNESS, ORKNEY

The geese are back, and in great numbers. But not everyone is celebrating their return

They came straggling in overhead – a loose skein of perhaps four dozen geese. They stretched apart then came together again with elastic ease; clear, brassy voices. They're back.

Every winter, Orkney plays host to about 70,000 Icelandic greylag geese. They cruise in towards the end of summer, the cold weather closing in behind them, and stay until spring. You'll find them everywhere – paddling in the shallows, floating in rafts on the ruffled inland lochs. Most of all, however, you'll see them in the fields: more birds than livestock, all gathering in great flocks to graze.

There are curlews too, poking around with their curving proboscises. Starlings lifting in shivering masses, alighting on fences, power lines, then back down in the grass. Rooks all in an uproar, bickering in the low evening light. But it's the geese that get the farmers going. It's their sheer force of numbers, their voracious appetites. They trample the fields, eat the crops, nip the fresh new grass before the cows can get to it. Disturb them and they rise up as one cacophonous wave, a thousand adenoidal complaints echoing off the hills.

They're new here, relatively speaking. There were no geese in the 1980s, either visiting or resident. A few trickled in during the 1990s, to make 300 breeding pairs by 2002. By 2008, there were 10,000. Now 25,000 or so live here year-round – and then there's the Nordic hordes. It's thought that rising temperatures allow them to settle further north, saving them effort during their annual migration.

Farmers use many strategies in their resistance: scarecrows in fluorescent jackets, air cannon firing late into the night, shooting parties at dawn. For a while there was a full-time 'goose scarer', who pursued them through the fields, shaking rattles on a pole. It was to little avail. Earlier this year, NatureScot announced that it would cut funding for 'goose management'. It looks like they're here to stay.

Still, for the unlanded, the skeins can be a guilty pleasure. I like to watch them fly over: time's arrows, shooting in from the north. Heralds of the cold weather to come.

Cal Flyn, 2021

How four crates can feed a hundred thousand

SANDY, BEDFORDSHIRE

Each seed potato, planted five months ago, has grown offspring a dozen or so times its own weight. Now it's time for them to come up

Spuds, tatties, taters – the time to unearth these magic tubers has come. Summer's heaviest harvesting is under way in billows of dust, rolling tractors and trailer upon laden trailer, bound for welcoming barns.

Almost five months before, I stood at this same field corner looking over newly ploughed soil, the fine tilth sculpted into a corrugated landscape of hillocks and hollows. A pair of yellow wagtails flitted from top to top, and in any other year those lemony migrants from Africa would have been the highlight of my walk.

But that day I gained more exhilaration from a quartet of wooden crates parked at the end of the field. Each of the waist-high tubs was filled to the brim with seed potatoes, and each peach-sized pellet was destined to be sunk into the soil to grow offspring a dozen times its own weight. On that day, when the supermarket shelves were empty of flour, pasta and rice, and in that period of perpetual doubt, I glowed in the certainty that, come autumn, there would be mash for tea.

Over spring and summer, I watched this crop get watered by farm irrigators and downpours. I walked its length and width to estimate how many potatoes lay beneath. When the plant tops were raked off by tractor, I knew there was a fortnight to go, fourteen days for the buried skins to harden.

Two tractors come down the lines in parallel. One is the taker, the other the receiver. The former, with wheels in the gutters on either side, uses spinning wheels to throw up the banked earth into a pouch. The contents bounce on to a quaking conveyor belt, which shakes off the soil and nudges the potatoes up its crane-like stem. At the end of the belt, a funnel sends a stream of tatties raining down into a trailer pulled by the accompanying tractor.

Two small potatoes have spilled out on to the concrete track. They are in the path of huge tractor tyres that will crush them as they turn. I scoop them up – just enough for a lunch. In the field before me are a hundred thousand dinners.

Derek Niemann, 2020

Mystery built into the dry-stone walls

ABNEY, DERBYSHIRE

What a job it must have been to work in all these
narrow apertures – you'd need a good reason, surely

The track north-west of Abney is an old one, a packhorse route linking the village of Bradwell with Ashford. Here it reaches its high point before dropping steeply into Bradwell, an exposed spot, often harsh on a winter's day and sometimes on a summer's one too. I found myself leaning into a strong breeze that pushed across the moor, shaking the hairgrass and ruffling the yarrow and selfheal growing prettily against a long dry-stone wall that bordered the trail and offered me some shelter.

Abney Moor is a fine vantage point to consider the endless miles of these 'Derbyshire hedges' and how varied they are in function and form: how in one direction they can seem pleasing and complementary to the landscape, following the rise and fall of steep pasture, like a cast net; and yet in another appear angular and stern, laid ruler-straight with no feel for the ebb and flow of the hillside.

Built into the footing of the wall next to me were remnants of a medieval cross that once marked the boundary of three parishes, shown on the map as Robin Hood's Cross (named after a local baron and not the outlaw).

Rather than follow the track down to Bradwell, I cut left along Bleak Knoll, its crest split down the middle by an unusually high wall – over six feet in places. And along its length, every 15 feet or so, roughly a rod in old measures, a small rectangular aperture had been built into its base a few inches off the ground. It must have been the devil to work in so many of these things, and the obvious question is why.

Holes in dry-stone walls have a plethora of names that sometimes explain their purpose: 'lunky' is common in some parts of the country, 'hogg hole' in others, a hogget being a yearling sheep. But these gaps seemed too narrow for all but the youngest lambs. Wallers might also build in a 'smuse' or 'smoot' hole for rabbits, to trap them as they passed through or stop them burrowing underneath and weakening the structure. This seemed more likely; a hundred years ago, a rabbit farm nearby was supplying a London furrier.

Ed Douglas, 2020

There's a telltale musky smell beneath the plum tree

CAISTOR ST EDMUND, NORFOLK

Badgers have marked out their territory by anointing their droppings with scent from glands under their tails

The last of the Victoria plums are rotting on the ground. I step around them, avoiding the sticky mess and gorging wasps. The air has a sweet, alcoholic tang, like the day after a big party. Peacock butterflies and red admirals flit from fallen fruit, drinking the fermented juices. Docile and plum-drunk, a peacock lands on my hand, wings all tatty now.

I scavenge a couple of partly edible plums still hanging on the trees, making sure to check for maggots before biting. Many of the fruit have been affected by the pinkish caterpillar of the plum moth, *Grapholita funebrana*, which burrows into the flesh to feed around the stone. When sated, they will spin a cocoon hidden away in the bark of the tree, to emerge as a dull greyish brown moth in May next year.

Looking up at the branches, rather than the ground, I nearly squish my summer-sandalled foot in something. There, beneath a tree, like vomit outside a nightclub, is a pile of dark purple excrement, dotted with plum stones and nestled in a scrape: it's a badger latrine. It has a musky, sweet but feral smell – and to another badger it is a social message.

Badgers anoint their droppings with scent from the glands under their tail, typically to mark territory or indicate mating status. The badgers visiting this orchard were most likely from a sett about a mile away; their faeces mark this spot as theirs. Odour is an important part of badger communication, and a community will also set scent on each other. Known as allo-marking, this produces a combined, communal perfume that is different from that of neighbouring clans.

The fallen plums signal the dying days of summer. This change of season always weighs heavily on me, like a hangover. Already I miss the swifts screaming overhead. The third brood of swallows are nearly ready to leave too. All that is left is the alcoholic tang of rotting fruit and the sweet knowledge that badgers have been here. Now, I must turn my face to autumn.

Kate Blincoe, 2020

To the Widecombe fair, with
Uncle Tom Cobley and all

WIDECOMBE, DARTMOOR

People sit about on straw bales and enjoy the show,
including moorland ponies, folk singers, and Austin 7s
bouncing slowly across the bumpy ground

A one-way system directs traffic here, across the commons and along steep, narrow lanes edged in granite walls, towards the autumn fair. In the sheltered Webburn Valley, overlooked by Honeybag, Chinkwell and Bell tors, is the show ring, trade stalls, the Great Close car park and ranks of animal trailers that have brought precious horses, sheep and cattle.

Yesterday's 'liquid sunshine' (rain) is replaced by blue sky and white clouds casting shadows on the surrounding pastures and hedgerows. Spectators relax in the warmth and admire the many classes of moorland pony and their smartly attired riders; in contrast, elegant Anglo-Arab horses prance around the ring, while fairies, mounted on placid 'unicorns', await the fancy-dress class. Downslope, beneath oak and ash, judges inspect the sheep entries, dominated by the hardy greyface and whiteface Dartmoors with tightly curled, weatherproof fleeces; the rams have curved horns that appear polished for the occasion.

Nearby, enthusiasts' tractors and renovated machinery – including a hand-operated seed fiddle – assemble prior to their lumbering turn around the ring to demonstrate the variety of implements that were necessary for forage crops before modern-day operations. Other parades include lightweight Austin 7s bouncing slowly across the bumpy ground, sedate classic cars and prize winners who will be awarded from a table loaded with sparkling silver trophies, all supervised by Mr Deeble on his grey mare, Lilly.

In the village square and on the green, beneath turning leaves of chestnut, beech and sycamore, folk singers and morris dancers entertain yet more people sitting about on straw bales, bollards and ledges. Within the church, high above the granite floor slabs and pillars, painted medieval roof bosses include green men and a tinners' rabbit (three hares racing in an endless circle). An automaton, made in 1959, portraying Uncle Tom Cobley and his famous companions riding to this very fair, is out for the day, displayed by the history group near the beer tent.

Virginia Spiers, 2019

With a delicate flutter, the season has turned

WENLOCK EDGE, SHROPSHIRE

Autumn is the time to feed addictions,
obsessions and enchantments

A comma butterfly settles, head up, on the trunk of a crab apple tree. We are on the turn: the harvest moon, a big brass lamp, rises through oaks above the Severn Gorge and lights the ghostly breath of mist caught in the hazels arching over lanes; bats jink against the blue even-glow of a sky stretched taut as nylon, and a hawk-moth purrs against your cheek; out in the stubble fields, before the ploughs return, there is a stillness that smells of sleeping horses.

In woods by the priory, tawny owls recite the most beautiful of old forest languages with an excitement not heard during laconic summer nights; leopard slugs the size of severed fingers draw silver roads through cut grass, and earthworms slip backwards under torchlight; a toad, badly injured, walks stiff-legged from an unseen trauma towards some dark place where it can retreat into the jewel inside its head. Put out of harm's way, it was found later, flattened on the road, paying the harvest debt of John Barleycorn.

Mornings are nippy, washing over faces like stream water as mizzle slips from branches into the soil, leaving an ochre residue in the crowns of lime and birch. Puffballs and ceps have bitten chunks missing, like foam-rubber toys found under a hedge.

Gossamer tripwires of orb-weaver spiders glint as the sunlight enlivens, animates, shines the surfaces of stone and wood like shoes, magnetises insects to tremble with new powers; they – the wasps, bees, hoverflies and true flies – come flying in to rooms of light, chasing intoxications of fruit, nectar, pollen and unmentionable juices, in this the season to feed addictions, obsessions and enchantments.

There is a quickening of creativity in the air, a nation of the imagination, something bright as gold, loamy as humus, dark as shadow, free as fungal spores; these colours composed on the wings of a moment poised in a glimpse of being.

A comma butterfly settles, head down, on a crab apple tree. We have turned.

Paul Evans, 2019

The village phone box is gone –
but not without a fight

COMINS COCH, ABERYSTWYTH, CEREDIGION

*All that is left now is a hole filled with topsoil where
the box once stood. I might plant some native
wildflower seeds there*

The valley below the house has been choked by mist in the early
mornings, the cool approach of autumn obvious as you step outdoors. Hedgerows and orchards are heavy with fruit, dropping so
many windfall apples that the local blackbirds are having a hard
time keeping up. Robins are again becoming vocal, their songs
from the high branches cutting through the clear, suddenly chill
air.

With young birds fledged and nest sites abandoned, the sound of
chainsaws echoes around the village as those who have held back
from serious gardening, to protect the occupants of their hedges,
try to restore some order before the weather turns. Logs are cut to
length for the stove and stacked to dry.

Another harvest has occurred, long anticipated but still a surprise when it came. The sole village telephone box, shorn of its
technical components almost a year ago, was finally removed one
weekend by a pair of genial workers with a lorry. While not one of
the classic, treasured designs, the box had served us on the corner
of the lane for decades – its light often the only illumination in the
village once the scattered streetlights had gone out.

Aside from its vital utility in the days before telephones were
ubiquitous – one friend recalled using it to summon a midwife
when they had no landline – the phone box was useful for navigation in a settlement where many houses lack a number, or even a

street name; and as a destination for late-night taxi drivers, it was succinct and unambiguous. Many of its ilk have found a new rural role as a defibrillator – but, sadly, not ours.

The old phone box put up a fight. It took a while to get it and its heavy concrete base airborne on the hoist, then swung aboard the lorry. The broken-tooth hole it left was filled with rubble and topsoil – it's easy to miss the fact that anything has happened. I might wander past with some native wildflower seed to give the new patch a good start. Something red would seem appropriate.

John Gilbey, 2018

Ivy isn't just a plant, it's a habitat

STAMFORD, LINCOLNSHIRE

Ivy wasn't always a pariah, more a blessing.
It protected houses from demons at times
when spirits were close

A glove of ivy grasps the lower trunk of a mature silver birch. It's long been a thing of parasitic charm, this stuff – English ivy on trees, houses, walls. It's bad, isn't it? Weakens brickwork, cancers bark, kills trees. Get rid of it, they say. But it's so pretty, you say.

Ivy's life cycle is vividly imagined. Juvenile, it grows in woodland and hedgerow, along the ground until it finds a tree trunk, or whatever else. On touching the tree, its roots change shape to fit the surface, then secrete a glue-like ooze to attach. Root hairs emerge, find gaps, slide in, then lock, like a climber attaching gear into a rock face. If it's on your house, by the time you pull it off the wall the damage is done.

But ivy wasn't always a pariah, more a blessing. It protected houses from demons at times when spirits were close, like Christmas and All Hallows. Milk drunk from ivy wood cups were said to cure whooping cough.

I notice that the trunk beneath this ivy is dark, as if ink-dipped. Above, it is silver only in patches. Nevertheless, the tree looks strong. I part the ivy leaves. Cobwebs bridge delicate spans, caught with debris. Here are generations: grey cables of branch wired into the trunk alongside more verdant brown, some of it hung with rows of desiccated roots like millipede legs. Still deeper, there are knots thick with cobwebs. A few late-season, cold-slowed wood ants loiter. It's dense, microscopically so, but clearly a layered shelter for insects. Insects bring birds. In autumn it flowers. That means more birds. More life. This isn't just a plant, it's a habitat.

But what of this tree? Autumn's here, winter is coming. The canopy will thin, sun will find the ivy and it will grow. But it won't kill. Ivy doesn't strangle, nor does it pull nutrients from the bark. It might weaken a feeble tree or compete for meagre nutrients at ground level. But the tree supports the ivy, just as it's meant to.

And it is pretty. It's a windy day, and the ivy catches it, sending the whole thing frantically aplay. And just for a second, if you let yourself see it, the tree shivers.

Simon Ingram, 2018

A log of our apple orchard spans the decades

ALLENDALE, NORTHUMBERLAND

The early entries are in the erratic lettering of an old typewriter, then in my mother's blue ink, and lastly my teenage handwriting

The sun's already up and the chamomile edging the path is covered in dew. Droplets trickle down the reddening apples on our young tree, 'Winston', self-fertile and a good doer for the north. It's a bountiful year in our valley, thanks to the cold, late spring and a lack of frost at blossom time. Thrushes scrabble, frantic among bird cherry branches. Pears ripen on the tree by the house wall and wasps cluster on eaten-out plums.

Apple trees have good and bad years. I take down the Orchard Book on my childhood garden; its records go back to the 1950s. There's the smell of old paper, and its cover is mould-speckled and torn. A fabric-covered ring binder costing 3 shillings and 9 pence, loose threads dangle along its cracked spine. The early entries are in the erratic lettering of an old typewriter, then in my mother's blue ink, and lastly some in my teenage handwriting.

Fluctuating between 'poor crop' and 'too many to pick', the yield was measured in bushels. We filled large crates and lined the wooden racks in the cold cellar, where, spaced apart, they would last a winter. I relished their names: 'Peasgood Nonsuch', 'Worcester Pearmain', 'Laxton's Superb', 'King Pippin', 'Winter Greening'. The earliest of all, 'Beauty of Bath', a pink-flushed apple I delighted in eating straight from the tree. 'Charles Ross', particularly productive, grew next to the seep of the septic tank.

Problems are noted in the book: 'sawfly', 'codlin' and 'rot'. Some fruit was bought by the grocer: 'Sold to Mr Dearlove at a shilling a pound.' Each tree listed in the book was identified by a white number painted on its bark. If one fell in a gale or was cut down because of canker, a line was drawn across the page.

I would climb lichened trees which were knobbly from pruning, and hide among the leaves. My favourite was 'Baumann's Reinette', an ancient espalier said to be 150 years old when I was a child. My mother's comment in the book in those waste-not years: 'a very good apple, in perfect condition for eating at Christmas'.

Susie White, 2018

OCTOBER

A strange but perfect autumn day*

THE MARCHES, SHROPSHIRE

*A rainbow's feet touch the earth beneath black
vanilla clouds, one end at Wat's Dyke, the other
at the nearby hospital*

'It gives showers for today,' says the man, poking an errant sprig of privet back into the otherwise immaculate face of the hedge. This micro-fidget sends a ripple, strikes a tone – there is something weirdly perfect about today. It appears in a rainbow, its feet touching earth beneath black vanilla clouds, with one crock of gold buried under Wat's Dyke – a ghostly linear earthwork of the northern Welsh Marches – and the other under the orthopaedic hospital in Gobowen. As the sky lifts to a pale autumnal blue, the middle of the arc fades, but the remaining colours are vivid fragments of a lucid dream.

Black sheep in the centre of the hillfort are alert and all staring in the same direction, as if some spectral dog lopes along the fence-line. These are Iron Age sheep with hard mouths and sharp eyes that shaped the hill country long ago – a captive audience from pre-history that is indifferent to human drama. The birds are quiet and distant, even the invisible ones within spitting distance in the hawthorn and oak scrub, their conspiratorial chatter bright as berries, coded into their own frequency.

The far hills are hazy; rains stalk them. Whatever gathers there is beyond this one place, floating free of pervading horrors; even

---

* This entry is dedicated to John Vidal, who died on Thursday 19 October 2023. John was the finest environmental journalist of his time, a great *Guardian* figure, and a dear friend to us for nearly fifty years. This entry was written from John's home patch; his magnificent enthusiasm for life is sadly missed.

the shadows we cast don't touch the ground. Then an apparition materialises out of the thin air through which it flies, to alight on a bracken frond. Blacker than a rook, redder than a rosehip, whiter than smoke from the chipboard factory at Chirk – it's a red admiral butterfly. Perhaps not the last, but certainly the most pristine of the many red admirals seen this year, it adjusts itself on the frond as if aligning to magnetic north.

As it does so, the perfect mystery – of a butterfly and unseen birds and black sheep under a rainbow during a moment smoothed into a hedge – is uncannily strange and familiar at the same time. This is ecological beauty.

Paul Evans, 2023

The brown trout lurks in dusky pools

UPSTREAM FROM LOUGH NEAGH, COUNTY ANTRIM

*There's trouble in the watercourses here, as
pollution worsens. But for now, the native trout,
and the anglers, endure*

Dusk. Along the bank there's a trail of worn grass beaded with patches of bare earth, where the fishermen stand and wait. 'The tug is the drug,' says Jim Gregg, of the Six Mile Water Trust. This charity was formed in 2008 to protect the river after a catastrophic fish kill, when tens of thousands died. The anglers speak in wondering tones about the river's recovery from that still unsourced pollution. 'We call it the Phoenix river,' says Michael.

There have been other fish kills since. And now there's more bad news downstream, where the Six Mile Water disgorges into

Lough Neagh. For months, that freshwater 'inland sea' has been laced with toxic algal blooms. Up here, however, it is possible to believe that all is well. As darkness closes in, the river flows like black silk. A delicate V-shaped wash is agreed to be an otter on the move. Overhead, the flitter of a Daubenton's bat.

The anglers are out at this hour in the hope of catching dollaghan. This variety of brown trout, *Salmo trutta*, is endemic to Lough Neagh and its tributaries. At this time of year, the adults are leaving the lough and returning to their native rivers to spawn. Preferring the cover of darkness, they lurk in gloomy pools during daylight. 'They're dour,' says Andy. The others laugh softly. The men show me their lures. Tiny feathery works of art weighted to sink below the surface, deep into the water column.

As stars emerge, the Plough stations itself above the nearby stone bridge. Reels crackle. Lines swizz. Ethan's muted excitement announces a tug. His head torch glares. As the net scoops, braced splashing turns into a muscular blade of freckled gunmetal and gold. The dollaghan is laid on the grass for a quick check, then released back into the water. Later, on our return across the bridge, we lean over the wall to look at the river. It rushes silver under our torchlight. Suddenly, there's a dart between the water crowfoot. A dollaghan – this big! – flickers bluish as it crosses an open channel to speed upstream.

Mary Montague, 2023

A nearby farm may never be worked again

LONG DEAN, COTSWOLDS

*It's up for sale, but such is the premium on land here,
it's unlikely to remain in agricultural use*

I'm just back from the dairy farm up the hill. Unfailingly helpful, John has agreed to collect a 10-foot roller we've bought from another neighbouring farm that is on the market, with its equipment being sold separately. I'll repay John with sausages, our customary form of exchange.

The roller is needed for our soft river meadow, where hooves compress the soil, leaving it dented and uneven. Access from either end is laborious, so to keep one permanently in the field is ideal. The solution of the roller, however, is bittersweet.

The farm we bought it from is known locally not by its name, but by that of the family who have farmed it for decades – the people, with time, having become synonymous with the place. They were of a different generation, though nonetheless forward-thinking in their equality. His pride was the tractors, hers the livestock, and their stories endure: the way he would tuck their baby under the hedge while he ploughed; the farrowing sow that went for her ('because I was in my nightdress, see'); the favourite cow that leaned out of its stall at market to lick her as she passed.

They now lie buried together in a field opposite the house, and various factors have forced a sale. We won't see their like again – and it is also possible we won't see their farm worked again either. Such is the premium on land in this part of the country, it will command a price well beyond the affordability of anyone who wants to run, as they did, a modest family enterprise.

Like a local estate that was recently divided following a death, land here increasingly is passing out of agricultural use and becoming an 'amenity', or merely a tax-benefiting investment. So much is impoverished by this, not least the core identity and cohesion of the traditional rural community.

Someone expressed concern to the farmer at the idea of a tractor passing over his grave, which he quickly dismissed. It would be a far greater sadness if one didn't.

Sarah Laughton, 2022

The passing ravens are to be watched, not photographed

KILFEAGHAN, COUNTY DOWN

Such awe-inspiring birds – one comes so close
I can almost feel the beat of its wings

Two miles up a boreen – a single-track road – I'm cradled in the bosom of the Mourne Mountains, sitting outside a cottage with a view to Carlingford Lough. The mountain silence is interrupted by a whooshing of wingbeats, and I know that a raven is about to fly over my head.

No camera in hand, I can feel its stout wings swimming through the morning air, its beady eye shining in the morning sun as it weighs me up, before an updraught sends it high and off towards the skyline, where it is joined by two peregrine falcons. Minutes later, I hear a raven call again. This time I have my camera, but I'm so in awe as a pair of the boot-black wonders glide overhead that I just watch.

It's another special moment in the townland of Kilfeaghan, with its dolmen (megalithic tomb) with 35-ton capstone, the most beautiful wild chicory and the tiny Killowen Distillery half a mile down the road in an old cowshed. I have a glass on hand to toast three Irish hares, an adult and two youngsters, which every morning lope down from the heather and gorse and vanish into the lush pasture. Likewise the peregrines – now four, so probably the parents and a couple of this year's offspring – which hug the contours of the ridge and rise up to the clouds, before dropping like a stone in a stoop at some imagined prey. These are practice flights for when they need to feed themselves completely.

I am soon joined by a family of five hooded crows, a buzzard, the peregrines again, my bold heroes the ravens and, finally, a small group of swallows that alight on the gravel in front of me. Once again, the camera remains on the table as I watch – but no matter, the image is cached. Serendipity has always been my writer's touchstone, and the latest happy accident of landing in the Mournes has proved to be quite exceptional.

Sean Wood, 2022

There's magic to the woods when it rains

STANMER WOODS, EAST SUSSEX

After a summer of drought, the rain has felt special,
and nowhere more so than here

It's raining in Stanmer Woods, great fat droplets tap-tapping on leaves while a thousand rivers stream down tree trunks. I wonder where the rain has come from, when it last made land, and which trees and leaves it has known before.

Autumn is just beginning here. I walk in the shadow of the weather, crunching beech mast and kicking the first of the fallen leaves. The woodland floor is dappled with patches of the brightest orange, while stubborn greens hold tight to trees. There are mushrooms to gawp at: jelly fungus on a stump; sulphur tuft and King Alfred's cakes on logs. I search, in vain, for earthstars and amethyst deceivers, take photos of others I've yet to know. Bracket fungi helter-skelter up a tree that stands dead among the living.

There's magic to the woods when it rains. Something otherworldly, Narnia-esque; I can't imagine why anyone would want to be stuck indoors. It's wet, but not too wet – the rain falls on leaves above me and most of it channels along branches and trunks. There are few people here, and I can stop and look at things without being noticed. Blackbirds turn leaves; robins sing a sad song; there is, briefly, a chiffchaff.

The woods seem cleaner, fresher during rain. Dust and other residues wash off leaves until they glisten, water pools among the tree roots, and the rest is swallowed by grateful earth. Everything feels new, including me. Is this forest bathing?

After a summer of drought, the October rain has felt special. I leave windows open at night so I can wake when it falls, I obsess over water butts, I watch frogs leap across the garden. Sometimes I catch myself humming or whistling when the water comes; it truly makes me happy. As the kettle boils in the first light of morning, I crouch beneath the shed roof and watch it fall.

In the woods, the pattering of raindrops on leaves is music, the pools of water in tree roots are wine. I know that rain can be just as deadly and miserable as drought, but for now this human and a thousand trees are savouring every drop.

Kate Bradbury, 2022

I console myself that robins sing only of the future

SANDY, BEDFORDSHIRE

In between hospital visits, I go for a walk,
accompanied every step of the way

Dusk came on unawares. A cry against the dark triggered our last conversation. 'Can you hear the blackbird?' I asked. 'Magpie,' she said. My mother has been dying by degrees this autumn, as surely as the shortening of our days. Perhaps this is a fitting time to bow out for a May child, named after the life-giving month of her birth. My own life-giver's final journey accompanies me on every walk, colours every observation.

First light on her last day? A song jerks me out of solemnity, robins in stereo, one left, one right. One more from a bush a few steps on, another by the biggest oak.

Over the past few weeks, I have wondered what it is that I register in the song of these highest of sopranos. Is it melancholy, wistfulness or hope? Each time, I pull myself up and remind my indulgent self that birds have only the future in their throats. Robins have purpose without a past, and their new season has begun – one that demands territorial challenge, assertions of position, the preliminaries for breeding already under way. Though the song tinkling out on all sides lacks the fluency of spring, these little assertive spits have a fervent energy. Whose spirits would not lift at such statements of intent?

A dog walker acquaintance rounds the corner and offers pulling leads and knowing kindness, since he is aware. But I'm all eagerness, and share my elation at the robin abundance. 'Wouldn't know a robin if I heard it,' he says.

Down at the riverside, another robin leads the way, its legs so thin, and the morning light still so murky, that its rounded belly appears to float above the path. It keeps a safe distance, flutter and stop, flutter and stop, then veers off into the meadow.

Shortly, I will go back to the hospital for what I know will be my final visit. But I'll never forget these fleeting moments of solace with the robins, nor our last words together when my naturalist's exactness didn't matter.

'Magpie,' said my mother. 'Magpie,' I said. And the blackbird fell silent.

Derek Niemann, 2022

An explosion of colour before winter's gloom

BADENOCH, CAIRNGORMS NATIONAL PARK

The landscape at this time of year is dominated by the radiant dying of foliage, in front of ever-changing hills

'October is the coloured month here,' wrote Nan Shepherd in *The Living Mountain*, her meditative hymn to the Cairngorms written in the 1940s. For me, it seems a month that grasps the whole spectrum of colours in its eager hands, before November winds blow them away and December darkness falls.

The great oaks still hold most of their leaves, and are still mostly green, though tinged with yellows and browns. The birch leaves are a soft shower of lemon and lime, gradually thinning to reveal more of the cross-hatched white trunks and the spindly black branches. The aspens, meanwhile, are the showgirls of the forest, shimmying in cascades of gold to the rustling of their own applause. Their cast-offs carpet the trails, each leaf as brightly splashed as an artist's palette before being trodden into the mud.

In the forest, the solitary rowans do their own thing. Some are still verdant with feathered green leaves and fat bunches of berries, red as postboxes. Others have gone bald early, their fruit blackening, while yet others have sunny yellow clusters set against leaves turning scarlet. On the tier below, the dying bracken is shifting from gold to copper to bronze, while further down on the woodland floor, the mosses thrive in fresh, immodest greens, fungi sprouting among them in colours of temptation and poison.

At the edge of the trees, the river holds the sky, sometimes grey as doves, or gunmetal, or silver, sometimes blue as a dream. Moody days of darkness and fleeting rain are transformed by rainbows, light piercing the water veils.

Beyond the river, the fields are dotted with cattle and geese, the grass glowing in the low sun till it meets the border of deep evergreen forest. Beyond that, the hills. Their curving flanks change colour with every mood of the weather, and never more so than in October, with the radiant dying of foliage and the coming of storms.

The Cairngorms are 'most opulently blue when rain is in the air', said Shepherd. Today they are a brooding indigo as cloud foams off the plateau like a cauldron. High on the tops, the dark mountains are speckled with the first of winter's snow.

Merryn Glover, 2021

A fox flickers on to the old railway track, an unexpected flame

Only saints dare to tame foxes. My dog and I
are content to just watch in awe

We walk the Belfast Greenway near our home together, the dog and I. We both pay attention, though our interests diverge: he prefers the low-down scents, while I tend to look upwards, searching for birds and squirrels.

We were out, mid-morning, on an overcast, ordinary day, following the long-abandoned railway track between the trees. Pink patch of wild orchids on one side, a high bank of ferns and nettles on the other. Behind us, Samson and Goliath, the city's iconic yellow cranes. Suddenly, a fox trotted out in front of us. We stopped. His coat was a rich, luxurious copper, tinted with gold and dipped darker brown towards his paws. Perhaps he was marking his territory, expanding his boundaries in preparation for winter breeding.

He flickered across our path like an unexpected flame then paused, glowing, to look directly at us. The triangles of his ears and snout gave his face a contoured symmetry. His amber gaze, complete with vertically slit pupils, was more feline than canine: frank, appraising and fearless. The dog looked up at me, mouth agape in astonishment, and I could feel myself do the same. Only the tod kept his muzzle shut. No gekkering today.

The ancient Irish, my myth-loving ancestors, believed foxes were descended from the dogs of Vikings, possibly because of their red hair and wild fighting spirit. Only the saints among us would ever dare to tame foxes: Saint Brigid is a rare example of a fox whisperer extraordinaire. Meanwhile, over in ancient England, it seems that foxes were revered, even worn, long before the execrable fox-fur coats of modern 'fashion'. Several thousand years ago, Lindow Man was fox-cuffed before his body was settled in a bog. Perhaps vulpine accessories would make him quicker in the next world, capable of outfoxing the gods.

The cunning of foxes certainly makes them natural Celtic symbols for diplomacy, in this country bogged down by its past. In the mid-Ulster dialect of my youth, 'cunning' enfolded an older verb form, kenning, which suggests having clear-eyed, deep knowledge. 'I ken ye,' adults would say with a piercing stare if we tried to blag our way out of any task.

We felt kenned by the fox too, before he swept away his glorious, white-tipped brush, leaving us glowing in his wake, gilded by encounter.

Anne Baillie, 2021

Not just a waterfall, but a glorious, multi-sensory assault

JANET'S FOSS, NORTH YORKSHIRE

The light at this popular spot plays with the air around you, as the water burns the skin

I forget that October brings a relief as potent as April. I forget that summer gets just as old and weary as winter, and that autumn begins with birds in new plumage, freshly motivated to sing.

I forget that on some mornings the sky will be so blue and sharp you could cut yourself on it. That the season starts with scarlet hips, haws and rowanberries. That beeches begin their farewells with outbreaks of amber and gold months before they actually shed their leaves, while ash foliage drops early and green, no ceremony, like the friend who slips from parties without saying goodbye.

Similarly, I forget the magic of this place until I go back. The beauty of Janet's Foss, in the Yorkshire Dales, is no secret. Everyone stops for a picture, but the light here does things their camera will struggle to record: it tinkers with water, gilds mist and turns gnats into flecks of airborne fire. Even if you manage to photograph all that, and to record the complex fog of sound, much will be missing.

Then there is the tactile burn of cold water – a sensation we interpret as pain purely because we rarely stimulate the largest organ in the body in its entirety. And the smell: just as the water here is clear enough to be its own true aquamarine colour, it is also clean enough to have its rightful scent. Fittingly, for a flow that will become the River Aire a few miles downstream, the smell is equal parts river and atmosphere: the simplest of ingredients pounded to an aerosol by a pestle and mortar of gravity and rock.

I find the aroma has a brainstem effect – like the skin of a baby or a lover; like petrichor; like the sea; like a sweet wild rose. It stops me in my tracks, sharpens other senses.

I taste it and feel it, on inner surfaces and outer ones, and I hope I never tire of being reminded. Seasons and places, like friends old and true, are always best met in person.

Amy-Jane Beer, 2021

After the sun showers, a surprise visitor in the Wharfe

BURNSALL, YORKSHIRE DALES

A whiskered head pops up in the river, prompting shouts of excitement in the bankside pub

There are some days in early autumn when a kind of second spring occurs; the world is slipping into dormancy, but there are poignant reminders of when life was resurgent.

As the chlorophyll in them breaks down, the lime-green leaves on the ash trees overhanging the River Wharfe have the same gem-like translucence as when they were new. The weather is a volatile brew of warm sun, roving downpours and rainbows. Vibrant green pastures shine against backdrops of bruise-dark cloud. Our hemisphere is tilting towards winter, but in the quality of light, and the echoes of vernal freshness, it has briefly met April coming the other way.

Darkness is closing in, but autumn has its own kind of hopefulness. The swallows and sand martins of Wharfedale departed for Africa weeks ago, apparently taking the warmth with them, but there is another kind of wild energy at work now: a cold alchemy, the power of which draws in salmon from the Atlantic and flocks of fieldfare from the Arctic.

After our walk, which takes us through a series of drenching, dazzling sun showers, we stop for a pint outside the Red Lion in Burnsall, where the beer garden overlooks the Wharfe. A man at the next table spots something in the water and shouts in excitement, prompting a dozen or so people to stand up to see what the fuss is about.

'It's an otter!' someone says. I wonder if it might be something less secretive, like a mink, but then I see it for myself – an unmistakably large, whiskered head, right in the middle of the water, looking in our direction. It dives back into the current with a serpentine slickness, bobs back up a little further downstream, disappears and reappears a few times, before submerging for long enough that we return, slightly stunned, to our tables.

Later, just as we're leaving, it pops up again several times, apparently fearless. It is a remarkable, unexpected, unearned glimpse of a notoriously elusive creature. A little flare of joy before the cold to come.

Carey Davies, 2020

Into the woods, where all is thick with life

COED Y CWM, ABERYSTWYTH, CEREDIGION

*The deep leaf litter beneath my feet creates an
acoustic like that of a softly furnished library*

The three families of swallows that nested in the abandoned stone shed on the edge of the farm have long since departed, leaving the lane quiet and poorer. Thick skeins of bramble stem, with mature growth the colour of dried blood, have wound through the hedgerow between the very last of the sloes – now looking polished and iridescent.

Skirting the top fringe of the wood, which is stunted by harsh weather from the south-west, I pick my way through the dense holly understorey. From the deep shade, a wren loudly objects to my intrusion before whirring away through the colour-edged foliage. Patches of light, filtered between the higher branches, highlight the layer of moss that smooths the rough bark of the trunks.

Lockdown prevented my usual spring visit to the wood, one that is timed to enjoy the flowers and rich scent of the wild garlic. Where the path crosses the steep track that bisects the wood, that broad patch of ground – which in May would have been a shin-high raft of thick fragrant leaves – now feels derelict and is rank with sour, matted growth.

Deeper into the wood, a hollow in the hillside has given enough protection for the beech trees to reach their full height. Despite the apparent lack of wind, the smaller branches move insistently, leaves generating a swirling warm sibilance punctuated by the occasional sharp creak from the larger boughs. The deep leaf litter beneath my feet soaks up other sounds, creating an acoustic like that of a softly furnished library.

I follow the main track westward across the hillside towards the sea until my route is blocked by the back wall of the old quarry, then cut back towards the crest of the hill. This seldom-used path meanders through a carpet of ivy, the flowers still pale and immature. At the sharp, upper break of slope, a wooden stile leads me from the trees into an open pasture cropped tightly by sheep. To the north, the chain of familiar hills along the Llŷn Peninsula – capped with white, buoyant afternoon clouds – rises into view as I walk up the field towards home.

John Gilbey, 2020

The enigmatic magic of magpie inkcaps

WENLOCK EDGE, SHROPSHIRE

*This phallic, monochrome mushroom is full of
contradictions and unknowables*

'One for sorrow, two for joy' goes the old magpie rhyme, but
these are not birds, these are mushrooms – *Coprinopsis picacea*,
the magpie inkcap. There have been changes since the last time I
walked this path between field and wood: a new wire fence erected, low-sweeping branches of an old oak lopped, debris and scrub
cleared, pasture tidied and improved.

In a patch where something has been disturbed under the fence
is a cluster of amazing black and white fungi; fruiting bodies in
various states of growth and decay. In this one patch, an egg pushes
out of the ground; a dark bell-end with white feathery patches rises
upwards on a stalk; at a foot tall, its cap rolls up and melts into a
black inky gloop. 'Three for a girl and four for a boy . . .'

The magpie inkcap is unusual and, although found in Britain and
Ireland, throughout Europe and in North America, it's rare to find
such a strong group. Scientifically described in the eighteenth century as *Agaricus picaceus*, its name was changed to *Coprinus* (an
eater of dung) *picacea*, which looks like *Pica pica*, the magpie; it
was renamed *Coprinopsis* because of DNA differences with other
Coprinus species such as shaggy inkcap, but it still retains *Coprinus*
as a synonym.

Magpie inkcaps feed on tree and grass debris in woodland on
calcareous soil; it is inedible and is said to have alarming poisonous
effects. Despite this, it has also been found to contain chemicals
that may have the potential to be anti-neurodegenerative and anti-
cancer drugs. 'Five for silver, six for gold . . .'

Although most of this fungus lives invisibly in the soil as a gauzy network of filaments decomposing plant life, its fruiting bodies are outrageously exhibitionist. This phallic monochrome mushroom, much more animal than plant, is an enigma. Why is it so strikingly pied? Why so poisonous? Why so uncommon? And why does it turn into a substance that not only looks like ink but can be used as such, in a process called deliquescence, to carry its spores? The poet Gerard Manley Hopkins gave praise for 'all things counter, original, spare, strange' in his poem 'Pied Beauty'. The magpie inkcap is all these things. 'Seven for a secret . . .'

Paul Evans, 2020

A tireless sheepdog that lives for these hills

EDALE, DERBYSHIRE

At this time of year, man and dog use their intimate knowledge of the moors to bring down the sheep

Outside the old barn where our daughter had danced the night before with her new husband, I watch mist spill off the cloaked plateau of Kinder Scout. Nearby, one of our younger guests is playing in the yard, a small explosion of energy and white-gold hair that draws the attention of Mac the sheepdog. Mac's sudden appearance prompts squeaks of alarm, and his owner emerges from the workshop to see what the fuss is. With Geoff's reassuring presence, girl and dog become best friends, and she soon has Mac racing round the yard collecting a tennis ball.

Geoff was born on this estate; his dad was estate manager here years ago, although the grazing is let now. Even so, Geoff still turns out to help at busy times of year, and now is one of those times: the sheep are being brought off the moor for winter, all the estates together, all on the same day. Geoff had already done a dozen miles on Kinder that morning, helping round them up.

'The fog slowed us down,' he says. 'Can't see 'em when it's like that.' Now we stand and watch as whole flocks flow down the hillside like a creamy-white wave breaking up the dale. A shepherd sprints across the distant skyline, chasing some unseen excursion by renegades making a break for it. 'They know every inch of that moor,' Geoff says, with feeling. 'Holes in the wall and so on. Escape routes. All they want is to be up there.'

To entertain my young friend, Geoff sends Mac up and down the nearest field with a series of whistles and shouts. Mac pays close attention, starting and dropping with intelligent precision. He's not far off four, when he'll be available for breeding. Geoff's knowledge of this dog's forebears reaches back over many generations. He taps his head. 'I've got this immense family tree in here,' he says. I've often thought of this valley's human stewards, passing Edale's secrets from one generation to the next. Now I realise there is a canine equivalent, as wedded to this valley as the sheep: a marriage made in heaven.

Ed Douglas, 2019

A golden morning with flocks to match

DAWDON, COUNTY DURHAM

Bounding goldfinches set against a sparkling sea,
the wild calls of pink-footed geese – these are
surely moments to savour

A charm, the collective noun for a gathering of goldfinches, is nowhere near adequate to describe the flock of more than a hundred that we followed along the cliffs near Hawthorn Dene this morning. Our experience of these little finches was one of pure elation.

They were feeding in thistles and knapweed, shredding seedheads, sending thistledown drifting out to sea. Their liquid, twittering calls brought to mind a schoolyard full of children at playtime. That sound rose to a crescendo when we came within twenty paces, before they rose into the air in a panic of whirring yellow-barred wings that flashed in the sunlight, then faded again as they settled back to earth.

This stretch of coastline is fine goldfinch habitat, with impenetrable gorse and blackthorn thickets for nesting along the clifftops, and a mile-long strip of limestone flora that provides enough seed resources to last well into winter. The huge flocks that assemble here are one of the most exhilarating sights of early autumn, especially on a fresh, golden morning like this, with a clear view to the North Sea horizon, where sea and sky meet with razor-sharp clarity.

The sounds of flocks of birds can have a profound effect on mood. From the south we could hear the faint but unmistakable clamour of geese. When we turned to look, other cliff walkers were gazing at the sky. A skein of migrating pink-footed geese passed overhead, flying in a ragged V formation towards Northumber-land, probably heading for their winter feeding grounds.

There is something about their wild calls that sends a little shiver down the spine and stirs the soul. Long before clocks and calendars, when the passage of the sun across the sky and the celestial orbits of the moon and planets were the only measures of time, this spectacle would have been a portent of change, a time to prepare for the turning of the seasons.

Soon they faded from view, trailing in their wake a reminder that fine autumn mornings like this, with bounding flocks of gold-finches set against a sparkling blue sea, are moments to savour. All too soon, winter will be here.

Phil Gates, 2019

It's stockpiling season on the forest floor

MIDDLETON PARK, WEST YORKSHIRE

Jays and grey squirrels fill their caches, ready for leaner times, keeping an ancient engine running

It's been a good year, I think, a good last gasp of summer for red admirals, those big and devilishly handsome butterflies that cruise the nettle-tops and browse the rain-drenched ivy, all in black save for dashing red-and-white epaulettes. According to Vladimir Nabokov, these were the 'butterflies of doom' in pre-Soviet Russia, so called because a sudden abundance coincided with the assassination of Tsar Alexander II in 1881 (though Nabokov was quite wrong in insisting on the name 'red admirable', which is an affectation).

Here in the woodland there's a sense not quite of impending doom, but certainly of hardship. Of lean times to come. It's stock-piling season. The grey squirrels – it seems like there are dozens of them – are intensely busy. Rake-thin and hyper-alert, they cover the leaf-strewn forest floor in Pepé Le Pew bounds, before leaping to take their spiralling squirrel-routes up the trunks. Acorns (the only nut that wears a beret, someone said this week) are abundant, and the squirrels are filling their caches for winter.

The jays are doing the same, stowing their precious nuts under the maturing leaf mould. A single jay might hide as many as five thousand acorns in a single season. Partly, they're preparing for the cold weeks ahead; and partly, without meaning to, they're helping the woodland replenish itself. Many of the cached acorns will go unrecovered, and some, eventually, will germinate. This broadleaf sprawl just south of central Leeds is one of the biggest semi-natural woodlands in the county, and oak is its mainstay species; the squirrels and jays help sustain the chugging of the forest's ancient engine.

There has always been treasure under the ground here at Middleton. The paths I walk wind through the remains of old coal-mines, sunk beneath the oak roots in the early 1700s. You can still see the shaft openings among the trees – still see, even, the weary circles trodden in the soil by the ponies whose labour drove the pit engines. There's one place I know of where you can kick the topsoil and send fragments of coal skittering into the pit hollow.

Richard Smyth, 2019

Long lines of geese feast after a transatlantic flight

Most of the world's brent geese are here in this moment, squabbling over the eelgrass

The sun rises above the drumlin sweep of the Ards Peninsula, brightening the sky to a vast expanse of silver and azure that glazes the mudflats. Across the bay, and below Scrabo's folly, the hum of rush hour fades under the fluting yodels of oystercatcher and hysterics from redshank. There's a sudden flourish from a freshwater channel. Trailing black legs with pistachio-green feet, a little egret floats off to settle on a mess of mustard-coloured wracks.

A faintly off-key throb draws my gaze further out. I adjust the spotting scope. Out of the mudflats' matt and slick, a smudge resolves to become a flock of light-bellied brent geese (*Branta bernicla hrota*), the noise a constant of their contact calls.

Strangford's tidal lough is currently hosting three-quarters of the brents' world population. The non-breeders have been here since late August, after an almost unbroken journey from their summer grounds in Arctic Canada. Thousands more have flown in since, latterly family groups, with their goslings learning the route across the Greenland icecap and through staging areas in Iceland.

At my feet is what they've come for after the arduous Atlantic flyover: eelgrass (*Zostera*), swirling around the lugworm-decorated blisters of sand. Long lines of geese are heads down, zealously pecking for protein-rich rhizomes. Families with the most muscle monopolise the best swards, and there's a fair amount of hustling.

As a new skein arrives, the muttering ratchets up. A goose strains irritably skywards to defend its patch, and a hapless black-tailed godwit flusters away. Curlew, interspersed among the flock, seem unperturbed by the tensions, though it all becomes too much for some of the geese. A small stampede takes off, skimming away to seek less coveted ground. I straighten from the scope and watch their brindle-buff plumage flicker through the autumn light.

Mary Montague, 2018

Helter-skelter red squirrels race round a tree

ALLENDALE, NORTHUMBERLAND

The woodland floor is so springy and quiet,
I can hear all the signs of life

With its openness and regularly spaced trunks, this place makes me think of Winnie-the-Pooh's 'enchanted place on the top of the forest'. Scots pines, thinned out some years back, have furrowed boles that are bare and straight. They turn ruddy brown towards the crowns, from which swoop graceful dark branches. Sunlight filters between the trees, flecking the mossy woodland floor. There are waist-high fronds of male fern and the ground is spongy with needles.

I pick up the remnants of a pine cone. It has been efficiently deconstructed, scales chewed apart to extract the seeds – a sign of feeding squirrels. These female cones start tightly closed and emerald green. They take two to three years to develop, until dispersal stage, when their ripe contents fall to the ground. Take a cone indoors into the warmth of a house, and it will expand so the winged seeds can be tapped out.

The sound of my footsteps is absorbed by the springy floor, so I can move quietly through the wood. I hear the high-pitched calls of goldcrests, though I can't spot them. They move restless-ly through the treetops, using their thin beaks to pick insects out from between the pairs of pine needles. There's the sudden clatter of distress calls, and a sharp *kee-wick* in response, as small birds mob a tawny owl. A screech of jays, a woodpecker call – but so far, no red squirrels.

Domes of fly agaric, scarlet with flaky white spots, have been scraped by teeth marks. Though these storybook fungi are toxic to humans, red squirrels are able to eat them, often leaving them to dry on a high branch before adding to their winter stash. A scratching sound makes me look up, and there they are, two squirrels chasing helter-skelter around a nearby trunk, auburn fur glowing in a patch of light.

Fluid, lithe, there's an exuberance to their movements as they spiral up and down, oblivious to my presence in the energy of the moment. Their hold here may be fragile, but it's a thrill knowing that it's still possible to see red squirrels in Allendale.

Susie White, 2018

NOVEMBER

A space where a gap should be

HADRIAN'S WALL, NORTHUMBERLAND

I know that the great Sycamore Gap is not there any more, but its absence in this landscape is still a shock

Pumpkin-orange, burnt umber, rust: the beech trees at Steel Rigg car park are a frenzy of colour, despite the day being dreich. I set off east along Hadrian's Wall, well wrapped up. Ahead is the massive outcropping of the Whin Sill, its columnar rocks as grey as the heavy clouds above. It's a familiar sight. I came here years ago to work as a site planner on a Roman dig and have lived in Northumberland ever since.

The path twists up the steep stone steps of Peel Crag. The wind whips hair across my face as I pause to study plants. There's wood sage, honeysuckle, ivy, bilberry and wood sorrel – remnants of a once tree-filled landscape. By a gate at the top, a group of shaggy black cattle are grazing the southern slope. Waxcaps gleam in the tufty grass – glossy, bright red buttons and wavy, buttery forms.

This section of the wall, running along the crest, is capped by turf and wildflowers. Diminutive leaves of parsley piert, yarrow seedheads, sprawling rock-rose. Wild thyme spreads along the stones, and it was here that I once filmed for a gardening programme about herbs.

That sense of continuity has been disrupted. I'm heading for Sycamore Gap, tramping the switchback of hills till I reach the top of the far rise. Although I know what to expect, it's with a jolt that I look down into the empty space where the famous tree once stood. It had fitted so perfectly into the bowl of the land, so graceful and balanced, a place for kestrel and thrush in an otherwise treeless landscape.

Now just a stump remains, boxed in by a fence like a museum exhibit: here stood a tree. Its absence is a shock, and I'm glad no one else is about. There's a quietness to feel its loss and, into this still moment, the sky briefly clears and a rainbow arcs the sky.

The low sun throws the shadow of the hill across the field, across the crumpled mass of twigs and branches that are left behind. What's missing is the shadow of a solitary sycamore.

Susie White, 2023

Footpath furniture can be a work of art

BISHOP AUCKLAND, COUNTY DURHAM

The stiles and gateposts we clamp our hands on in the course of a walk are worthy of closer attention

This high stile, beside Coundon Beck, would be a challenge for anyone with ageing hips and dodgy knees. But after the recent first snow of winter, ice and mud made its steps doubly hazardous, so thank you to whoever had the foresight to install a stout pole beside it.

I hauled myself up, pausing to admire the top of the post, a rough-hewn hemisphere worn smooth by the grip of countless ramblers. Collectively, they've created an accidental work of art, smoothing the wood's exquisite pattern of concentric annual rings, polished by their palms to the glassy patina of frequent use.

I've experienced a similar kind of fellowship with unknown walkers in parts of Weardale. Near Wolsingham, there is a rickety old gate that opens with a springy iron latch, forged by a blacksmith in the distant past, and closes with a satisfying snick. The winter sun highlights a pattern in the metal surface, like shallow craters on the moon, created by hammer blows, though at the top, which curls like a shepherd's crook, the scars have been worn smooth by the hands of passers-by who have pulled on the latch. How many generations has it taken for flesh to polish away signs of the blacksmith's hammer? Thinking about that question, a superstitious hiker laying hands on the latch might imagine walking in the company of a pageant of ghosts.

Dale footpaths used to be full of gates with handmade iron fittings, everyday minor work for village blacksmiths: hooks, eyes, chains, hinges, drawn cherry-red from a forge then fashioned by hammer on anvil. As this footpath furniture falls into disrepair, when wooden gates and gateposts crumble, it's replaced by factory-made, galvanised-metal substitutes – but even these sometimes have character.

One such, on a path across the flanks of Chapel Fell, is closed by a spring-loaded bolt that shoots home into a hollow, tubular post. When a south-westerly wind blows across the bolt hole, the post becomes an organ pipe. A mournful sound, rising and falling with the gusts and lulls, drifts across the fell, oddly in tune with calls of golden plover and curlews that will return there to nest in spring.

Phil Gates, 2023

Leaf colour changes by the week,
and by the instant

SANDY, BEDFORDSHIRE

One moment the lime tree is ablaze in early-morning
yellow-gold. The next, the fire is out

This shifting season paints itself in two trees outside my window. I rootled in a bag of coloured pencils at half-term for lime and sycamore, and began to draw. Though my sketching skills are limited, I have learned to see colour changes by the week, the day, and even in an instant, with the parting of clouds.

The old lime to the right is at the end of a line that once marked the boundary of a Victorian villa. Two weeks ago, my drawings would have given it a strong mid-green base, for only the leaves on the outermost twigs curled and furled, all their chlorophyll sucked back into the core. This marked the patchy beginnings of a brief golden age, when previously subsumed carotenoids and xanthophylls gave the lime its first hues of autumn.

At dusk two weeks later, the whole tree is flushed dark bronze, though the hue deepens towards copper in the fading light. At dull dawn, the lime is cloaked in rust – but such subdued colouring can deceive. When the rising sun's rays break through and slant in from the south-east, all is yellow-gold, so bright that it quickens my pencil and fills me with elation. But just an hour later, in this most changeable of weathers, a cast of cloud dampens the fire once more.

The sycamore to the left has proved slower to turn and has a stubborn north-west face. One whole bough flaunts a mostly emerald outpost, while the rest of the tree has retreated uniformly into amber. The sycamore's giant, fingered leaves have that maple family durability, holding their shape, resisting any tendency to curl. Now, and only now, are they starting to drop – in my childhood, sycamore leaves rained down over half-term. Has the season rolled back to later in the year?

The picture will fragment in the gales. Seventeenth-century British settlers crossed the Atlantic and retained an older name for this season, one that was already going out of favour here. We have impenetrable autumn, America has fall, sketching a picture of tumbling leaves with a single word.

Derek Niemann, 2023

The serious business of a Herdwick meet

BUTTERMERE, CUMBRIA

This breed of sheep is not just part of the landscape here, there are cultural events based around it

The late-autumn shepherds' meets are quiet shows that focus solely on sheep, with perhaps a fell race or a shepherd's dog competition as well. Sheep are a serious business in the fells, and at the Buttermere meet there are classes for every age of sheep, as well as sheep shown in show-red and natural colour, and sheep with the best mouth. But there is only one breed: Herdwick.

Herdwick are not only part of the landscape here, there are cultural events centred around them. The meets held at this time of year may be entered by any shepherd from the parish of the meet or any adjoining one. They were originally set up for shepherds to walk to with their tips (their rams; they're called tups in some parts of Cumbria, tips in others). They will then sell, swap or hire them.

The tips here are getting restless. They know that soon it will be time for them to be 'loused' among the yows, who will quietly grow lambs over the winter ready for springtime. Today at Gatesgarth Farm the sheep are contained in a long run of metal hurdles, and every couple of minutes there is the sound of metal crashing as the tips try to get to the yows in neighbouring pens.

From a picnic table bending under the weight of silver cups, the classes are shouted out in turn, and shepherds skilfully guide the correct sheep out of their pens for that class. 'Best group of eight, then three yows natural colour.' The sheep are brought out, and the judge looks at each one in turn. There is no rush, no hurry, very little chat. Everybody waits quietly until the rosettes are handed out.

The final class of the day is for the Overall Champion. All the winners from the previous classes go head-to-head in the final. Johnny Bland from Yew Tree Farm in Borrowdale wins, following his victory at Borrowdale last week. He looks delighted as he calls his whole family over for the prize-giving. It's been a successful day.

Andrea Meanwell, 2022

This beach is ever-changing. Today it is black with sea coal

ALNMOUTH BAY, NORTHUMBERLAND

Once dumped in the water as waste, the coal returns
in waving patterns, transforming the view

On this windy day, the sea is powering across the sands between Marden Rocks and Seaton Point. Light bounces off the shining beach, and it's hard to look at the water for its brilliance. Wiggly piles of lugworm casts lie in neat coils, and oystercatchers probe with mud-tipped red beaks. Just a few dog walkers today, but plenty of birds taking advantage of the turbulence. Wheeling flocks of golden plover are flashing green-gold then silver as they turn in unison. Redshank and turnstone work the sea's margin, and starlings scrabble among the seaweed.

Every time I come here, the beach has a different character: washed flat and empty; lumbered with boulders; metre-deep in seaweed, redolent with oozing black liquid that I wish I could bottle for my garden.

Today, though, the whole sweep of the bay is transformed by a finely textured black grit, scuffed by dog prints to reveal the sand beneath. The retreating water has left waving patterns, branched like tree roots, flowing like river systems seen from above. This is sea coal, something regularly washed up on the Northumberland coast, due partly to erosion of underwater seams but mostly to historical dumping of waste from coalmines.

Back in the 1970s, when I lived in a damp rented farm cottage, we'd burn this cheaper coal, its sea-sculpted rounded lumps splitting and exploding in a red-hot fire. 'Seacoalers' made a tough living from gleaning what the tide washed up, using horses and carts instead of easily corroded motor vehicles.

Further down the coast, a community of seacoalers lived next to the Lynemouth power station. Their harsh way of life was captured in black-and-white photographs by Mik Critchlow and Chris Killip, and was the subject of 1985's *Seacoal* by Amber Films. In 2000, the country diarist Veronica Heath wrote of visiting her sea-coaler friend.

Today, the beach is nearly as black as the closing scenes in *Get Carter*, as black as the cormorant standing atop a red warning pole. Yet next time I come, the beach will be different once more.

Susie White, 2022

Swimming with the starlings

HAYLING ISLAND, HAMPSHIRE

Our group of sea-swimmers is hesitant about taking the plunge; so, it seems, are the birds

We arrive at the beach just after sunrise, though there is no sun to be seen. Dingy grey stratus clouds blanket the sky, and on the other side of the Solent, the Isle of Wight is obscured by mist.

Sewage-overflow alerts have kept us landbound for several weeks, so we dawdle on the shore, contemplating the water, murky with what we hope is now just stirred-up sediment. For the first time this autumn, there is a noticeable chill in the air, and though the sea temperature has only dropped one degree since our last swim, we are anxiously anticipating the cold bite of the water.

As I pull on my neoprene boots and gloves, a squadron of starlings wheels overhead. While starling murmurations, thousands-strong and amorphous, are one of the most breathtaking wildlife spectacles at this time of year, I'm just as entranced by this modest gathering of about sixteen birds. Swooping in, they line up on a wall, whistling and chattering to one another. One scruffy individual hops down and waddles over to a large, shallow pool that has formed in a depression in the shingle. It dips its toes into the water, hesitates for a moment, then takes the plunge.

Its breast and belly submerged, the bird rapidly dunks its head, shimmies its body and flicks its wings, showering its back with droplets of water. This is the signal for the rest of the flock to pile into the communal bath. Spray flies in all directions as they jostle and splash, a frenzy of activity.

Field guides often describe the starling's white-speckled winter plumage as dull, but as they perch atop the beachfront restaurant's sign to preen and dry their feathers, there's a hint of the rainbow-reflecting metallic gloss of their breeding finery. Two juveniles are still in transition to adult plumage, their dull greyish-brown heads and spangled bodies giving them the appearance of children trying on their parents' clothes.

Spurred on by these enthusiastic avian dippers, I leave them to their toilette and lead our intrepid flock of 'Bluetits' swimmers into the surf.

Claire Stares, 2022

A room of one's own – then in flew a chiffchaff

*For ten minutes it was just the two of us: me at my
desk, the bird exploring with purring wings*

A ruffled vibration, like running a thumb across the pages of a book, comes from the open window. I register it, distantly, thinking of the goldfinches who like to peck cobwebs from the lintel. But I don't look up. The fanning becomes louder, but I'm busy writing and still don't look. Now the quiver is inside the room. The air ripples and the stirring grows.

I look up. A chiffchaff in my bedroom whirrs its wings, taking no notice. Rapid olive feathers beat. A palette of green and brown, moss and pine, brings the woodland directly into the house. Its pale eye-stripe flashes like a thread of sun. One of the first migrants to arrive in spring, the chiffchaff's song is often what makes it memorable. The familiar, disyllabic *chiff-chaff* heralds warmer days and a swell of birdsong.

There is, therefore, something dissonant about its voiceless presence in November, with the only song coming from purring, woodwind wings. Inside when it should be out, quiet when it should be loud – these broken patterns shake me out of my routine as, for around ten minutes, we build a gentle camaraderie, working side by side in the new normal.

Since an increasing number of these traditional summer migrants are now staying through the UK's warming winters, it's not so unusual to find it here. With more of my work taking place in the house, it's not so surprising to meet different neighbours.

As I write, it explores the room with a series of sorties, interspersed with intervals of treading air. I stretch periodically, as it hangs there, neither of us moving towards cover.

We are getting used to one another. It is only when I reach for a camera that it stirs and flits out of the window. Perhaps this gesture towards surveillance breached an unwritten code. I'm still learning what working alongside a chiffchaff is like. I hope I did some things right.

When I touch the keyboard and resume, all the air seems to have been let out of the room.

Elizabeth-Jane Burnett, 2021

The autumn frog dreams of spring

HOVE, EAST SUSSEX

When evening comes, so does the low croak of the male, bringing a little magic to the damp of my allotment

It's a November dusk on the allotment. My least favourite times of day and year. It's cold, and I'm wearing two pairs of socks and thick-heeled boots to stop autumn's sog and rot leaching in. I'm also, however, holding out for a peculiar magic that can be found in this damp, overgrown space.

I work quickly to stay warm, and quietly to not disturb birds. I plant broad beans and garlic in uneven rows. Distantly, I can hear traffic, but I'm more tuned in to the closer late-day rush for food and roosts. Starlings gather in rooftop groups and chat excitedly. There's a rush of wings above my head, and hundreds make their way to Brighton's piers for murmuration, their huge sunset dance in the sky.

I pack up, then sit on my makeshift bench by the pond. There's a closeness to near darkness. Do I feel more because I see less?

A fluffed-up magpie sits on a fence post; a thin plume of bonfire smoke drifts over silhouettes; midges dance.

Then I hear it – what I've been waiting for. The low, rumbling croak of a male frog. It's quiet at first, as if shy, then gains confidence and belts out its song as if there isn't a grinning human two feet away. No one knows why frogs croak in autumn, but I see it as a party invite for spring shenanigans. Males overwinter near or at the bottom of ponds, presumably so they can be first to the party in spring. Why wouldn't they make sure the females know which pond they've chosen?

The grass around the pond is long. I could be sharing it with a thousand frogs and I wouldn't know, except for this one, reminding me that it's not just me dreaming of spring. I close my eyes and the world smells of damp grass and decay. But there will be frogspawn in this pond. There will be mating and eggs and tadpoles. New life. Spring will be here again. The frog says so.

Kate Bradbury, 2021

In rural Britain, some signs are more polite than others

CROXTON PARK, CAMBRIDGESHIRE

While nature reserves ask, private estates demand

Yesterday it was 'Please stay on the path', a polite request on a charity nature reserve, duly obeyed. Twenty-four hours on, 10 miles away and a world apart, the inscription reads 'Shut & fasten gate'. Private estates do not ask; they demand.

For at least eight hundred years, villagers have walked through the back entrance to Croxton Park in supplication. They have bowed, not to the landowner of the day, but to a higher authority, for the parish church of St James is located at the very heart of the estate. There is but one path to God here, and all the tempting offshoots are barred with 'Keep out', 'Private', 'No entry'. It feels like old-style National Trust, with visitors expected to know their place.

Today, a welcoming committee in the form of a small flock of sheep has assembled, peering at us from the other side of the gate. We shut and fasten and leave it behind, and the curious sheep inch forward towards us over odd bumps and earthworks of grassy antiquity, until their high heels click-clack on the drive. The dense, curly coats of these dark-coloured Ryelands give them a koala-ish look. Behind them, cattle graze – black-nosed British whites, and beef shorthorns with light brown flanks flaking like old paint to reveal creamy undercoats. No run-of-the mill Holstein Friesian milk machines here.

Further along the cowpat-splatted, sheep-dunged drive, the grand Georgian house becomes visible over the fields; a *Pride and Prejudice* Pemberley, always out of reach. A cattle grid marks the transition to classic parkland. In the pasture, well-spaced veteran trees spread their branches down to cow-muzzle height. The oldest oaks, however, have succumbed to age and their whalebone carcasses lie where they fell. They are a reminder that the preservation of continuity requires constant change. Where are the young and maturing oaks, the ancient trees for the twenty-third century?

The drive ends at the lychgate, a portal to the churchyard. A metal plaque bears the inscription 'Please keep the gate shut'. And it is open.

Derek Niemann, 2021

Wild weather brings out the best in the birds

WENLOCK EDGE, SHROPSHIRE

Jackdaws and wood pigeons surf the westerlies,
opening their wings fully as gusts burst over the trees
and hurl the birds down the dip slope

There are wild energies in the air: wraiths of Atlantic weathers twisting and unthreading the sky, warping through trees, poking into thickets.

Galvanised and illuminated by these energies are birds. A parcel of linnets unwraps into a field, a blue tit pole-dances on a briar, blackbirds and redwings scuffle into hawthorns, long-tailed tits flick around high boughs. A covey of partridges makes for fields of shining tilth from which all memory has leached, leaving the piety of clay. The five of them plait through a hedge, neat and tidy.

Up on the Edge, jackdaws and wood pigeons surf westerlies, opening their wings fully as gusts burst over the trees and hurl the birds at a dangerous lick down the dip slope towards shelter. Ravens find their battle cries in the wind to challenge buzzards, which blow hard on rusty whistles.

On this blustery November day, flashing with sunlight, the broken column of a rainbow leans under a shelf of cloud sliding east. In the turbulence, birds' familiar skyways are unravelling and they travel through the vortex as explorers of a perilously shifting airspace, beautiful and reckless. Some take refuge in trees and hedges; rebellious yellowhammers pluck up courage to bounce above the blackthorn tips, then dive back in before they are swept away from their anxious clan.

Flight gives birds something more than mobility; it gives them an enhanced way of being, with an emotional, physical and psychic liberty unavailable to pedestrians. In windy weather, they seem to test the limits of this liberty and are aware that others are doing this too. Birds in flocks, charms, murmurations, and all their collective nouns, have complicated relationships and a shared awareness of kith in place. Even solitary birds must be conscious of belonging to the kin of the air. What then does it mean for a bird to be alone? Does wild weather remove the utility of flight and loosen the bonds between birds so that they fly as individuals, experience ecstasy, get lost in the flow, freed from each other, freed from themselves?

Paul Evans, 2020

Crowds gather for the homecoming salmon

STAINFORTH FORCE, YORKSHIRE DALES

People come here from miles around for the salmon run display. The fish have travelled a little further

It leaps from the churning water a few minutes after I arrive, startling me mid-sentence. Red-tinged, hook-mouthed and huge, the returning traveller from the Atlantic rises clean of the maelstrom by several feet, hangs tantalisingly in the air, then falls back into the curtain of the waterfall – a heroic effort, but not quite enough to clear the lip of Stainforth Force.

'Got it!' exclaims the photographer I was talking to, another picture of a leaping Atlantic salmon (*Salmo salar*) in the bag. 'I came last year, and it was like those Alaskan nature documentaries. They were almost jumping into my feet.'

These fish were born in the Ribble and are on their way 'home'. After surviving as many as four winters feeding and growing in the North Atlantic, they have navigated back to the mouth of the river (near Blackpool), made their way up through Lancashire, and are attempting to reach the exact place they were born, to spawn, recognising their home stream by its specific smell. Now, to get to the higher reaches of the river, they must overcome these falls, which are regionally famous for the salmon run display. Each leap prompts gasps and clicking shutters from the gathered spectators – then a return to watchful silence.

A small percentage of the salmon will return to the sea and spawn again, but the return migration exerts a huge physiological toll on the fish. For most, the cost of making life will be the loss of their own.

It is tempting to see an anthropomorphic nobility or dogged-ness in this, but that implies an unlikely level of individual agency; more probable is that the salmon's instinct to reproduce is a force of nature almost as blind as the waters they drive up against. But it makes me think about the instinctual undertows in our own lives, and the degree of freedom we have to swim against them. Walt Whitman comes to mind: 'Urge and urge and urge / Always the procreant urge of the world.'

Finally, a fish leaps up and, somehow, just about flops over the top. We all cheer.

Carey Davies, 2019

No better companions for a fungal foray

DURHAM UNIVERSITY BOTANIC GARDEN

*My granddaughters are my students
for the day, and I theirs*

Before I retired from university teaching, I brought undergraduates to this valley at the bottom of the botanic garden to demonstrate the rudiments of mycology. It's a perfect location for a fungal foray: deciduous beech and oak woodland on one side of a small stream, a conifer plantation on the other, with plentiful fallen timber.

The site is managed for mycological diversity, allowing dead branches to decay where they fall, entering an afterlife where wave after wave of fungal hyphae slowly reduce them to humus. As that great woodsman Oliver Rackham once said: 'A horizontal tree – alive or dead – is at least as good a habitat as an upright one.'

Today my students were my granddaughters, aged two and four, who raced under the entrance archway formed from 10-foot-tall toadstool sculptures. With their elegant picture-book simplicity, the giant metal fungi are a perfect gateway to the magical world of mushrooms and an open invitation to storytelling.

The imagination of small children knows no limits. We agreed that tall, grey-capped toadstools were dinner tables for the forest folk, and that the puffballs that sent up smoky eruptions of spores when they tapped them with a stick must be chimneys of their hidden underground homes.

When we discovered stumps covered with grey and black threads that resembled extinguished candlewicks, the children's instant question was: 'Can we come back at night and see these candles burning?' That image that they gifted, of a nocturnal woodland floor flickering with tiny lights, will come to mind now whenever I find this common candlesnuff fungus (*Xylaria hypoxylon*).

In years to come, perhaps they too will become undergraduates, pondering the mystery of how the minute white **threads**, finer than human hair, that we discovered under a rotting **log** organise themselves into the elegant architecture of the toadstools we found today. For, surely, curiosity begins with the joy of discovery, which triggers the need for an explanation and leads to an endless journey to find better answers. Along the way, it's good to listen to the innocent imagination of a child, to recall where it all begins.

Phil Gates, 2019

Searching for the source of the Fishlake floods

SNAILSDEN EDGE, SOUTH YORKSHIRE

*As I shelter from the biting rain I scan the
vast landscape, looking for clues*

Sploshing along under Snailsden Edge, the light rain angling in from the north turned to sleet; white bands of it stung my face. Fed up with this mild torture, I ducked into the lee of a high stone wall to wait for a patch of clear sky. My view was wide but darkly ominous: across to Dead Edge Flat, where the moor was seamed with black gullies cut by rain into the peat; then grandly rightwards to Withens Edge, where Derbyshire, South Yorkshire and West Yorkshire meet, the watershed between east and west; and below it the top of Great Grains Clough, source of the River Don.

Where I stood was little more than 30 miles from the flooded village of Fishlake, on the banks of the Don and a name now familiar from news reports. You can't turn back the clock to witness first-hand how and when people lose their way, but you can with rivers. Were there any clues as to the Don's downstream delinquency in what I could see now of its infant flow? Rivers, like people, are complex, and the Don's catchment covers more than 700 square miles, so it would be risky to jump to conclusions. But I could see some signs of early dysfunction.

Across the moors were ranks of black boxes: grouse butts. Several hundred yards away, I watched an all-terrain vehicle – the preferred means of transport for the modern gamekeeper – patrolling the moor. In the 1840s, Snailsden was one of the first places to develop driven grouse shooting, and since then these moors have been burned to promote the growth of young heather shoots, which the grouse eat. This landscape is wild and elemental, but there's little natural about it.

The impact all that burning has on how quickly water runs off these moors is contested. But in the same week that Fishlake flooded, Yorkshire Water, which owns thousands of acres of moorland hereabouts, announced new guidelines for those who lease its land for shooting, including, for the first time, a presumption against burning. The news felt to me like the first rays of sunshine after weeks of rain.

Ed Douglas, 2019

May the barnacle geese be protected from all unkind fates

PENRHYNDEUDRAETH, GWYNEDD

What a flood of pleasure it was to see them descend
on to the farthest shore to feed in the dimity light

Idling down to Abergafren on a dank autumn evening, I heard the calls high above – a yapping and yelping like a litter of young Pekingese dogs, a sound that used to be one of the identifying features of this lovely estuary of the Dwyryd.

Reaching the shore, I took out my glass and focused on a flight of seven birds, gliding down towards Glastraeth. Their faces were white-masked; barred wings flickered stroboscopic silver; pale bellies and rumps glowed in the dimity light. Barnacle geese (*Branta leucopsis*) – among my favourite birds, down from their breeding grounds in the Arctic.

Thirty years ago I used to walk here daily, often with my good friend and near neighbour, the sculptor and writer Jonah Jones. We'd encounter on a regular basis huge flocks of barnacle geese, curlew, pintail. Whether through climate change or disturbance by the very active local wildfowling fraternity, I don't know, but none of these species is now present in anything like their former numbers. I do know the flood of pleasure I experienced as I watched the ragged little band's descent to the sandy rhines and samphire pastures on the farther shore.

These beautiful, medium-sized geese have a strange presence in medieval bestiaries. Folklore had it they were the adult form of goose barnacles. The priest and historian Gerald the Welshman wrote in 1188 that 'Bishops and religious men in some parts of Ireland do not scruple to dine off these birds at the time of fasting, because they are not flesh nor born of flesh'. Pope Innocent III whipped the recusants into line early in the thirteenth century, noting with sound good sense that since in all particulars they behaved like geese, geese they must be, and therefore were not to be eaten during Lent.

I like the passage from the ancient Chinese text *Book of Changes*, which describes cries of the wild geese as 'like the red threads that bind us to our fates'. May the geese be protected from all unkind fates!

Jim Perrin, 2018

Postcards from the trenches

COTEHELE, TAMAR VALLEY, CORNWALL

While the woods here are once more in full autumn palette, an exhibition is under way to commemorate those locals who fell in the First World War

We head towards the woods, skirting the valley garden, with its stew pond and dovecote with mossy domed roof. A swamp cypress appears to be on fire, sparse scarlet leaves cling to acers, witch hazel is in flower, and a kousa dogwood sports strawberry-like fruits. Further on, orange beech, yellow chestnut and burnished oak contrast with the undergrowth of holly, woodrush, male and hard ferns, and the lurid green pastures on the opposite bank of the Tamar.

Few old trees in this steep woodland date from before 1891, when the great blizzard uprooted thousands of mature specimens. Some of the timber was used by James Goss, a shipbuilder of

Calstock, and my great-grandfather at Morden Mill commissioned an account desk made from fallen chestnut.

Trees also cloak the precipitous sunny side of the bank: bare grey branches of ash wave about above yellowing thickets of willow and hazel; swags of old man's beard benefit from lime brought in the past to sweeten acid soils; collapsed packing sheds are overwhelmed by bushy ivy.

Views open up, past the bridge over the derelict incline railway, back towards Cotehele House. In addition to the Christmas garland already strung through the Great Hall, this year a collage covers the walls, which are usually hung with armour and antique weapons.

Designed by the artist Dominique Coiffait to commemorate the centenary of the end of the First World War, the collage consists of 20,000 paper flowers cut from his lino prints by volunteers, and is embedded with images of, and postcards from, locals who went to fight in the trenches.

One of the photos shows young Stanley Breen, holding a rifle and seated on his horse. He survived to become a tenant on the home farm, where, with his wife, Sheila, he milked cows, reared pigs, geese and turkeys, and stored straw and hay in the big barn, which was later converted into the National Trust's restaurant.

Virginia Spiers, 2018

When does winter start? Let the trees answer

CLAXTON, NORFOLK

*In the name of research, I turn my attention to two
clumps of poplars and some oaks near the marsh*

It was my wife who inspired my last few weeks of village excursions, when she asked what marks the beginning of winter and autumn's close. It's not as straightforward as you might expect. 'Meteorological winter' opens on 1 December (and runs until 28 February), but 'astronomical winter' has to wait until four days before Christmas for its own beginning (and until 20 March for its end).

I soon learned that official writ doesn't really run in our parish. I used the trees as my best index of season and began research on the marsh, where there are a couple of clumps of about twenty mature poplar trees. Throughout summer they are equal-sized domes of heraldic green, but by 6 November the more exposed of the two was stripped out. The other, meanwhile, had retained about 50 per cent foliage on that same date, although within a week its half share was largely gone. I estimate that it had kept no more than perhaps 10,000 leaves of June's 5 million. By the third week of November, both were bare.

Then I enquired of the oaks on the track to the marsh – and they confused the picture completely. One in particular is a tree I photograph repeatedly, to capture its cycling metamorphoses. It is now about typical for late November – that blend of fading green and decayed iron that makes up the quintessential cold flame of autumn oak. What is shocking is that the smaller one by its side is still completely immersed in summer green. For this indefatigable plant, not even autumn has arrived. Meanwhile, a third mature oak across the dell, despite its enclosed location and perfectly good health, had shed its entire 200,000-leaf load. It is winter personified, but half hidden in the wider copse.

As 1 December approaches, I conclude that our society likes to deal in fixed generalised categories. We call the whole thing a 'season' or a 'landscape', but in fact every small spot has its very specific portion of nature's total genome. It may obey a wider, inexorable cycle, but each keeps its own hour and knows its own season.

Mark Cocker, 2018

Fly agarics everywhere, and of startling variety

SUTTON BANK, NORTH YORKSHIRE

I turned my back on a view of the Pennines
for this – but it is worth it

I've just walked past a fingerpost directing walkers to 'The Finest View in England'. This was the opinion of the writer and local vet James Herriot, and round here, that's as good as gospel. On this blue dome morning, though, it's a reasonable claim.

I'm on the North York Moors plateau, where the vast wall of Whitestone Cliff towers over the wooded escarpment of Sutton Bank, fiery with autumn colour. There's blue in the looking glass of Gormire Lake, and far away, beyond the Vale of Mowbray and the eastern Dales, are the great knobbly whalebacks of the Pennines.

But I'm here for a spectacle on a different scale altogether, though one that comes with an equally compelling recommendation: 'Mummy, you *have* to see, it's Fairyland.' So I turn my back on the finest view and plunge into the blue-green air that gathers around spruce. Immediately, I see what he meant. The hummocky ground is splotched with scarlet. I've never seen so many fly agarics (*Amanita muscaria*) in one place.

The caps are startlingly variable: some picture-book-perfect hemispheres, others ranging from golf balls to dinner plates, a few inverted into bowls. Some are regulation white-spotted, others washed plain. The overripe ones are purple and brown, liquefying, and the oldest are engulfed by the thread-like hyphae of other fungi.

I was taught that fly agarics are deadly, though reliable records of fatal poisonings are all but non-existent. It seems they're not even that effective in seeing off the houseflies they're supposed to kill when left crumbled in a saucer of milk. What they *are* is powerfully psychoactive – with a range of effects, including the Alice in Wonderland delusion, where objects appear alternately much larger and smaller than they really are.

But I don't need to ingest any to see what every child knows is here. I crouch, and there it is: the architecture of an archetype, ready to be peopled at will with fays, or smurfs, or gruffaloes.

As I wind my way out, chainsaws start up nearby, because of course, in Fairyland, there must also be woodcutters.

Amy-Jane Beer, 2018

DECEMBER

Life has returned to these bits from the Blitz

CROSBY TO HIGHTOWN, MERSEYSIDE

The fragments of wall and chimney here were once the stuff of Liverpool's homes. Now they protect the coast and are home to sea beet, plovers and turnstones

Crosby coastal path lures winter walkers north towards Hightown, where the River Alt, after meandering across north Merseyside, joins the Mersey to spill out into Liverpool Bay. Sandwiched between estuary, beach and scrub, with a ribbon of fixed dunes, there is much to tempt the senses here.

It is bitterly cold today, harsh and penetrating, yet invigorating. The sky is cloudless and luminous, as only a winter sky can be. The scrubby sward, floral and fecund in summer, is now flattened and frost-embossed. A vole scuttles through the grass, its progress aided by the rigid archways of frozen plants.

Crosby Beach is like no other: this is 'Blitz beach'. Two miles of debris covering the sand, so rich in pattern, texture and colour, artefacts of one nation's hatred of another. There are doorsteps and lintels; bits of walls and chimneys; curlicues, fleurs-de-lis and gargoyles; signs of lives lived before. This chaff of the 1941 May Blitz on Liverpool and Bootle was brought here seventy-five years ago to protect the coast against Mersey storms. Now it is washed, eroded and remoulded, clays returning to river sediment.

History and nature converge here, as wartime relics anchor plants and harbour roosting birds. And despite the season, this is not a habitat in hibernation. Sea beet grows profusely among the fragments. Cormorants fly overhead; anxious redshanks call. Oystercatchers pipe while turnstones sift among remoulded bricks. Stonechats, in great numbers, dash from erect frozen stems to fence posts, their radiant rufous breasts as warming as mulled wine.

What draws the eye most is an unusually large flock of grey plovers. They line the lower margins of the beach, wing feathers outlined porcelain white. Clustering in such numbers provides warmth and protection from predators, and as the rising tide encroaches, the birds shuffle en masse further up the bomb-scree for temporary refuge. As the tide bites further, there is no leeway left for roosting; with a rush, they take flight, a hundredfold choreography of white rumps and black 'armpits'. The cold persists, but I am warmed.

Jennifer Jones, 2023

A ghostly, freezing day in the Cairngorms

ABERNETHY FOREST, STRATHSPEY

Temperatures have plummeted here, transforming the sights and sounds. Only the joyful redpolls disrupt the stillness

The first snows of the winter have been followed by overnights of −10°C, and the trees and grasses are filigreed with a thick coating of frost. Near to home, a flock of chaffinches are cooried up in a birch, and I check for bramblings, a bird I'm always delighted to see. Our feeders are busy with coal, blue and great tits, goldfinches, woodpeckers and a solitary crested tit, the latter another sure sign of winter, though I wonder where the siskins are.

In the past few days there has been a flock of finches a hundred or more strong, coming and going, landing on the topmost branches of the birches and pines at the far side of the field, and I can't tell if their restlessness is part of their modus operandi or because of our local marauding sparrowhawk.

In the afternoon, the temperature rises to –7°C, and I go for a walk. My footsteps seem loud, and grasses, mud and leaves that have been soft underfoot are crunchy. Puddles crackle. When I stop, the place is silent, and it's easy to forget how the snow shifts the quality of both light and sound. In this early gloaming, a soft mist envelops the valley, casting everything in a soft pink-grey.

I cross hare tracks and follow mice or vole prints that criss-cross like an intricate dance, heading up towards where I know there are pinewoods, even if today they are invisible, then ghostly. It's just 3.15 p.m., but sunset is in about fifteen minutes, so I head home. The mist thins just enough to see a hint of blue above. I hear a loud chattering, then see the finches again – redpolls – in a birch just in front of me, skittering and chittering, hanging upside down on the branches like Christmas decorations.

When I get to the tree, the snow underneath is confettied with birch seeds, so I follow them to another and peer up, amazed at their acrobatics, how they disrupt the stillness of the afternoon, smiling as they shower birch seeds and snow on my head.

Amanda Thomson, 2023

Close (and not so close) encounters
with the rooks

KIRKCUDBRIGHT, DUMFRIES AND GALLOWAY

The flock is a swirling black snowglobe,
a thousand strong

The Liverpool-born poet Richard Le Gallienne wrote: 'I meant to do my work today / But a brown bird sang in the apple tree.' These words are very dear to me, as Fairy Hill Croft here in sub-zero Galloway is full of things to turn the head.

The resident badger clans have dug a total of forty-seven latrines down the lane and near my wood shed. Most of the badgers hit their target, but a few have missed the hole completely, and not one backfilled. With my white beard developing nicely, this Santa also rescued a roe deer trapped in a fence, tripped over a squat woodcock (such clever camouflage), watched 200 Holsteins navigate the milking parlour and disturbed three blue tits that were roosting in a deserted house martin's nest.

Most memorable was the sight of hundreds of rooks that lifted from the top field this week – think Hitchcock – sunlight picking out their characteristic baggy trousers, grey ceres and the bootblack sheen of their feathers as they returned to the cowpats for a good feed.

My new year resolution is to identify which individuals rise first when they see me. A tough task when faced with a swirling black snowglobe in an instant. The rooks, well-dressed parliamentarians strutting their stuff, have a complex hierarchy of bosses and lackeys. Older birds are responsible for the majority of nest building, breeding and parenting, but it is thought that they whip subordinates into action to help raise the young, leading by example in foraging, defence of territory and other behaviours.

At this stage of the year, with nesting duty imminent, some of the yearlings still try to obtain food from their adults, dropping their wings and opening their gapes, but are given short shrift and even pecked.

Living among the birds, I am rewarded with close encounters, like the single rook that purred almost like a cat. He caught sight of me and offered a regular caw before joining another group on the electricity wires. As my one-time neighbour Robert Burns wrote: 'Gie me ae spark o' nature's fire / That's a' the learning I desire.'

Sean Wood, 2023

Four seasons on one twig

WOLSINGHAM, WEARDALE, NORTH PENNINES

After being utterly captivated by a flock of long-tailed tits, I go to see what they were foraging for

The annual ride on the ferris wheel of the seasons was approaching its lowest point: the winter solstice, the shortest day. Dank preceding days of fog, relentless rain, mud and dawn-to-dusk grey skies brought the temptation to curl up on the sofa and enjoy nature vicariously through the pages of a good book.

But then a north-westerly Arctic wind delivered today's crystalline frost, frozen puddles and blue skies. A shivering, brisk-walking sort of day, until a small flock of birds had me frozen to the spot. Long-tailed tits, a dozen or more, bounding along the hedgerow in my direction. A troupe of avian acrobats, searching every twig for food morsels, never still for a second, like excited schoolchildren on a class outing.

Soon they were all around, oblivious to my presence, so close I could hear the rustling wings and soft contact calls. Could there be a more heartening end to a year than to be surrounded by these hyperactive balls of fluff? One bird, so close I could have reached out and touched it, dangled upside down, holding on with one leg while it picked out something lodged between the toes of the other, before moving on to join the flock.

There's an anthropocentric temptation to interpret all that frenetic energy as exuberance. Really, it stems from their dire need for food. After they'd gone, I looked for what they might have been seeking on those lichen-covered twigs. A five-minute search yielded only a small spider, a couple of aphids and what might have been insect eggs – meagre fare in these short, freezing days of winter.

There was something else uplifting in that blackthorn hedge: four seasons on a single winter twig. A few purple sloes, the product of flowers pollinated nine months ago, some lemon-yellow autumn leaves still clinging on and, among them, tiny, tight flower buds – spring pre-packaged, ready for warmer, longer days when this hedge will be white with blossom, not frost.

The ferris wheel of the seasons slows but never stops, and will soon be picking up speed again as the days lengthen after the solstice.

Phil Gates, 2022

In the long, dark winter, a beam of golden light

MAESHOWE, ORKNEY

*When the entrance of this ancient cairn begins to
fill with the solstice sunset, around 2.30 p.m.,
the genius of its neolithic creators is manifest*

Near the village of Stenness, a strange conical hillock snouts up from a grassy field. Shrouded in rough grass and encircled by a ditch, it is both a part of the landscape and unmistakably artificial. This is Maeshowe, a 5,000-year-old chambered cairn, best visited at this time of year, when the days are at their shortest and the genius of its neolithic creators might be viewed to full effect.

Inside, at 2.30 p.m., a crowd of strangers stand together in the gloom, waiting. We discuss the cairn's construction – the long, low passageway that leads into the dark, the great slabs of stone tightly corbelled to create the arching roof – and the runic graffiti scratched into the walls in the twelfth century by Viking raiders. These runes are slender, branching figures, their meaning not dissimilar to what you might find in any bus shelter: who Thorni was bedding, adjudication of the shapeliest widows, who woz 'ere in 1153.

Outside, the sun is dipping below the Hoy hills. We lapse into silence, watching the warm yellow light creep up the passageway. Then I spot it, what we're all here to see: a pencil-thin band of light appears on the far wall. It spreads, claiming the stone inch by inch, until it forms a square window of gold, like a portal into another world.

This eerie illumination can be witnessed around the winter solstice, when sunset comes into line with the stone entrance. The full significance of the cairn's astronomical alignment is not fully understood, but the passing of midwinter must have been of great significance to our ancient predecessors – as it is for us.

Winter here is long and dark and wet. On a clear night like this, one might hope to catch a glimpse of the Northern Lights in its dance of the green veils. But more often we are clouded over, wrapped in a blanket bearing rain and sleet. The bright days of spring feel a long way off. But the light show at Maeshowe promises they are on their way.

Cal Flyn, 2022

A wild and contradictory place

MALIN HEAD, COUNTY DONEGAL

Giant energies meet here, at the most northerly point of the island. I may even see Islay thicken out of the gloom

Through the wind's bluster, I hear strident calls. But as I scan the shelves of fields behind Ballyhillin Beach, there's no sign of the barnacle geese that fly from Greenland to winter along this coast. My gaze lingers on the knuckles of land that show how, at the end of the last Ice Age, the shore rose as a glacier melted away.

So much of Malin Head is like this. Shifting. Contradictory. Hinting of a vast elsewhere, with giant energies hissing at the brink. When I first came here, decades ago, my parents teased me with this riddle: how could we be at Ireland's northernmost point yet still be in – as the Northern Irish commonly refer to it – 'the south'? But anything seems possible in this place. Islay might just thicken out of the horizon's massed clouds. Like the child I was, I hunch forward as I squint. *Maybe.*

Turning my back on Scotland, I head for the shoulder of Altnadarrow (from the Irish *ailt na dtarbh*, 'the ravine of the bull'), where landfall brunts a seething ocean. To my right is Banba's Crown, a promontory named for a mythological goddess, Banba. Her sister, Ériu, bequeathed her name to Eire, while Banba only managed to retain this small, if vital, point. Still, a flight of fancy could hold a jealous sibling responsible for the huge white letters of EIRE that are carved into the crown's rim. A firmer mind clings to the conventional story: the graffiti is a warning to Second World War pilots of the republic's neutrality.

Banba's Crown is topped by what looks like a truncated hennin, the tall headdress worn by medieval noblewomen. This is the derelict signal tower, built in 1805 by the British admiralty to help thwart a Napoleonic invasion, and later used for early transatlantic telecommunications. This historical importance finds its refrain in the echo of Malin's name through what poet Carol Ann Duffy called the 'radio's prayer', otherwise known as the BBC shipping forecast.

The bluff is pitching me towards the Atlantic's shrugs of white-laced grey and jade. I stop to catch my breath. A gannet spears itself into the heaving swell. Beyond, the offing flattens to a vast disc that pans uninterruptedly to the Arctic.

Mary Montague, 2022

The farm rolls on, regardless of day or year

LONG DEAN, COTSWOLDS

Before dawn I'm out feeding the cattle,
deep in the seasonal routine

It is the final day of the year, but the farming cycle, governed by season and not calendar, makes the significance of tomorrow almost arbitrary. Not until the herd is on spring grass, new calves 'at foot', will it feel as if we have truly turned a corner.

Now we are deep into winter, with its unchanging daily routine, and I am out before it is light, as I have been every day – Christmas included – since the cattle became dependent on supplementary feeding. They're waiting for me, just as they always are, for the most part stoically patient, but one or two with a peremptory shout. Devons are known for being vocal.

The bull, true to character, stands silent. Head raised expectantly, he raises it a little higher as he scents his breakfast. I toss the bale into the ring feeder and climb in after it. A steer pushes forward, catching his hoof on the rim with a metallic clunk.

Not being a big farm, we don't have the capacity to handle large, round bales, so our cattle are fed twice daily with a series of small ones. I cut the twine with a knife and carefully pocket it, then begin pulling the hay apart. Conveniently, this feeder has a partition bar missing, creating a larger slot to accommodate the bull's neck. As I work, his great, woolly head brushes against me. I am mindful of him, but so, it seems, is he of me, deferentially turning to one side as I bend. He has the softest patch of fur, just below his eye, smooth where the rest is curly.

The hay smells sweet. I am always amused by the juxtaposition of the two points in time of its handling. When hauling it, freshly made in the heat and glare, this coldly dark dawn feeding is beyond the imagination – and vice versa. But as I break the bale I see a speck of yellow, a desiccated flower, summer's promise preserved. Tomorrow will not mark the start of my new year, but I know it will come.

Sarah Laughton, 2022

They drive you out, your mum and dad

SANDY, BEDFORDSHIRE

Winter is a dangerous time for a young
swan who is yet to fly the nest

A *tuk, tuk* from the water below draws us to the side of the bridge. We look down through the crown of a leafless willow. Despite weeks of negligible rainfall, the spring-fed Ivel keeps a brisk flow. No amount of scanning the bankside will bring the moorhen – if that is what it was – out of cover.

A bird does indeed appear, as if propelled from under our feet. A young swan that I haven't seen for weeks has turned a lighter shade of pale, though it might not be in time for a pure white Christmas. In its autumn moult, the bird trades, quill by quill, the unassuming greys and browns of its juvenility for the brilliance of adulthood.

And therein lies peril. Dark plumage advertises innocence in swan world; whiteness constitutes threat. And this bird rests uneasily. Something in the way it sits in the water: perhaps it's the neck, raised beyond the habitual bend of relaxation.

A second swan bursts out from beneath the bridge, every feather conveying aggression. Who taught a male swan to 'make yourself look big', wings billowed, fanned and arched to present its opponent with a wall of fury? Neck thrown back so that the next move of its loaded head will be a thrust and stab?

Though the youngster paddles a swift retreat, the adult male rises out of the water and extends his neck. Slap! He strikes the surface with both wings. The young bird scrabbles to take flight. Slap! The male has caught up and may be trying to bite. Slap! The juvenile is flying now. It flees round the bend, and the cob settles.

What kind of triumph is this? The adult has driven off its young, a bird he tended ever since it was an egg on his female's nest. She sails up, wings also bowed in anger, a co-aggressor. The territorial pair have banished their offspring, a necessary cruelty of winter.

Derek Niemann, 2021

Storm Arwen battered the valley, but the barn owl survives

ALLENDALE, NORTHUMBERLAND

It is small relief that, for all the damage done, the owl is gliding once more, low over the snowy field

It was back in September at dusk, a time of uncertain light, that I thought I saw a white bird. In that fine autumn, there followed other evenings of gardening late, but it was several weeks before I saw it again. A barn owl flying low across the field, quartering the long grass; I hadn't imagined it.

The variety of habitats in the valley where I live makes for good hunting: a mixture of wood pasture, tufty grasses and marsh. This rough land provides cover for small mammals and, in particular, field voles, a barn owl's main diet. Since that first sighting, the owl has become a regular, recorded in my notebook morning and evening, a pale floating shape, backlit as dawn comes over the hill, wings tinged apricot as the sun sets.

Barn owls are crepuscular birds, so the short winter days give a greater chance of seeing one. Their soft, silent feathers have little waterproofing, and they rely on hearing to locate their prey; on wet, windy nights they go hungry. One ear set higher than the other enables them to pinpoint sound.

I saw it again recently. The owl hovered low, feathered legs dangling, claws folded, before dropping into the long grass by the river. It lifted off again, gripping a vole, and took it to a half-hidden spot in the lee of a conifer wood. Mantling its prey, it tugged for five minutes before peering round and flying into the dark trees. One morning there were two barn owls circling each other, hinting at possibilities for next year.

Then Storm Arwen came; I looked for the owl the day after. All around the valley, roads were blocked by fallen trees, and many people had no electricity or water. Gales of nearly 100mph had been recorded in Northumberland. I hoped it had hunkered down in some barn or hollow tree.

A relief, then, to see it glide over a field patchy with snow, its cream and golden-buff wings matching a landscape now white with straw-coloured grasses. I stood under the crook of a hawthorn, watching. The barn owl had survived the first major storm of winter.

Susie White, 2021

The naked mystery of the winter tree

WENLOCK EDGE, SHROPSHIRE

This old field maple, stripped of all its butter-yellow
leaves, seems to be floating in the dim light

The day goes on as it begins: a wet flannel across the face that smells of mould; a mizzle, violet tinged; December's dimmer switch stuck on three, from what might have been dawn to what might become dusk. Beautiful.

Looming from this foggy myopia is a tree. It is a field maple, *Acer campestre*, ancient, with a great knot of roots that shows how the field has eroded from weather and sheep. The root-knot, of Medusa's petrified snakes, supports a single straight trunk, clear for about 6 feet, then opening into an irregular-shaped canopy 20 feet tall and almost as wide. The butter-yellow, five-lobed maple leaves have fallen and its winter nakedness is an intricate tracery of twigs bearing brown buds, raindrops and vivid daubs of lichen. It is a smaller tree than the ashes and oaks, but probably older.

This field maple is solitary, enigmatic, magnetic and sheltering. There's something odd about its position in relation to the earthworks under the sod, which may belong to a field system from its monastic past or earlier. Nothing in this light gives away its age, identity or place, nothing feels tethered to this strangely floating land. A swan periscopes above pool reeds, redwings speak scratchily in an old ash, and in the hedge along the lane the brambling are restless. These birds burst from the kale patch like a feathered cannonball, spread into hazels, regroup in high trees, then dive back into the field when they've forgotten what it was that spooked them.

But even the hair-trigger paranoia of the brambling is muted in this delicious murk. The feeling is that things are going on that the physical senses can't detect, mysterious things. I received a Christmas card with a quote from Richard Wagamese's novel *Medicine Walk*: 'I sorta think you gotta let a mystery be a mystery for it to give you anything.' At 3.30 p.m., jackdaws start gathering to roost. In these solstice days of the guttering year, winter trees give off their own beautiful mystery.

Paul Evans, 2021

The fleeting magic trick that is hair ice

FOREST OF AE, DUMFRIES AND GALLOWAY

Coiffed and with a parting, it is perfectly named, yet crumbles to the touch

Mist is rising from the Water of Ae tributary, turning gold as the dawn light slips across the valley through the forest of birch and pine. Fieldfares clatter down the path at our presence and a goldcrest calls sibilantly through the still air. Under the mist, a dipper stands up to its shins in the flow of clear water. I want to clamber down the bank and stick my finger in the river, but by the bank I stop. A white branch catches my eye. I reach out a fingertip to feel that instead, and it crumbles to my touch like fresh snowfall.

Hair ice. Uncommon, but a speciality here. It is one of nature's finest magic tricks, the freezing temperature revealing invisible processes. It needs damp air and a fungus, *Exidiopsis effusa*, to form. The fungus expels moisture along the radial rays of the wood, then when this moisture meets the freezing air, it turns to ice. The wood keeps expelling water that freezes into thin wispy filaments, strands of ice that are almost invisible individually, but which together form a thick fur.

I hold a branch up to the sun: tiny water droplets are suspended on the hair-like strings of ice. They burn white in the light, a cold blue in the shade. Best of all is how the name fits perfectly. The ice is coiffed. It has a parting. On either side of the branch the strands diverge, curling around the twig and ending up facing the same direction, as if styled by the night air.

Perhaps the greatest trick of all is in its disappearance. When we return down the path an hour later, the golden morning sunlight has crept across the river, warming our side of the bank. The ice has vanished, leaving only wood, damp from the thaw, clear of bark and moss. And I realise then something I've wanted to know all year. The clarity of ice is this: that nothing lasts forever. The real trick is how to make the most of it.

Stephen Rutt, 2020

Ghost ponds still haunt the marshland

MARSHWOOD VALE, DORSET

These lost pools come and go, but once materialised,
they can reveal long-buried secrets

The Marshwood Vale's many ponds stand out most clearly in winter. Water puddles naturally on the thick grey clay, forming pewter mirrors over slurping marsh. They look bare and lifeless now, but this dormancy is an essential part of their seasonal life cycle. Some of the spores and seeds they contain require cold to trigger germination in the spring.

There used to be more ponds here. Almost half have disappeared over the years – silted up, or filled in an attempt to make the land more productive. But these lost pools still haunt the landscape, materialising in shallow outline when the fields are waterlogged.

'Ghost ponds' can be priceless botanical time capsules. Restoring them disturbs buried seed, which may germinate, bringing back plants not seen in a century. One of the UK's rarest wildflowers, grass-poly (*Lythrum hyssopifolia*), was recently found growing on the banks of a re-excavated pond in Norfolk. The seed had lain sealed in the mud for decades until it was brought back into the light.

Similar restoration projects are happening here in Dorset. The new owners of a local farm have created four ponds as part of Defra's Countryside Stewardship scheme, two of them in an area where a pair of hobbies (*Falco subbuteo*) often nest. These fast-flying falcons prey on dragonflies as well as small birds, and prefer sites near water where insects gather.

I think the fourth pool may be a re-excavation of an old site, a materialised ghost. I visit on a changeable, topaz day, with the sunlight flashing rainbows and a salty wind flying in from the sea. Filled with autumn rain, the pool glimmers amid a small copse of oak and thorn, previously a dumping ground for broken machinery and plastic waste. Its banks already sprout the first growth typical of disturbed ground – sow thistle, spear thistle, broad-leaved dock and creeping buttercup. Tracks in the mud show that deer, pheasant and fox come to drink.

As the light fades and dusk falls, the copse pond feels as if it is brooding. Out of sight under that opaque surface, a whole world of new plants and invertebrates is being incubated.

Sara Hudston, 2020

The hunched silhouettes of roosting ravens

BUXTON, DERBYSHIRE

*On an eerie, undark evening, I hear their shuffling
sounds as they settle into the pine canopy*

Lightwood Reservoir is well used by dog walkers and seldom a place you can have all to yourself until well after dusk. During the recent snow, however, with all its glorious ambient glow, the witching hour – when the darkness, solitude and arrival of Lightwood's roosting ravens converge – was put back to a later slot.

At 5 p.m. there was still a residual apricot layer on the western horizon, and from the snow across the woodland floor emanated an almost pink-white light. It had the strength to reveal each tree as a chiselled silhouette, and even the boot- and paw-impressed paths were threads of grey in the wider blanket.

The two ravens cleaved the valley and passed at low elevation, almost as if to avoid any projection of their flight outlines upon the starlit inky blue overhead. The contact calls were soft, and mingled with the churn of Hogshaw Brook. But I could hear the shuffling sounds of the birds as they settled into the pine canopy close to their nest tree.

I imagined their day in this whitened landscape. Snow, of course, is no enemy to ravens. Their survival skills kit them out even for the high Arctic, where they routinely draw up fishing lines from unattended ice holes to steal the catch. The kills made by other predators – foxes or eagles – supply them with rich pickings. Arctic wolf cubs emerge blinking into a world of perpetual daylight and the unfailing attentiveness of black birds. One study indicated that wolves lost up to 20 kilos of meat a day to ravens.

I adjusted my position to watch the roosting birds. If their hunched silhouettes offered no profound insights, at least the deep black of their outline was a true measure of this strangely undark night. The company of ravens also yielded this warming thought in a frozen land: such is their early breeding season, the nest above my head could be lined with brown-scribbled blue eggs in just a few weeks.

Mark Cocker, 2020

The tiny king of darkness

OTLEY, WEST YORKSHIRE

I'm woken by the volley of noise that is a singing wren, vivid and defiant in the early-morning black

A noise invades my dreams. I wake to the dark void of a December night and the bright, quickfire trill of a bird.

The complex song, with its rapid, rat-a-tat volley of notes – unmistakably that of a wren (*Troglodytes troglodytes*) – sounds for a second time. It reminds me of the dawn choruses of early spring, except this is a lone voice, and instead of early dawn light filling the room, all is black obscurity.

During the breeding season, this tiny bird, which weighs about as much as a pound coin, produces a noise so loud and reverberant that it seems to defy physics. Today's is more muted, perhaps because of the energy-saving demands of winter, but it is still vivid and defiant, its piercing clarity accentuated by the silence. I listen, finding it a comforting reminder of life in the darkness.

Not all wren-induced awakenings have been looked on so kindly. In Ireland, various myths involve the birds singing at a bad time:

waking up a jailer as Saint Stephen was trying to escape, or betraying warriors trying to sneak up on an enemy camp.

Such stories justify the (no longer literal) tradition of 'hunting the wren', which still continues in a few places across Europe, particularly in the west of Ireland and Isle of Man. Such festivals always take place in midwinter, often on 26 December (the feast of Saint Stephen), when the bird's song is conspicuous amid the general lifelessness.

These traditions could be seen as mere persecution, but they are also imbued with a kind of veneration. Irish rhymes accompanying the custom refer to the wren as 'king of the birds', a title that goes as far back as *Aesop's Fables* and is reflected in its Dutch name: *winterkoninkje* (winter king).

I get up, part the curtains and look outside. In a bitter easterly wind, silhouetted bare tree branches sway against moonlit clouds, and dry leaves scrape across flagstones in the garden below. Winter is punishing for wrens, and one in four of them won't last until spring. But, for now, my tiny king of the cold still sings in the dark.

Carey Davies, 2019

Hope on a New Horizon for the English elm

CAISTOR ST EDMUND, NORFOLK

An arguably morbid gift to my father will help this beleaguered species towards a new chapter

As I head out of the deciduous woodland of Foxes' Grove, I spot it, tucked away near a small conifer plantation. Tall and skinny, with a few sprigs of growth sticking out from the slender trunk, this sapling is newly planted and decorated with shiny deer protection round its base. It appears insignificant, yet the reddish-brown buds of this young elm contain a secret, as if tightly wrapped in brown paper.

I am standing on Elm Bank, which in the 1950s was crowned with English elms. They were the largest trees on the farm, reaching up over 30 metres high. Those trees are gone, dead before I was born, after a virulent new strain of Dutch elm disease arrived in the 1960s. The disease, spread by elm bark beetles, has removed more than 60 million trees from our countryside, and counting. In the end, the dead wood of those massive trunks was blown up using dynamite. Today, aside from a few evergreens, I am surrounded by open grassland.

The sapling was a present to my father from his children. It could be considered a sinister gift, the elm being linked in folklore to death and the underworld. It was also commonly used to make coffins and is now synonymous with loss and disease. However, like my father, it is no ordinary specimen.

This young tree is an *Ulmus* 'New Horizon', specially bred in Hampshire for resistance to the deadly fungus. Immunity should persist as it reproduces, via a strong and far-extending root system, reaching out suckers underground that then rise up to become resistant offspring.

The sapling is first and foremost a gift for my dad, but it is also intended as a gift for this tenanted farm, and for the white-letter hairstreak butterfly. *Ulmus* is the sole host and food plant for this rare species, which has consequently experienced massive decline as we have lost elms. I hope it is a legacy for future generations on this borrowed land that will unfurl over the coming decades.

Kate Blincoe, 2019

Unexpected treasures on a dark day

EYAM, DERBYSHIRE

*Winter has two faces here: some days are crispy and
frosty, others need saving from the thick gloom*

As I neared the top of Sir William Hill, it started to rain. But if the
outlook was bleak, the view was compelling. From the hill's crest,
nibbled at for quarry stone by labourers in some distant past, I
looked out across to Abney Low in the middle distance – a lovely
hill, curved and green, with a grid of white limestone walls laid
across it like fishnets. Beyond it, above the village of Abney, was
the darkly brooding dome of Offerton Moor, now quickly disappearing behind gunmetal clouds.

Winter has two faces in the High Peak. Some days are crisp
and frosty, with golden sunlight slanting in on its low trajectory,
the bracken bronze and the gritstone crags etched against a blue
heaven. On days like that, there are plenty of smiling faces to greet
you. More often, though, it's like today: warmer but wet, the rolling hills so blanketed in grey that colour has drained from the
moors and sheepwalks, as though the land's blood was pooling in
its boots. Crows in a nearby line of beeches were all in silhouette,
snipped from black crepe.

There's something dispiriting in such thick gloom at the fag end
of the winter solstice. On days like this, crows and dank sheep are
often all you'll meet. The greyness and lonely tug of the wind can
settle on your soul like ashes. So as Abney Low followed Offerton
behind the blank cloud, I wondered to myself what I was doing
there.

Then shreds of mist began racing up the moor towards me from
the valley below, and everything changed. Rocks and trees disap-

peared as a silvery veil was thrown across them, then suddenly re-appeared as the strengthening wind ripped the veil aside. A prospect that only moments earlier had seemed flat and dull was now textured and brimful of energy, the perspective closing and opening by the second. Around me, glistening with pearls of moisture, the red moor grass seemed to catch fire, so vibrant in the half-light that I could almost hear it humming. Even on the darkest days, there can be unexpected treasures.

Ed Douglas, 2019

Tumbling lapwings, foraging rooks, a cruising harrier

OTMOOR, OXFORDSHIRE

Before the spectacle of the starlings begins, these pre-roosting hours on the reserve are rich with interplay

The sky today is shifting, moody, oceanic; the light is accordingly mercurial. It's not long after midday, but at times it feels like the near edge of dusk.

Otmoor is a wetland reserve, a sodden, low-lying sweep of reed bed and heath north of Oxford. But the key habitat here often seems to be the sky. The overhead traffic is constant: flocks of lapwing in characteristic tumble; straight-necked wildfowl beelining for the crowded ponds; starlings on sharp-winged manoeuvre; the burly silhouette of a peregrine against the barely-there sun; rooks stirred from their companionable foraging in the drenched fields; golden plover in their hundreds; wood pigeons, always alone, criss-crossing the daubed impasto clouds. 'Traffic' is the right word.

Here, more than most places, there is a sense of interplay, networking, of the Otmoor birds' busy lives as nodes in a complicated web.

A sparrowhawk corkscrewing through the hawthorns panics the winter thrushes foraging among the blackthorn (the fieldfares, with their throaty warning rattles, are flighty today – maybe it's this unpredictable light). In the damp air above the reed beds, rooks fall from the sky to mob a cruising marsh harrier. Greylags at pasture look up as three honking Canada geese make a steep descent from the murk.

In a little while, up to 50,000 starlings ('A lart, ennet?' mutters a local in the reed-bed hide) will assemble here to roost. It will be an entrancing spectacle, but I'm just as enthralled by these low-key afternoon musterings and manoeuvrings, these lowering pre-roost hours in which the birds watch the sky with a cricketer's weather-eye, feel the tick of their inner clocks, perhaps hunt out a supper of sloes or leatherjackets, perhaps form into flocks to idle away the afternoon (ornithologically, if uncharitably, this is known as loafing).

I leave before the murmurations begin.

Richard Smyth, 2018

About the Introducer

Ian McMillan is a poet, journalist, playwright and broadcaster. He has written comedy for radio and plays for the stage, and worked extensively in radio and television. He currently presents *The Verb* on BBC Radio 3 and appears as a regular on *Coast*, *BBC Breakfast*, *Countryfile*, *Pick of the Week*, *Last Word* and *The Arts Show*.

About the Illustrator

Clifford Harper is a self-taught artist and illustrator. He has worked for many radical and alternative publications, the international anarchist movement and almost all of the UK national newspapers.

His Country Diary drawings first appeared in the *Guardian* in November 1996. A collection of this artwork, *Country Diary Drawings: 36 Drawings by Clifford Harper*, was published by Agraphia in 2003 and is available for purchase from online retailers.